ABERDEEN UNIVERSITY STUDIES SERIES

NUMBER 152

ST. NINIAN'S ISLE
AND ITS TREASURE

VOLUME I

TEXT

ST. NINIAN'S ISLE

AND ITS TREASURE

BY

ALAN SMALL, CHARLES THOMAS
AND DAVID M. WILSON

WITH CONTRIBUTIONS BY

KENNETH JACKSON, HUGH McKERRELL
AND T. B. SMITH

VOLUME I

TEXT

PUBLISHED FOR THE UNIVERSITY OF ABERDEEN

BY

OXFORD UNIVERSITY PRESS

1973

Oxford University Press, Ely House, London W. 1

GLASGOW NEW YORK TORONTO MELBOURNE WELLINGTON
CAPE TOWN IBADAN NAIROBI DAR ES SALAAM LUSAKA ADDIS ABABA
DELHI BOMBAY CALCUTTA MADRAS KARACHI LAHORE DACCA
KUALA LUMPUR SINGAPORE HONG KONG TOKYO

ISBN 0 19 714101 3

Printed in Great Britain
at the University Press, Oxford
by Vivian Ridler
Printer to the University

Preface

To his students the late Professor Andrew C. O'Dell was not only a teacher but an adviser and friend. It was his own deep interest in the historical geography of Shetland, on which he had written extensively, along with his interest in his students, that led to what at first appeared to be a straightforward excavation of a medieval church. Five seasons of excavations revealed a multi-period site and culminated in the uncovering of the St. Ninian's Isle treasure, one of the most important discoveries made in Scottish archaeology this century. It is tragic that Professor O'Dell's heavy commitments, both local and national, and his untimely death in 1967, prevented his completing the excavation and publishing the results.

On his death Mrs. O'Dell asked me to publish a report of the results, and I have followed his own wish in inviting a number of specialists to write on various aspects of the work. To these colleagues, who have given unstintingly of their time, I am deeply indebted.

ALAN SMALL

Contents

CONTENTS

VOLUME II

Acknowledgements

Aᴌᴌ contributors to this volume wish to express their gratitude to Mrs. O'Dell, without whose help this publication would not have been possible. They are indebted to Miss Nisbet for generously providing her personal diaries for their use. Thanks are due to the Carnegie United Kingdom Trust for financial help towards the cost of field work and publication; and to Mr. Tom Henderson, of the Shetland County Museum, for his generous assistance in many ways.

Alan Small wishes to thank Professor Kenneth Walton for much advice and encouragement.

Charles Thomas wishes to thank his former colleague, **Mr. Malcolm Murray**, for accompanying him to Shetland and taking all the photographs which illustrate the section on the sculptured stones and crosses.

David M. Wilson wishes to thank the following: Professor Julian Brown, Mr. P. D. C. Brown, Mr. C. E. Blunt, Miss P. Butler, Miss V. I. Evison, Mr. P. Fett, Dr. John Fletcher, Mr. James Graham-Campbell, Professor David Greene, Mr. J. Hopkins, Miss K. Hughes, Professor K. H. Jackson, Dr. A. T. Lucas, Mr. E. McKernan, Dr. H. McKerrell, Mr. E. W. McKie, Mr. K. R. Möllenhus, Miss H. C. Nisbet, Dr. Olaf Olsen, Mr. B. Ó Ríordáin, Dr. R. I. Page, Mr. K. S. Painter, Professor C. Peschek, Dr. C. A. R. Radford, Dr. J. Raftery, Mr. J. G. Scott, Professor D. B. Strong, Mr. A. E. Truckell, Mrs. L. Webster, Dr. A. E. Werner, and Mr. G. Willmot. He also wishes to express his gratitude to his wife for her many drawings. He is grateful to Miss P. Henman for typing many drafts of his section and for much secretarial help. His greatest thanks are, however, due to Mr. R. B. K. Stevenson and Miss A. Henshall, who supported innumerable requests and gave so very much of their time during many visits to the National Museum of Antiquities of Scotland; without their co-operation it would have been impossible to carry this work through to its conclusion.

T. B. Smith wishes to thank the Editor of *Acta Juridica* for permission to use material already published in that journal.

The copyright of the following is acknowledged: Ashmolean Museum, Oxford, pl. xxxvii *a*, *b*; Bergen Historisk Museum, pls. xl *c*, *d*, xli *b*; British Museum, pls. xvii–xxvii, xxix–xxxv, xliv *d*, xlvi *a*, lii *b*; Burgh Museum, Dumfries, pl. xliv *a*; City of Glasgow Art Gallery and Museum, pl. l *e*; J. R. Coull, Esq., pl. i; Department of the Environment, pls. l *a*, liii, lv, lvi; Ipswich Museum, pl. xlix *c*; Professor K. H. Jackson, fig. 29; Mrs. G. Keiller, pl. xlix *a*; National Museum of Antiquities of Scotland, pls. xxxvi, xxxvii *d*, xxxviii, xl *a*, *b*, xli *c*, xlii *b*, *d*, xliii, xliv *b*, *c*, xlv *a*, *c*, xlvi *c*, xlviii, xlix *d*, l *b*, liv; National Museum of Ireland, pls. xxxix *b*, xli *a*, xlii *e*, xlvii *a*, *b*, xlix *b*, l *c*; Public Library and Museum, Campbeltown, pl. xlii *a*; A. Small, Esq., figs. 1–5; Stavanger Museum, pl. xxxix *a*; Society of Antiquaries of London, pls. xxxvii *c*, li, lii *a*; Professor A. C. Thomas, figs. 7–13; Victoria and Albert Museum, pl. l *d*; Mrs. Eva Wilson, figs. 14–28, 30–2, 34–42, pl. xxviii; Universitetets Oldsaksamling, Oslo, pls. xlii *c*, xlv *b*, xlvii *c*; University of Aberdeen, fig. 33, pls. ii–xvi; Shetland County Museum, Lerwick, fig. 6, pl. lvii.

I *The site: its history and excavation*

ALAN SMALL

S T. NINIAN'S ISLE (Lat. 59° 58′ N., long. 1° 21′ W.), some 22·4 km. south-south-west of Lerwick, is a small, now uninhabited, treeless island about 1,600 m. from north to south by 1,250 m. from east to west lying off the south-west mainland of Shetland, to which it is connected by a 550-m.-long tombolo of white sand built up by the tides of the Atlantic sweeping round both ends of the island (pl. i, fig. 1). The site which was excavated lies at an altitude of 20 m. just west of this tombolo. At the present time the tombolo provides an easy crossing for tractors and lorries to the island at practically all seasons; it is only for short periods during very high tides accompanied by north-westerly gales that it is covered over by the tides. The geomorphological history of the tombolo is not clear, and one cannot be precise about access to the island at specific periods in the past. There is a large body of evidence supporting the view that sea level has been rising in Shetland at least over the past 7,000 years; evidence comes not only from several archaeological sites which are now below high-water mark but also from the discovery of land-peat at the bottom of Lerwick Harbour.[1] This drowning of the old sandy shorelines could account for the fact that no mesolithic sites have so far been discovered in Shetland, of the coastal type found in north-east Scotland. The sand blowing up from the tombolo has covered over the archaeological remains on the eastern half of the island to a depth of 6 m. in places. The marks of former turf layers in the sand suggest that the build-up of sand on the island has been an intermittent process, but there is no evidence to suggest that the structures of any particular period were suddenly inundated by sand to such an extent that they had to be deserted. The pre-Christian horizons all lie on a clay soil formed from the underlying grey schists which are the bedrock of the island, and there is very little sand in the profile until the immediate pre-Christian period; this suggests that as late as 2,000 years ago the tombolo did not exist or was only beginning to form. Tombolos and other similar accumulations are somewhat transient features in the landscape; their cycle of development and decline is related to the equilibrium profile of the sea bed and the availability of material to

[1] Hoppe (1965), 195.

feed them. Because of the rising sea level there has been extensive coastal erosion on the western shores of the Isle and the Shetland mainland, and there is no shortage of eroded material for deposition. Active erosion is most marked in the north bay, Bigton Wick, which is a poor anchorage with several sunken rocks only 3·7 m. below the surface.[1] The south bay, St. Ninian's Bay, is a much more sheltered haven with a sandy bottom; this suggests southward movement of material. Thus it would seem that in prehistoric times St. Ninian's Isle may have been a true island approachable only by boat and it was not until the early Christian period that there was any natural causeway to it.

For a site which has a strong local tradition of being the Mother Church of Shetland there is surprisingly little early documentation of the structures. As Goudie[2] reiterates, oral tradition suggests that the church was built by shipwrecked mariners in pre-Reformation times,[3] or alternatively constructed by the Udallers of the area for their own convenience. The first tradition is repeated *ad nauseam* in various parts of Shetland to account for the ruins of many unexcavated early churches, and may be dismissed without comment in the light of the archaeological evidence. No pre-Reformation documentation exists, and the church[4] is not included in the list of Shetland churches submitted to the General Assembly of the Church of Scotland in 1586 by the Lord Clerk of Register.[5] Nor was there ever a Reformed minister of St. Ninian's Isle.[6] The earliest references to the island appear in legal documents. In 1576 Arthur Sinclair declared that he possessed the heritable title to St. Ninian's Isle,[7] and in 1588 Laurence Sinclair of Houss had a disposition from Robert, Earl of Orkney, of the lands of St. Ninian's Isle in Dunrossness.[8] The island is again mentioned (as Sancttrinyeanis Yle) in the Court Book of Shetland for 1 August 1603, in a case dealing with the fishings off the isle,[9] but there is no reference to a church in any of these documents. It follows that, since there is no pre-Reformation record of the island, it cannot be stated with any degree of certainty that the medieval church was ascribed to St. Ninian, and there is no justification whatsoever for attributing a Ninianic dedication to the Dark Age building.

The first documentary evidence of a church appears on Pont's map of the Shetland Isles prepared about 1608 and published in Blaeu's atlas (1654). A church is indicated in nearly the same position as that found during excavations, but no indication is given whether it was still in use or in a ruinous state. Nearby a house or settlement is marked of which no trace was discovered during the excavation probably because the area

---

[1] North Sea Pilot.
[2] Goudie (1912), 41–2.
[3] Edmondston (1809), ii. 116.
[4] I am indebted to Professor J. S. McEwen of the University of Aberdeen for help on this point.

[5] Peterkin (1839), 304.
[6] Scott, H. (1915).
[7] Goudie (1904), 204–5.
[8] Grant (1893), 289.
[9] Donaldson (1954), 106.

examined was not sufficiently extensive. The island is named *S Tronons Yle*, which may possibly be a misprinted St. Ronon's Yle or indeed St. Tronon's Isle (St. Ninian has been known in other areas as St. Trinyon).

James Kay, writing about 1680, states that there is a church on the island, but gives no indication whether it was in use or of its condition;[1] he also notes the difficulty of access to the isle during north-westerly gales, adding the interesting point that horses were specially trained to wade across at high tide. The Revd. John Brand, who visited the site in 1700, comments: 'To the North West of the Ness lyes St. Ninian's Isle, very pleasant; wherein there is a Chappel and an Altar in it whereon some superstitious People do burn Candles to this day. Some take this isle rather to be a kind of Peninsula, joyned to the Main by a Bank of Sand, by which in an Ebb People may go to the Isle, tho' sometimes not without danger.'[2] This description is copied virtually verbatim by several later writers, notably Martin and Sibbald.

In 1744 one John Bruce (Stewart) obtained the property on his marriage to Clementina Stewart,[3] and is stated to have demolished the remains of the chapel and built the retaining wall which still stands (though it is no longer an effective barrier to cattle straying on to the island). The Revd. Mr. Low, having inspected the site in 1774, noted that: 'the remains of an old chapel is still to be seen. . . . The lower storey of the kirk may be distinctly traced, which having once been vaulted, is supposed to have served for a burying place.'[4] This statement is reproduced in Hibbert's book in 1822.

The late eighteenth century was a period of extremely stormy conditions in northern Scotland, and it was probably during this period that the ruins of the church were finally covered over. Thomas S. Muir, who visited the site in 1861, reported that all trace of the church had vanished. The soil profile also suggests rapid accumulation of sand at intervals: the upper 1·5 m., all of which has accumulated since 1750, is completely immature and shows many traces of sand movement after short periods of fixation by vegetation. This sand movement may account for the local tradition that the altar was still visible within the lifetime of people who died twenty or thirty years ago; the sand may have shifted to expose the altar for a short period after Muir's visit. The last few decades of the eighteenth century also saw the depopulation of the island; it is tempting to connect this depopulation with difficulty of access to the island in the more stormy conditions of the time, but there is no conclusive evidence to support this view. The last recorded child born on the island was one James Sinclair in 1771, to William Sinclair

[1] Kay (1908), 31.

[2] Brand (1701), 84. During excavation a late seventeenth-century copper coin was found wedged in the altar.

[3] *Henry Blair* v. *J. B. Stewart*, Condescendence in Process, 18 Nov. 1783.

[4] Low (1879).

and his wife Ursula Leask, but although the island was uninhabited the churchyard continued to be used for burials until the mid nineteenth century.

When Gilbert Goudie, the well-known Shetland antiquarian, visited the site in July 1875 with the specific objective of seeing whether any trace of the structure of the chapel could be found, he was unsuccessful. He found the area in an extremely unkempt state: 'There was some difficulty in prosecuting a search, the cattle contesting possession of the ground and tossing the skulls and trampling the bones which are strewn about the sand-blown surface, or protruding from beneath.'[1] Little wonder he draws attention to Sir Walter Scott's use of the site as a setting in 'The Pirate' for the grotesque scene of Norma of Fitful Head searching in the sand for the bones of her ancestor Ribolt Troil. Goudie's survey revealed an ogham stone, which is now in the National Museum of Antiquities of Scotland in Edinburgh;[2] the stone is broken, and Goudie reported the presence of other fragments on the island, but diligent search in modern times has failed to recover them.

The excavation

Preliminary excavation began in 1955 under the direction of Professor Andrew C. O'Dell assisted by members of Aberdeen University Geographical Society and continued for five summer seasons. Mr. J. Budge, the landowner, readily granted consent to excavation and materially helped the success of the project. There was no local tradition of buried treasure on the island, and the objectives of excavation were simply to find the remains of the medieval church in order to establish its plan and date of construction.

Since there was no exact record of the location of the site, excavation was begun with a series of test trenches in the general area where local tradition suggested that the chapel had been. A confused mass of bones was unearthed from the relatively modern churchyard, and later a section of the medieval church wall was located. Professor O'Dell then decided to excavate on the principle that structures were the only significant feature on the excavation; he argued that, since the whole area of the church and its surroundings had been repeatedly used for burials right up to the middle of the nineteenth century, there would be no significant stratification left on the site. Consequently thousands of medieval interments were removed rapidly without record and reburied to the west of the church. The density of burials tends to confirm the tradition that the church served not only the island but also the neighbouring part of the mainland, and it is surprising that the treasure had not been found by earlier gravediggers since interments had been intruded within a few inches on all sides of the hoard.

[1] Goudie (1904).   [2] Goudie (1912).

It is never easy to write up an excavation which someone else has directed, and in this case the matter is further complicated by the methods of recording used on the site. There is no master grid for the site, and small finds are frequently recorded by the name of the excavator rather than by their specific location; it is thus impossible to relate them to specific horizons. No site diary can be found nor a comprehensive finds record, with the result that most of the prehistoric account in this volume is based on the recollections of the author and his former fellow students who have kindly lent him notes, photographs, and personal diaries.

The first indication of pre-Christian occupation came during the third season of excavation, when a small area about 2 m. × 2 m. was excavated in the centre of the nave to ascertain whether the medieval church had had a crypt and also whether there had been an earlier church on the same site. This section produced the one fragment of *porfido verde antico* and at a slightly lower level a disturbed mass of domestic and funeral debris. For the same purpose a small area excavation about 12 m. × 8 m. was attempted on the south side of the church in 1959, which revealed an extensive complex of pre-historic walls, pavements, and graves; all the structures extend beyond the limits of the excavated area, and it is impossible to ascertain their true nature. It is indeed unfortunate that Professor O'Dell never had the opportunity to finish the work as he wished, and much prehistoric material remains undisturbed below 6–7 m. of sand.

The area below the nave

The excavation of this area, started in 1957 and completed in 1959, revealed an extensive complex of fragments of paving and walls some two metres below the medieval foundations. Most of the structural evidence had been completely destroyed by the intrusion of later pre-Christian and Christian burials and also by the several periods of rebuilding in the pre-Christian phases. This area was trowelled over carefully, and a mass of pottery discovered; that which can be assigned to specific points confirms O'Dell's view that the stratification had been badly disturbed by later burials. From Miss H. Nisbet's personal diary it is clear that at least two short stone cists were un-earthed in this area; no dimensions are recorded, but both contained fragments of two urns. One grave also contained numerous small well-rounded quartz pebbles apparently set in a clay floor, and both cists contained burnt and calcined bone, suggesting crema-tion burials. From Miss Nisbet's description I have been able to isolate the rim fragments of one of the urns (fig. 2); it is a thick-sided, fine-textured vessel with a roll rim, which has numerous parallels in Shetland, e.g. at Jarlshof,[1] Clickhimin,[2] and Underhoull,[3] and

[1] Hamilton (1956), 44.   [2] Hamilton (1968).   [3] Small (1966).

appears to fit well into a Broch-period context. This would suggest that the confused domestic remains in which these cists were found must at least partly pre-date the Broch period. O'Dell's notes suggest that he identified at least four phases of occupation, but on the extant evidence this cannot be confirmed or refuted. An examination of the remaining pottery supports the hypothesis of occupation over a fairly long span of time. Some of the sherds bear close resemblance to those from the late Bronze Age phase at Jarlshof, while others continue the sequence through the Broch period at least into the Wheelhouse phase.

Although the area was trowelled over and all fallen stone removed, none of the fragments of structure was disturbed. These were planned (the plan will be deposited in Shetland County Museum) in the hope that they could be linked with structures found when the areas outside the church were excavated; O'Dell's untimely death has made this impossible. The whole area was then filled with sand to bring the level up to the medieval foundations, so that shoring could be removed without disturbing the medieval structures.

The area to the south of the church

In the western section of this area there is an extensive paved area as shown in the plan (fig. 5); large flat stones are carefully laid on a clay base, and the interstices between the stones packed with clay. From the north-eastern corner of this paved area a narrow flagged path rises north-westwards with the natural ground slope towards another paved section which continues beyond the excavated zone. From the large quantity of pottery sherds recorded from this area it is clear that these are the fragmentary floors of at least one and possibly two huts; the pottery suggests a Broch period or Wheelhouse date (figs. 3, 4). Overlying these structures in the south-west corner, with a clear stratigraphical break, is a later kerbed and flagged pathway some 1·3 m. wide rising steeply to the north-west; since only 3 m. of its length was excavated no conclusions can be drawn as to its purpose.

There is no clear stratigraphical link between these structures and those in the eastern part of the area, where the dominating feature is a dry-stone wall running north and south across the area. This wall, 1·2 m. wide, and constructed of two facing walls and rubble core, extends beyond the limits of excavation at both ends, and was badly collapsed in the south. Dug into the top of this wall and clearly post-dating it was a short cist containing an adult skeleton in a crouched position but no grave goods; each end of this grave consisted of two large parallelopiped stones set on end, and the sides were of thinner slabs set on edge. Two other cists were noted within this complex.

One had thin stone slabs forming three of its sides, while the wall formed the fourth; the grave measured 1·4 by 0·4 m. and contained only charred human bones. Lying to the south of this cist and also against the wall lay a rectangular box 1·2 × 1·5 m. and about 20 cm. in depth; thin stone slabs formed the remaining three sides of the box, which was filled with shells. To the west of this a further small cist of similar construction measuring 1·1 by 0·5 m. was in a somewhat ruinous state but contained human bones. The area to the east of the wall was not completely excavated, but the only available site-plan redrawn as fig. 5 shows a number of box-like structures formed by stones set on edge which suggest further burials.

The most important find recorded from this area is a necklace of seventeen bone-and-antler beads (fig. 6); this was discovered below the north/south wall, and consequently may belong to the earliest period of occupation of the area. A fair quantity of pottery was recorded from this area, but the recording system is not sufficiently precise to relate particular sherds to specific structures. However, looking at the pottery as a whole, one finds no sherds which do not fit happily into a Shetland Iron-Age context. It is impossible to put precise dates on the complex, particularly as there is no justification for sacrificing any of the complete beads of the necklace for radio-carbon dating, which would have given an approximate base date, but the early Christian graves in the north-east corner of the excavated area, which are separated from the earlier structures by a clear stratigraphical break, provide satisfactory confirmation of the deductions from the pottery.

In the lower levels of the site the earlier structures are set on a gleyed soil with no evidence of sand in the profile. Sand does not in fact appear until the barren horizon below the dark-age graves. This points to St. Ninian's Isle being a complete island at this time, the formation of the tombolo coming later.

In conclusion, this chapter can do little more than prove the existence of a multi-phased Iron-Age complex of both domestic and sepulchral remains beneath the church on St. Ninian's Isle. The small finds are insufficient to delineate the various phases of settlement, and the excavated area too limited to give any real picture of the nature and extent of the communities.

II Sculptured stones and crosses from St. Ninian's Isle and Papil

CHARLES THOMAS

A TOTAL of no less than twenty-two worked stones came from the St. Ninian's Isle excavations. Many are of quite exceptional interest, including those which formed part of two double-compartmented composite stone shrines of the 'corner-post' class. Discussion would, however, be incomplete without reference to a smaller, and similar, group of stones from the old kirkyard of Papil, on West Burra. The Papil stones also include parts of at least two composite stone shrines, and culturally and chronologically they must be seen as comparable with those from St. Ninian's Isle. Nor can the respective sites themselves be discussed in isolation, since they are clearly contemporary and probably connected in a variety of ways.

In attempting to describe, or to assign relative dates to, any of the St. Ninian's Isle stones one is handicapped by the absence of any contextual record. In the first section of this chapter, after the discussion of Papil, I have therefore had to attempt a partial and necessarily tentative reconstruction of the excavations (1955 to 1959), and of what I believe to be the most likely sequence of events. In the second section all the stones from both sites are grouped, and described, in terms of their ecclesiastical functions—as shrines, grave-markers, grave-covers, and funerary slabs—and are set against the previous discussion of early Christianity in Shetland. The third and last section is a very detailed catalogue of all the St. Ninian's Isle and Papil stones, including illustrations of almost all of them, where necessary showing more than one factor or aspect of each.

I. EARLY CHRISTIAN SHETLAND: AN OUTLINE

If Adomnán's life of St. Columba, written shortly before 700, be taken as an accurate source in this respect, Irish monks from Iona (and possibly other west-coast foundations) had reached Orkney in the latter part of the sixth century. It is, admittedly, a more difficult step from Orkney to Shetland than it is from the mainland to Orkney, and in the absence of any evidence, it is hard to think that the Christian faith reached Shetland before the seventh century. Radford has contended that certain of the very simple incised cross-slabs or grave-markers found at Skúvoy and at Kirkjubøur, in the Faeroes, 'date from c. 700 or even earlier' and 'cannot be much later than 700'[1]. While this may be pressing rather much weight on such simple and long-lived forms, it can certainly be argued that such cross-slabs are, in general, pre-Norse, and that an early eighth-century date for Christianity in the Faeroes argues for a date in Shetland in, at any rate, the latter half of the previous century.[2]

We should expect the earliest Christian sites in Shetland to assume the usual form of small, conveniently situated, monasteries, to which outlying hermitages would soon be added. The monasteries certainly, and the hermitages probably (at a secondary stage of their existence), would be accompanied by cemeteries for the local Christian converts and their families, and for the monastic brethren, whose tombs would by the eighth century tend to be distinguished in certain ways. We might also expect to find at least a few isolated 'communal hermitages' or 'eremitic monasteries'—the type-site is Sceilg Mhichíl on the Great Skellig rock, off Co. Kerry—where one would not normally expect to find graves of lay persons at all.

These sites are all represented in Orkney. The elaborate site on the Brough of Birsay, and on the east coast that on the Brough of Deerness, appear to be monasteries.[3] The more accessible 'hermitages'—which are what I have elsewhere[4] described as 'developed cemeteries'—should occur in some numbers—St. Tredwell's, Papa Westray, is a distinct possibility, and fieldwork would reveal others. Finally, Eynhallow[5] is conceivably an isolated 'communal hermitage'.

In Shetland, the detailed field-survey has yet to take place, but Papil, West Burra, is a very strong candidate for a monastery. Outlying hermitages or developed cemeteries include that at Mail, Cunningsburgh, where the sequence of grave-markers goes back to stones with both ogam and runes; probably the sites at Lunna, Nesting,[6] and Kirkaby, on Unst;[7] and one would now add that of St. Ninian's Isle. Some recent aerial photography in the North Isles has revealed, on isolated and near-inaccessible stacks which are not overlooked from the near-by land, what seem to be clear examples of isolated hermitages of the Sceilg Mhichíl class.

[1] Radford (1962), 163 and n. 3.
[2] Cf. Wainwright (1962a), 131.
[3] Radford (1962), 166–9.
[4] Thomas (1971), passim.

[5] Radford (1962), 169–70, 184.
[6] Macdonald and Laing (1967–8), 127–8, fig. 7.
[7] Ibid., 129–30, fig. 10.

Papil

The former kirkyard of St. Laurence's lies near the shore on the eastern side of West Burra. The visible, and abandoned, church was built in 1815, and went out of use in 1920; below the floor (1967) could be seen foundations which may belong to some immediately older structure (see fig. 7, a plan of the site).

The church stands on a low, widely spread, and distinct mound (pl. ii). The explanation is given by Moar and Stewart, in their succinct account of Papil and its sculptured stones.[1] Until its destruction, shortly before 1809, the older towered church known as St. Laurence's (or St. Lawrence's) stood north and west of the present building. It is assumed to have been somewhat like the twelfth-century church, with round western tower, on Egilsay (St. Magnus).[2] According to Moar and Stewart,[3] a third building 'is traditionally reputed to have been situated on the north side of St. Lawrence's Church'. The rough location of these last two is shown on the plan, fig. 7.

This is important because, whether or not the 'primitive building' was the ruined pre-Norse church, careful inspection of the kirkyard suggests that the present rectilinear enclosing dyke stands, more or less, upon an older bank enclosing a rhomboid. This is particularly noticeable along the south side. An enclosure of this shape is more likely to represent the extent of a Christian Norse cemetery, or monastic enceinte of that date, than an early (pre-Norse) one, as Radford has emphasized;[4] and Macdonald and Laing (1967–8) report the discovery of a 'sherd of late Norse pottery' on the inner face of this southern bank. One would hazard the guess that the pre-Norse enclosure was of much the same extent, perhaps a little smaller, but of curvilinear plan (cf. Birsay, Orkney, where the rectilinear enclosure can be seen superimposed on the older bank or wall).[5]

None of the cross-marked slabs found at Papil can be regarded as having been found *in situ*, apart from the virtual certainty that they had not previously left this particular cemetery. The various corner-posts and panels of the composite stone shrines, however, do seem to have been concentrated on the north side of the present structure, in a position which would place them east, or south-east, of the 'primitive structure' (see fig. 7); and Moar and Stewart's account, which specifies distances in feet, allows this degree of precision. This placing supports the idea that the 'primitive building' may, like the shrines, go back to the eighth century, even if the three stones from Papil Shrine *A* (see p. 25 below) were not, when found, in their original position *vis-à-vis* each other.

[1] Moar and Stewart (1943–4).
[2] Radford (1962), 182–3, fig. 33.
[3] Moar and Stewart (1943–4), 91–2.

[4] e.g. Radford (1962), 180.
[5] Ibid., 176, fig. 32; Cruden (1965), 23, fig. 1.

St. Ninian's Isle

The description which follows is drawn from a variety of sources. In 1958, in connection with a B.B.C. broadcast, I was able to discuss the first few seasons of excavation with the late Professor Andrew O'Dell, and to take a number of notes (with sketches) which he was good enough to look over and to approve. In June 1967, as part of my work as a Leverhulme Fellow, I spent some time in Shetland with my old friend and former colleague Mr. Malcolm Murray (Department of Archaeology, University of Edinburgh). We visited both Papil and St. Ninian's Isle, and made triangulated plans of both sites; we also put aside several days for work in the Shetland County Museum, and through the courtesy and help of Mr. Tom Henderson we were able to measure, draw, and photograph practically every aspect of every worked stone from these two sites. I have since had the advantage of hearing Mr. Alan Small's personal memories of the excavations, and of seeing certain plans and slides; and also of reading a series of notes, made at the time by Miss Helen C. Nisbet (Grant Institute of Geology, University of Edinburgh). My account, the imperfections of which are in no wise due to all these kind friends, should be read in conjunction with Mr. Small's, and is directed towards the construction of some coherent story for the ecclesiastical sequence.

Professor O'Dell's excavations took place from 1955 to 1959. At the start, the entire area was below the turf. The focus of the work was the (now visible) ruin of the medieval church, the remains of which were largely demolished some time after 1744. The general character of the structure was apparent by the 1956 season, and work was concentrated on the interior; on an extensive area to the south of the church; and on a smaller area to the west. Despite O'Dell's trial trenching, no trace of any enclosure could then be found, and in 1967 I was unable to see the slightest hint of any such.

The plan (fig. 8), which must not be taken as definitive, combines points of details from all the sources named earlier. The walls of the church, when uncovered, stood some 3 to 4 feet high. Bedrock, overlain by a thin layer of peat, was encountered some seven feet below the level of the wall footings. Immediately above this peat, and both inside and outside (to the south of) the church, crude stone walls, with rubble collapses, paved areas, and occupational debris, appeared to indicate (pre-Christian) secular occupation. Pottery, which I saw in 1958, was of the kind found in the Jarlshof wheel-house complex,[1] and this occupation must be labelled 'Iron Age', even if it belongs to the early centuries A.D.

A number of inhumations in short, or medium-length, slab cists constitute the next phase at St. Ninian's Isle. These are marked as *A* in fig. 8. Apart from one inside the church area, containing 'pottery and human bones' (H. C. Nisbet's notes), there were at

---

[1] Hamilton (1956), e.g. 66, fig. 35, phase III.

least six south of the church. One contained a crouched inhumation (adult); two others held skeletal fragments, one perhaps of a mother and child (?). Stratigraphically, these are slightly higher than the Iron Age walls and paving, and the large cist with the crouched burial appear to sit directly upon the top of a wall.

Subsequent phases (up to four) are all Christian. The long cists (marked *B* in fig. 8), outside the south-east angle of the church, mark the first Christian interments. These oriented long cists were, stratigraphically, from two to three feet higher than the short cists (those marked *A*). Normally one would expect them to lie east, or south-east, of a contemporary chapel or oratory, in this part of the world most likely to be stone-walled; I take this to be represented by the 'Earlier Walls' said to have been noticed below the footings of the medieval church.

It is extremely hard to make much of the visible church. It was apparently refaced, in parts even rebuilt, in the medieval period, and some restoration was undertaken in the course of the excavations. The church plan as shown in fig. 8, triangulated by Mr. Murray and myself, is at least accurate. Without pulling down the walls, we could not resolve, *in situ*, the nature of some of the straight joints. I would argue that the western half, Professor O'Dell's 'nave', was in origin a rectangular unicameral chapel, with a central west doorway and internal dimensions of the order of 16 ft. 6 in. by 22 ft. 6 in. (or longer). This was remodelled, when the east wall was broken, giving access (through a chancel arch, or a simple opening) into an internally rounded chancel. The odd external shape of this chancel[1] cannot be made out now.

The little masonry block, in the south-east angle of the nave, described as 'a side-altar' (O'Dell) is of poor construction, and is not, as previously published plans might imply, bonded into the wall at all.

A final phase, ending not when the church was partly demolished (after 1744) but when Christian burials at this site ceased to be made (about 1840?), must be regarded as post-medieval; to it should belong numerous burials within the (roofless) church, and perhaps some very late burials reported as having been made across the ruinous north wall.

Into this sequence must be fitted the various worked stones. Those whose find-spots can be ascertained, even approximately, are shown on fig. 8, marked by the arabic numerals which are used throughout this chapter. The seven shrine posts were all found within, or on the walls of, a curious little unroofed structure ('Founder's Tomb') lying just south of the apsidal chancel. This was stratigraphically high and late, and is probably no older than the medieval period.

[1] Cf. O'Dell *et al.* (1959), 242, fig. 1.

In summary, the St. Ninian's Isle sequence involves some six phases. Phase 1 is an Iron Age occupation, probably commencing in the first few centuries B.C. and lasting until the third and fourth centuries A.D. In the next two or three centuries (phase 2) the ruins of this homestead were used for a pre-Christian burial-ground of short-cist inhumations. The cemetery—perhaps the local burial-ground for a number of families— continued in use, but as a Christian one, with oriented extended inhumations in long cists, after conversion to the Faith (perhaps as early as the late seventh century, the burials probably by the eighth). The graves are almost certainly aligned on the longer axis of some accompanying stone chapel (this is phase 3). This 'Early Christian' phase may have been interrupted, even ended, around 800 by the first Norse raids and settlements, an episode marked by the burial of the silver hoard under the chapel floor.

After an interval, perhaps a considerable interval, a slightly larger chapel was constructed above the first chapel. This is phase 4, and I join with Dr. Ralegh Radford in regarding this as a reflection of Norse Christianity, unlikely to be older than the twelfth century. The succeeding phase 5 saw this chapel enlarged into a church, with the addition of an apsidal chancel. The surviving altar foundation (which I take to be an aspect of this enlargement phase) measures 30 in. by 53 in.; I have argued elsewhere[1] on the basis of a number of altars from very similar 'churches of lesser consideration' in Cornwall that dimensions and proportions of this nature indicate the final twelfth and early thirteenth centuries, altars of preceding and subsequent periods being of rather different proportions and sizes. In this case, a date some time after 1200 would be quite appropriate. The final phase (phase 6) marks the decay of the church, possibly from the Reformation, if that really affected it, until shortly after 1744.

This sequence is no more than a reconstruction, but it is in accord with the evidence that we have, and it is one that can now be demonstrated—often in its entirety—for a good many Christian sites in north and west Britain. The apparently continuous use of the cemetery from pre-Christian into Christian times is something that I have noted from a large number of places.[2] It could be argued, and it is wholly feasible, that this chapel and cemetery were in sporadic use through the ninth, tenth, and eleventh centuries, if only by a few surviving Christian islanders or Picts under the domination of pagan Norse landholders. There is no direct evidence for this, and one would expect rather more Christian graves than seem to have been noticed. Again, the cross-incised or cross-marked stones, all of which are grave-markers of one kind or another, appear to fall within phase 3, the pre-Norse cemetery (e.g., nos. *11* and *15*), or else to be as late as phase 4 (the supposed Christian Norse re-building—nos. *12*, *14*, and *17*, all significantly

[1] Thomas (1967a), 108.   [2] Thomas (1971), ch. 3.

of steatite). The others—like *18*—may be later. Our main concern must be with the composite stone shrines, which I shall suggest belong wholly to the eighth century A.D.

The last point in this discussion is one that I mention with some diffidence; it is one on which I long enjoyed a spirited but friendly argument with the late Dr. W. Douglas Simpson. It was the ascription to St. Ninian which, in the first place, led Dr. Simpson to suggest that the excavations should take place. I find it impossible to believe[1] that this dedication is any older than the twelfth century, in which case it would belong to phase 4. It is, by current beliefs, quite out of the question that Ninian or his pre-Northumbrian episcopal successors in Galloway had anything to do with the north of Scotland, let alone Shetland. By the same token, the dedication in honour of St. Laurence (presumably the Spaniard who was martyred on a gridiron in the third century) at Papil must surely be connected with the medieval round-towered church. The caesura in Christian life which followed the Norse incursions was profound, as we know, and it is a fair assumption that most if not all of the pre-800 dedications (in honour of Columcille, or Cormac, or Brigid, or some Apostle or universal saint) were lost. Most of the early Christian sites in Orkney and Shetland are known to us only by such labels as Birsay, Deerness, Eynhallow, Kirkaby, and Papil; these are Norse locative and descriptive terms, not Irish or Pictish names involving original patrons or founders. We do not even, as far as I am aware, know the proper name of St. Ninian's Isle.

Composite stone shrines—an outline history

From the fifth century A.D. in Britain there is evidence that the bodies of saints—the principal corporeal relics—were prepared for veneration as visible and accessible remains. This involved an action called, in Latin sources, *translatio* or *commutatio*. At a period after death which could be anything from a few days to a century, but was often from five to ten years, the original grave—an extended inhumation, in a cist or a simple 'dug grave'—was opened, and the skeleton, sometimes with a desiccated integument, was uplifted. The remains were then enclosed in some form of box or structure, which was not then reburied, but was designedly left above ground, and visible, and was frequently sited above the original, filled-in, grave. They were enclosed in such a way that, either by removing the lid, or by gaining access through some lateral or end aperture, the actual bones could be seen, touched, and venerated.

This, part of the pre-Constantinian 'cult of martyrs', developed very swiftly and widely in the Mediterranean. It was in those lands central to the development of much church architecture. The shrines or martyrial tombs, constructed over elaborate and

----

[1] Thomas (1968), 117, n. 12, with earlier references, *contra* Dr. Simpson's writings.

partly open graves containing martyrs' bodies, were surrounded by little yards, *cellae* or *cellae memoriae*. These *cellae*, each with the *memoria* of a martyr or saint as its focus, could be developed into funerary chapels, around which could grow the great martyrial basilicas. At this stage, there is some reason to suppose[1] that the idea of the open-air unroofed *cella* containing a form of shrine reached southern Ireland by the end of the sixth century;[2] but the shrine, of a class I have called 'slab shrines', seems peculiar to Ireland and the only extension so far suspected comes from Galloway, an Irish-settled area (Ardwall Isle).[3]

In Britain, we must suppose a second and probably separate introduction of this particular Christian practice at some stage in the seventh century—I suspect, via Northumbria. Unlike the state of affairs in the Mediterranean, and almost certainly in Gaul and Iberia too, where in so many instances the church grew up around the existing martyrial shrine (which would, for instance, tend to dictate the exact position of the main altar), martyrial tombs and subsequent enshrinements in the British Isles appear to have been added to existing churches. The extensive, near-contemporary, literature alluding to this British habit—for example, the writings of Bede—not only makes this clear, but confirms that this must be a comparatively late introduction. This explains why people like Aidan, Cuthbert, and Chad (Ceadda) were buried alongside an (existing) altar, instead of having altars erected over their graves or martyrial tombs.

The first British shrines that we can notice are wooden ones. Thus Cuthbert, who died in 687, was exhumed and enshrined in 698, in a full-length wooden reliquary coffin; fragments of this decorated coffin of course survive now at Durham. Chad, who died in 672 at Lichfield, was later exhumed and translated, his grave being covered by some form of roof-shaped wooden superstructure with an access-hole, possibly like a Germanic *Totenmemoria*[4]—Bede's account, usually mistranslated, is not entirely clear.

We see, appropriately at a period when free-standing wooden crosses were being replaced by stone ones, and when fashions in ecclesiastical architecture were shifting from timber to masonry, a gradual transition to the stone shrine. Dr. Radford's reconstruction of certain fragments at Jedburgh into a roofed stone shrine, which he would date to *c.* 700 and would assign to the remains of Cuthbert's mentor, St. Boisil of Old Melrose, opens the series. This is a fairly direct translation from wood-working, reproducing in its grooved stone panels the kind of detail (i.e. basal tongue-and-groove joints, rebated vertical corner-joints) visible in Cuthbert's wooden shrine or reliquary coffin. So far, the Jedburgh 'grooved shrine' remains unique. Its eventual successors in

[1] Thomas (1971), ch. 5.
[2] Cf. examples in Henry (1957), e.g. 82, 98, 101.
[3] Thomas (1967*b*), 141–2.
[4] Dannheimer (1966).

northern and eastern Britain are, I think, the 'solid shrines' which must have stood above opened tombs—the Hedda Stone (*c.* 800) from Peterborough, the ninth-century 'St. Leonard's School Shrine' from St. Andrews, Fife, and at some stage there is a cousinly relationship with the Anglo-Danish hogback tomb covers.

The largest class of multi-piece stone shrine, the class to which the Papil and St. Ninian's Isle fragments all belong, is one characterized by possessing separate corner elements and separate side and end panels. Unlike the Chad (Lichfield), Jedburgh, and subsequent 'solid' shrines, the lids or roofs may have been flat, or at the most very slightly coped; certainly not brought to a steep ridge, in imitation of a structural roof. This stems from the fact that these 'corner-post' shrines are not translations from wooden prototypes at all, but are based on a hypothetical, *ad hoc,* ancestor which was in no sense a skeuomorph of a church or funerary chapel or house-shaped portable shrine, but was related to the Early Christian sarcophagi of western Europe and the Mediterranean.

The corner-posts, which range from roughly shaped pillars of any locally available and easily worked stone to neat and finished blocks of regular and rectangular cross-sections, are easily detected. They exhibit, on one, two (contiguous), or three faces, long shallow grooves, cut or chiselled an inch or so deep, and an inch or so wide. These grooves do not run the full height of the post's face. They stop well short of the foot or bottom, as the lower quarter or fifth part of each post must have been socketed into the ground for stability. They also stop short of the top, implying that the heads of corner-posts could rise a few inches clear of the end- and side-panels, and of any lid or roof; and the schemes of decoration found on certain corner-posts confirm this explanation.

A normal ('single') corner-post shrine will possess four such corner-posts, each with two grooved and adjacent faces. These grooves take the lateral edges of the two shorter sides ('ends') and the two longer sides ('sides')—all known single corner-post shrines are rectangular in plan. The end- and side-panels, which are flat shaped slabs of appropriate stone, have their lateral edges cut down slightly from the full vertical height—by trimming out all four corners—and the 'tongues' so produced are further thinned or chamfered (or both) so that they will engage easily in the grooves in the corner-posts. I know of no instance in which any sign of mortar can be detected, and presumably a corner-post shrine, once fitted together, was held rigid solely by the fixed corner-posts.

A 'double' corner-post shrine is one divided, on its shorter axis, into two equal compartments. Excluding the lid, a single corner-post shrine has eight components—four posts, four panels. A double one has thirteen. There are the four outer corner-posts, and the two end-panels (six pieces). The sides are interrupted by two opposed median posts, each of which has not two, but *three* grooves. The additional grooves face inward, and take the median partition panel. Each long side thus has three elements, the median post and the two half-side panels, which, with the median panel, makes seven pieces to add to the six listed above.

The stone double shrines have, so far, been found only in Shetland. The diagnostic element is the three-grooved median post, and it will be clear that where, as on St. Ninian's Isle, there are no less than three such, there must have been two double shrines. A possible wooden predecessor is mentioned by Bede (*Historia Abbatum*, cap. 20). In August 716 Abbot Hwaetberht of Monkwearmouth exhumed the skeletal remains of his saintly predecessors, Easterwine (d. 684) and Sigfrid (d. 689), and placed *both* lots of remains in one single reliquary coffin, separated by a partition in the middle (*sed medio pariete divisa*); this was then laid in St. Peter's Church, close to the altar, no doubt as a visible and accessible shrine. Bede, who is usually precise in his terminology, used the word *theca*, instead of *sarcofagus* (= a one-piece stone coffin), and he implies something made of wood.

What exactly went into these single and double corner-post shrines? We have a very few side-panels, which fortunately allow some generalized estimates of length. When St. Cuthbert was exhumed in 698, his body—for reasons which need not concern us—was declared to be incorrupt; the skeleton was still articulated, the remains of the body itself desiccated. His wooden shrine or reliquary coffin, which is internally at least 5 ft. by 15 in.—it has probably shrunk through time—was designed to take a more or less full-length and relatively undisturbed corpse. This cannot be taken as the norm. In the acid soils of most of Ireland and Highland Britain, all that would be recovered on *translatio* would be the skull and a jumble of the major bones. The shrine would house these, and its greater dimension, the length, would need only be long enough to house the longest bones, like the femora, and then possibly set diagonally. This is quite clear from the Irish 'slab shrines', which cover little hollows only three to four feet at their longest. In the case of the corner-post shrines, we are dealing (as the few surviving panels indicate) with single shrines having an internal area of at the most 3 ft. by 18 in., and with double shrines that are certainly no bigger than twice this length. No individual human bones normally exceed 20 in. in length and a disarticulated skeleton would easily pack into such a space.

The basic device employed in corner-post shrine construction is the (not very precise) insertion of the lateral tongues on panels into corresponding vertical grooves in corner-posts. This is directly copied from the construction of (*inter alia*) low multi-piece chancel-screens in early churches in the Mediterranean, Gaul, and Iberia. It is a survival from classical architectural technique, and can of course be executed with great precision and skill in such media as fine-grained marbles. This later deflexion to a funerary context appears to be entirely a British phenomenon, and any question of the date, or origin, of the Shetland corner-post shrines must hinge upon the solution of this puzzle. (For discussion see Thomas (1971), 159–63.)

The early chancel-screen was composed of a number of small square-sectioned pillars, often with decorative knobs or terminals (*hermulae*), between which and into which were slotted the square screen panels, *cancelli* or *transennae*. These last were often richly ornamented with fretwork or the finest relief carving. Doubtless, as with most aspects of classical architecture, this rests on some prehistoric transition from timberwork to stonework, but this would have been at least a millennium before the first British corner-post shrines.

The idea of the chancel-screen itself, the low division between the sanctuary in a church and the rest of the internal area, probably reached Ireland in the seventh century through the intermediacy of Spain, but various allusions permit the belief that, for many subsequent centuries, this was in Irish churches always expressed in wood. We are concerned with the transmission of this idea in stone, and must look to an independent source in Northumbria in the latter part of the seventh century. The techniques and works of actual continental masons and craftsmen, introduced by such notable figures as Benedict Biscop and Wilfrid, provide the obvious explanation, even if unquestioned fragments of stone chancel-screens have yet to be identified from Hexham, Ripon, Jarrow-Monkwearmouth, and other relevant churches of this age.

The adaptation of the post-and-panel technique (which was also used for other early Christian features, such as the *ambo* or pulpit, and certain elements of the earliest baptisteries) to a corner-post shrine may involve only a few steps. In the first, a shrine of some simple variety stands within a chancel-screen which, as in many Mediterranean basilica, is not a straightforward north–south line across the church but encloses a three-sided area. In the second, an extension of the screen is detached to surround the shrine, and given some form of lid. In the last, this extension stands by itself and constitutes the shrine. With this hypothetical sequence in mind, the remarkable knobs on the top of some of the St. Ninian's Isle Shrine *A* corner-posts will recall those even more prominent knobs which surmount many chancel-posts (e.g., as shown by Stojkovic (1957)).

The present known distribution of corner-post shrines is entirely North British. The only possible Irish instances (two) are very devolved and uncertain, and one of them is apparently of full medieval date. On the assumption that the type had fully developed within the Northumbrian church by 700, we can explain fragments of two found in the lands of the Picts—a side-panel and corner-post from an ancient burial-ground at

Burghead,[1] and a corner-post from Monifieth, Angus[2]—as likely to belong to the middle of the eighth century, and as material reflections of the influence of Northumbrian Christian practices among the Picts after 710—these included, as Bede records (*Hist. Eccles.* v. 21), the dispatch of skilled Northumbrian masons, *architecti*, to the southern Pictish area, and Dr. W. D. Simpson argued that the surviving Romanesque tower at Restenneth Priory, Angus, includes eighth-century stonework connected with this episode.[3]

There are two very crude little corner-posts from Iona, both unfortunately recovered from modern stone-piles. These can hardly be argued to represent some independent Hiberno-Scottish evolution of the corner-post shrine, in view of the multiplicity of Iona's external contacts in the seventh and eighth centuries. All other mainland British fragments known to me, certain or dubious, are Pictish. At St. Vigean's, Angus, a large (6 ft. by 3 ft.) cross-slab appears to have been cut down to a significant shape which may, in some fashion, have allowed it to stand at the end of (or even to form the end of) a composite stone shrine.[4] From Perthshire, there are three possibly unfinished or incomplete side-panels at Murthly, Dull, and Meigle (no. 10)—the last-named is now lost.[5] Unquestionably the finest, and latest, corner-post shrine in the great sculptured monument at St. Andrews, Fife.[6] Various dates and artistic sources have been proposed for this, and only limited comment need be made here. The sheer complexity of this shrine makes it highly unlikely that it dates much, if at all, before 800, but Isabel Henderson's recent arguments for an early ninth-century date, and connections with the vigorous figure-carving schools of Mercia, are certainly persuasive. Dr. Radford's reconstruction,[7] translated into visible terms by the (now) Department of the Environment, is in my opinion open to some argument. The idea of the steeply ridged 'roof' or lid was drawn mainly from the supposed analogy of the earlier Jedburgh shrine, which is actually a different class of monument altogether. Such evidence as we possess on these points indicates that corner-post shrines possessed flat lids, or lids whose bases were flat, and one cannot exclude the suggestion that, in the present reconstruction, the gabled St. Andrews lid goes beyond the strict evidence.

The final point in this preliminary discussion concerns the relative location of these shrines. Where did they stand in relation to any church? We cannot argue from the Irish 'slab shrines' which, like the unroofed Mediterranean *cellae*, were intended as

[1] Allen and Anderson (1903), iii, figs. 138 and 141 = Burghead nos. 7 and 11.

[2] Ibid. 228–9, fig. 241 = Monifieth no. 1.

[3] Simpson (1963).

[4] Allen and Anderson (1903), iii. 268, fig. 278 = St. Vigean's no. 7.

[5] Ibid. 306, fig. 321; 315, fig. 329; 331, fig. 344.

[6] Radford (1955b); Henderson (1967); Allen and Anderson (1903), iii. 351–3.

[7] Radford (1955b), *passim*.

open-air embellishments to some cemetery. The early Northumbrian evidence implies that shrines were normally within a church, the most favoured position being alongside the altar (in the south-east angle). Nor can the 'Founder's Tomb' (fig. 8) at St. Ninian's Isle be used to support the idea of an external position, since this is no more than a muddled, and probably very late, repositioning of corner-posts from two distinct shrines. I suspect that those shrines whose schemes of ornament, on the panels or on the faces of the posts or on both, demand a unilateral viewpoint, stood within a church or chapel, and moreover they must have stood against a wall; this would have afforded the necessary extra support. One suspects, too, that the usual position would be against the south wall, but this is conjecture. Nor should one ignore the possibility that, notably at Papil, there might have been more than one church or chapel; is it arguable that Papil Shrine C (fig. 7), if really found *in situ*, points to the site of such an additional structure?

2. THE SCULPTURED STONES AND CROSSES

(*Note*. In the descriptive passages which follow, as in the subsequent Catalogue (p. 33), all stones are assigned a fixed (arabic, italic) numeral. These appear also on the two site plans, figs. 7 and 8. The numbers from *1* to *22* refer to St. Ninian's Isle, and those from *23* to *36* to Papil.)

The shrines

The total number of shrine fragments, mainly corner-posts and median-posts, is (from both Papil and St. Ninian's Isle) no less than nineteen, of which four pieces are now lost. From St. Ninian's Isle, we have five corner-posts and median-posts, all originally of rectangular cross-section with beaded angles and knobbed tops (three corner-posts, two median-posts); two fragments of a plain side- or end-panel, showing the lateral tongue; and two further posts, one with three grooves (a median-post) and one with two only (a corner-post). It will be argued that the first five posts and perhaps the two panel fragments belong to one double shrine (St. Ninian's *A*—the stones are numbered *1* to *7*), and that the other two posts (*8*, *9*) belong to a second shrine, St. Ninian's *B*, which may also have been a double shrine since stone *8* is a three-grooved median post.

The material from Papil is not quite so easily sorted out. It begins with the well-known pictorial side-panel (*23*), which is the long side of a single shrine, and a corner-post (*24*), which is the only post that can be fairly certainly regarded as part of this same shrine (Papil *A*). Two surviving three-grooved median-posts (*25*, *26*) indicate a second shrine, a double one (Papil *B*). Stone *27* is a corner-post which probably belongs to the Papil *A* shrine. There is what appears to be the (decorated) top of another corner-post, *30*, but there is insufficient of it to assign it to either shrine.

A third shrine, which would have to be Papil *C*, is indicated by a lost[1] median-post, no. *29*. This was not only found stuck in the ground, with a human skull by its foot— cf. the Papil site-plan, fig. 7—but into it, according to Moar and Stewart, were still fitted three panels (*28*, *35*, *36*). All are now lost, but one of them, here called no. *28*, was still visible somewhere in the kirkyard in 1943, and may well be recovered yet. It was 2 in. thick, and 14 in. square, the lateral edges being reduced to tongues by removing a corner (2 in. by $1\frac{1}{2}$ in.) at both bottom angles. These are careful and reliable measurements made by Moar and Stewart at the time and they constitute acceptable evidence.

We thus have parts of two double shrines (*A*, *B*) from St. Ninian's Isle; and from Papil part of a single shrine (*A*), of a double one (*B*), and apparently evidence for a third, also double (*C*). Nor is this affected by the demonstration (below) that both St. Ninian's Isle shrines may have begun as single ones, 'doubled up' in a secondary phase. By any standards, this is a remarkable assemblage of ecclesiastical stone monuments, unparalleled in either Britain or Ireland.

In reconstructing (on paper) these various shrines, I have worked from very detailed measurements (to $\frac{1}{8}$ in.) and from an extensive range of photographs. One useful principle is that the grooves, when opposed to each other in any reconstruction, should not only be of approximately the same length (to within an inch), but should also begin at approximately the same distance below the top of the post (top = flat shoulder, ignoring any upstanding boss, as in *1* to *5*). This at once has the effect of dissociating fragments that cannot possibly have fitted together, and thereby narrows the choice. The diagrams (figs. 9 to 11) are to scale, where the posts are concerned, but make no attempt, save for Papil *A*, to reconstruct the overall plan; stone *23* is the only complete panel. The drawings of the ornamented faces are mainly taken from rubbings, checked from photographs. In all subsequent discussion, faces will be cited as in the diagrams (figs. 9 to 13); thus, *5.a* means 'stone no. *5*, face *a*, as shown in fig. 9', and the same code is of course employed in the Catalogue and in the illustrations.

St. Ninian's Isle—Shrine A

The five posts assigned to this construction are of a light-coloured sandstone. All have been dressed to an approximate rectangular section, leaving the base rough, and the angles are emphasized by vertical channels or grooves just inside the edges. It is possible

---

[1] Cf. Moar and Stewart (1943–4), 94.

that the two panel pieces, *6* and *7*, belong to this, and in fig. 10 they are used to give the idea of the panel thickness only.

As set out, it is obvious that stones *1* to *4* form a set; stone *5* is the odd man out. The section of the grooves on *2.b* and *4.a* is shallower, more curved, less carefully executed than on all other grooved faces of stones *1* to *4*, but is matched by both grooves on stone *5*. Similarly, the actual grooves on *2.b* and *4.a* start much further down the faces, and are shorter. I would conclude that this shrine began as a single, four-post, one, to which two more posts (*5*, and the missing one) were added *en suite*—for *5* also has a shallow round boss on top—in order to make it into a double shrine.

In every case, the top of the groove stops well short, $4\frac{1}{2}$ to 5 in., below the flat shoulder. The implication is that this shrine had a flat lid, possibly as shown by the small fragment of a flattish slab (*20*) which is only just over 2 in. thick; fig. 10. This would have to be notched, as shown, to fit the shrine, and a new lid would have been required on the extension to a double compartment. The point is that a lid of this thickness would not obscure the upper ornamental panel on *5.a*, which must have been designedly visible.

The scheme of decoration implies that the short end formed by *1.d* and *3.b* was in some sense 'the front'. There is no trace of any ornament at all on *2.b* and *4.a*, and, as a single shrine, this end may have stood against a wall-face. The face, *2.a*, is decorated, and there must be at least an assumption that the corresponding face *4.b* was also decorated; but unhappily this face has been fractured, a great flake of about an inch in depth having removed most of its upper half. All the summit bosses are also extremely worn, that on *3* being almost wholly eroded, and only the boss on *2* now shows any ornament; but no trace of any can be seen on *1*, *4*, or *5*.

As a double shrine, one cannot argue that this stood against a wall, because *5.c* is ornamented. The two phases of construction—single, *1* to *4*; then doubled, with *5* and a missing one—may then imply two separate positions.

The ornament (fig. 12) is of great interest. It has all been carried out in a technique that I have called[1] 'the broad-pocked line', done with a mallet and some tool of the punch, rather than chisel, kind, the channel being then evened-out by rubbing or reaming. A good impression of the original effect is given by face *1.a*, lower portion, which seems to have been preserved by burial; most of the ornamented faces are sadly worn.

The disposition of the motifs preserves a subtle, and I think intentional, balance. Faces *3.b* and *1.d*, the 'important' end, both have S-scrolls, on *3.b* set vertically and linked by a neat junction, on *1.d* set horizontally. A rather inept double spiral, perhaps added, occurs below the S-scrolls on *3.b*.

[1] Thomas (1967*b*), 152–3, 176.

The two side-faces, flanking this end, are similarly not quite a balanced pair. Face *3.a* shows a pair of opposed 'S-dragons', as I have described[1] these beasts; they are sparring with each other, and their tails form *out-turned* spirals, two similar spirals being repeated below like additional tails. The corresponding *1.a* is terribly worn and is here drawn out with some reserve, from rubbings and photographs, but again it appears to show two S-dragons, whose tails are *in-turning* spirals; treating each tail as one 'leg', the other legs and the forelimbs are very crudely interlaced. Immediately below the dragons is a triquetra knot (fig. 12).

We cannot discuss the flaked-off face *4.b*, but on the side formed by posts *1* and *2* the scheme continued with a new emphasis. Face *2.a* has a schematic cross, indicated by four hollows set in a diamond shape, and below this are three smaller hollows, set two over one, an inverted triangle again like the placing of the triquetra on *1.d*. The new emphasis is thus the idea of *three*, and this is continued on the decorated boss of stone *no. 2*, which has a simple triskele-type motif (fig. 12).

The added corner-post, *5*, displays on the uppermost part of *5.a* a muddled little design, perhaps intended to be a double spiral, which, to anyone viewing the whole shrine from the end formed by stones *1* and *3*, is in general accord with the S-scrolls on *1.d* and *3.b*; and *5.a* was meant to be seen above the lid. The outer face of stone *5*, that is, *5.c*, has a simple cross, the sunken fields between the arms showing reserved pellets or roundels.

It must be said at once that this ornamentaion, even if necessarily here expressed in somewhat rough outline, points unhesitatingly in the direction of eastern Scotland and of Northumbria, owes little or nothing to the early art of Iona and the Irish missions, has distinct affinities with the styles seen on the Pictish Class II (cross-ornamented) symbol stones, and in my opinion is no earlier than the eighth century. For any ornament executed at St. Ninian's Isle, or Papil, before 700, we must look to a handful of the primary cross-slabs or grave-markers, which are (in contrast) executed in another technique. At this juncture, one might offer some comment on the iconography, as opposed to art-historical analysis *per se*, or to chronological inferences drawn from such analysis.

We are entitled, since the Cross began to appear on Christian grave-markers and other ecclesiastical stones in western Britain and Ireland around 600, to expect that a composite stone shrine of a century and a half later, housing the bones of a Christian saint, would at least display a Cross; and we have seen that it occurs twice (*2.a*, *5.c*). There is little point in speculating as to whether the triune motifs on the long side (*1*, *2*, *5*) possessed,

---

[1] Thomas (1961), 53–6.

then or later, Trinitarian significance, but I admit that the particular face *2.a* lacks parallel among several hundred examples of cross-marked stone faces. What is less easy to grasp is the import of the two faces (*1.a*, *3.a*) which display S-dragons. It is impossible now to grasp the thinking behind their inclusion, but a short digression may explain why even these odd beasts are not wholly irrelevant on such a monument.

The S-dragon is one of several composite animals—the so-called 'Pictish elephant' is another—found widely in post-Roman art in Britain and Ireland, and often quite at home in a bestiary[1] dominated by naturalistic animals and birds. In its seventh- and eighth-century North British guise, it is, as here, usually given a wide-jawed head, cross between dog and seal, short forelimbs, and a spiral tail; it is usually shown upright, and head, body and tail form a kind of vertical S-scroll. On metalwork (as opposed to stone), and generally in Ireland, the jaws become elongated, the eye large, and all four limbs appear, the spiral aspect being confined to limb-joints. Later still, when in pairs wholly or partially intertwined, S-dragons cannot be separated from 'interlaced animals' and are indeed the same thing, but one must now go back to the origins.

The North British, later specifically Pictish, S-dragon originates in depictions of the ram-horned or animal-headed serpent of pagan Celtic religion, an awesome Being who could be associated with the horned god *Cernunnos*[2] but who possessed some claim to independent divine status. This creature was taken northwards during the late pre-Roman Iron Age, and emerged in what is now Scotland in three-dimensional form as the great bronze armlets, with double terminals of long-horned serpents, of so-called 'Caledonian metalwork'[3] in the period A.D. 50 to 150. A parallel northern manifestation, also 'geminated' (i.e. having a head at either end), is seen in the well-known dragonesque brooch series.[4] In the earliest lithic art of the Picts, that of the Class I symbol stones, we find both the 'snake symbol', having cephalic bulges and markings which are neither eyes nor maxillae but vestigial flat horns; and probably influenced in shape and detail by such Roman and late classical monsters as the hippocamp and the stylized dolphin, the Pictish S-dragon as well.[5]

The appearance of two pairs of opposed S-dragons on the St. Ninian's Isle shrine goes directly with a similar pair on what may have been a shrine-panel[6] from Murthly, in Perthshire; and, singly or in pairs, on a large number of 'Pictish Class II' (that is, Christian) cross-slabs, dating from the late seventh and eighth centuries onwards.[7] There is a further devolution, on some west Scottish slabs and free-standing crosses of even later

[1] Thomas (1961), figs. 11 and 13.
[2] Ross (1967), ch. iii; 298, 344 ff.
[3] Simpson, M. (1968).
[4] Feachem (1951).

[5] Cf. Thomas (1961), 53–6.
[6] Allen and Anderson (1903), iii. 306, fig. 321.
[7] Ibid., figs. 29, 30, 162, 232, 310a, 318, 359.

date,[1] into mere S-scrolls without any animal or serpentine features at all. From Ireland, a fine pair of opposed S-dragons occur below an early cross-incised slab[2] at Caher Island, Co. Mayo.

What does this mean in understandably Christian terms? We are seeing, I think, this creature surviving the transition from paganism to Christianity because of its original and popular role; a role which, as Mircea Eliade, Anne Ross, and a few other percipient students have shown, was that of a *guardian*. The ram-headed serpent was the custodian of treasure, of knowledge, of the Sacred Tree; the averter of external and threatening evil, the avenger of wrongs done. This would at least offer an economical explanation for all the various forms of brooch and bracelet, all of which will have had an apotropaic function; in a much more developed form one sees this in the S-dragons, strung out around the periphery or enmeshed in the filigree panels, on such pieces as the so-called Tara brooch. On grave-markers and tomb-slabs, and *a fortiori* on anything like a composite stone shrine housing the mortal relics of some saint, these S-dragons are unswerving guardians. We see them, surely, on the St. Ninian's Isle shrine in this capacity, two vigilant pairs, obeying the unspoken command *Depositum custodite*.

St. Ninian's Isle—Shrine B

The second shrine (fig. 11) is represented by only two posts, which cannot be fitted into the scheme of Shrine *A*. They are assumed to go together, because, unlike all the *A* posts, they are of rounded section and have rounded tops, and as set out in the reconstruction are of the same thickness.

This again can be argued to be a shrine which began as a single one, *8* and *9* forming diagonally opposite corners, and which was converted into a double form by the groove on *8.c*. It must be pointed out that this last groove is all the evidence we have, and as it is of the same length and in the same position as the grooves on *8.a* and *8.d* it may be no more than an abandoned first attempt. Nor can it be shown, given that *8* and *9* form two corners of a rectangle, which way that rectangle's longer axis ran.

Papil—Shrine A

The first Papil shrine, characterized by the ornamented figure-scene side-panel (*23*), is a single one. Reconstruction has been confused by its discovery, as reported;[3] for, perhaps as a result of medieval piety, this panel had been incorrectly set up, its lateral edges slotted into *26* (which is part of Papil Shrine *B*) and into *27.d* instead of *27.c*.

---

[1] Ibid., figs. 118, 263.   [2] Henry (1947).   [3] Moar and Stewart (1943–4); and cf. fig. 13.

Only a partial reassembly can be suggested with the extant fragments (fig. 13). The lateral tongues of *23* are $13\frac{1}{2}$ (left) and $13\frac{1}{8}$ (right) in. in height, which excludes several posts and post-faces that possess grooves of insufficient length. As shown in fig. 13, the posts *27* and *24* are, despite the variation in size, both slightly and noticeably chamfered, and although the upper few inches of *24* are missing, it appears to have a groove (on *24.d*) of appropriate length, position, and shape.

The ornament (fig. 12) is impressive. On *27* there is one face with a reserved boss (*27.b*), while *27.a* has a design of a long-stemmed cross with expanded terminals, its upper arm flanked by the lower part of what I take to be a pair of addorsed (or opposed) and stylized S-dragons. This, with the broad-pocked execution, links this shrine to St. Ninian's Isle *A*.

The figure-scene on *23.a* occupies a slightly sunk area, roughly 35 in. across and 13 in. high, which commences only $1\frac{1}{2}$ in. below the slightly rounded upper edge. The scene is described and figured by Moar and Stewart[1] and has since appeared in a number of works. The ornament is reserved against a pocked-away background, about $\frac{1}{8}$ in. deep, and details have been incised; the reserved portions are partly in skilful relief.[2] Like many of the equally impressive scenes involving human figures on Pictish Class II stones, this cannot be mere decoration, but has a narrative tone. A distinct possibility is that it commemorates the introduction of Christianity to these northern regions, and may convey some such message as 'Holy men, carrying gospel books (or portable altars) in satchels, with an elderly saint (or bishop—the rider), came across the sea, to a place where they set up the Cross'. The continuous frieze of relief double-spirals, again recalling the motifs on St. Ninian's Isle stones *1*, *3*, and *5*, here portrays the waves, and it should be noted that the Cross itself, probably a stone one standing in its massive base-socket, would be among our earliest pieces of evidence for a free-standing cross of this size in pre-Norse times.

Papil: Shrine B

The two median-posts (fig. 13) numbered *25* and *26* are both quite plain. One of them, at least, must belong to a double shrine we can call *B*; and despite the difference in their sizes we must for the moment allow that they go together.

Papil: Shrine C

We are still obliged to explain certain other fragments. The median-post *26* was found in 1943 affixed to the panel *23*, to which it cannot really belong; it is so shown by Moar

---

[1] Moar and Stewart (1943–4), pls. v, vi.   [2] Ibid. 92, an excellent description.

and Stewart.[1] It is uncertain where *25* was recovered. The account[2] makes it clear that *five* posts in all were found—*24, 25, 26,* and *27,* and one now missing, which we can call *29.* This was a third median-post, with three grooves; and it, or else *25,* was found with three panels stuck sign-post fashion into its three grooves, and moreover with a human skull in one of the angles so formed. One of the panels was the small plain piece, 14 in. square with two lateral tongues, already mentioned (p. 21 *supra*), seen in 1943, and here numbered *28.*

This second double-shrine, involving the lost median-post *29,* the lost panel *28,* and apparently two further panels, also lost (*35, 36*), cannot be explained away. Its existence does not, however, account for yet another Papil stone, *30.* This is a neatly rounded top of a rectangular-section pillar, quite possibly a post despite its thinness (cf. St. Ninian's Isle *5*), and bearing, on *30.a,* a simple curvilinear ornament ending in two little spirals which is wholly in keeping with the decoration already discussed. It would be going beyond permissible inference to suppose that a fourth shrine existed, and *30* may belong to one of the shrines already listed; but there is no evidence as to which that may have been.

Chronology of the shrines

The evidence presented in fig. 9 and on p. 22 may be taken to support the idea that ornamented single shrines initiate the Shetland series—St. Ninian's Isle *A,* before extension, and Papil *A*—and that double shrines follow them. St. Ninian's Isle *B,* Papil *B,* and Papil *C* are all undecorated and are all, also, less carefully executed. This is, broadly, in accord with the Northumbrian evidence rehearsed earlier. Enshrinements, either in monuments of this class, or in wooden predecessors, were taking place in the later seventh and early eighth centuries, and we may perhaps possess stone fragments of such from Pictland proper. But these are all single shrines, and our first and only reference to a double shrine with median panel, and then in wood, comes from Bede for the year 716.[3]

The appropriate chronological horizons in Shetland would be the advent of Christianity—arguably in the early seventh century, more probably in the mid seventh, most improbably before A.D. 600—and the main phase of Norse settlement from the end of the eighth century. Enshrinements would, by their nature, not be primary events. One must allow the missionaries to grow old and to die, and then to rest in hallowed ground for a period. Arguments based on the art-historical element here represented tend to be little more than personal opinions, since they would take us back to the art of the

[1] Ibid., pl. v.   [2] Ibid. 94.   [3] Bede, *Historia Abbatum,* 20.

Pictish Class II stones, themselves by no means free from controversy as to absolute dates. On the other hand, I have explained at some length[1] why I regard the 'broad-pocked line' technique as (a) succeeding an incised-line technique, and (b) commencing in the eighth century, and it will be clear below that both techniques are represented in Shetland. The form of the S-dragons, the triquetra knot on stone 1, and even the incised outline cross on 15 (see below) cannot be far off A.D. 700. My conclusion, for the moment, is that the single shrines belong to the early or middle eighth century, the double shrines to the middle or later eighth century, and that the decline in workmanship could reflect the absence of skilled masons, the unsettled times associated with the first isolated Norse raids, or both if they are connected. If the art be predominantly Pictish, the shrines are an innovation from Pictish Christianity under Northumbrian influence, and on this last ground none may actually be earlier than *circa* 725 or so.

St. Ninian's Isle—primary cross-slabs and grave-markers

I have elsewhere suggested[2] that, in regions of Britain and Ireland where the tradition of the inscribed memorial tombstone was absent, physical commemoration of the Christian dead in stone begins only at the end of the sixth century. It can be argued that this may have been preceded by a phase of commemoration with forms of wooden markers, but this cannot be demonstrated archaeologically. The 'primary' stones, which are for the most part pre-Norse, are small and plain; they can be divided into *grave-markers*, usually pebbles or irregular fragments marked with a cross and laid over the head (?) of the deceased, and *cross-slabs*, similarly decorated slabs or little pillars which are thought to have stood upright at one end of the grave.

Unlike the composite stone shrines, this is essentially a western and north-western facet of post-Roman Britain, the source being apparently Ireland, and the spread a reflection of the work of Irish monastic missions. The crosses themselves[3] are of a limited range of linear forms, and are usually incised with a knife or point.

To this class must be assigned stone 10, a flat slab 14 in. by 8 in., which has a small incised linear cross with barred terminals; stone 11, which is a cross-slab 25 in. long, and was probably associated with the oriented long cists (see fig. 8); and stone 15, broken, but probably about 7 in. by 25 in. The last was found, face-downwards, over the silver hoard, and it thus affords a useful chronological terminus.

Stone 10 is an early form—some parallels are set out in the Catalogue—and may be as early as Christianity in Shetland; certainly *circa* 700, if not a little older. Stones 11 and 15 should belong to the eighth century, perhaps not before the second quarter; for 11 is

---

[1] Thomas (1967b).   [2] Ibid. 174.   [3] Ibid., fig. 37, top.

not incised, but rather crudely pocked; and *15*, though incised, bears an 'armpit' cross of Northumbrian type which is not likely to have been introduced until *c.* 725 or later.

Papil—primary cross-slabs and grave-markers

Only two stones from Papil can be regarded as gravestones of pre-Norse date, and neither is particularly simple. No. *32* is the rounded-off top of a slab, measuring perhaps two or three feet long by an average 13 in. wide and 1 in. thick. It was found in the region of the shrine components (fig. 7). There is an interlaced cross with a central ring and splayed terminals,[1] the general effect being very reminiscent, on the one hand, of the Northumbrian 'name-stones' (formerly 'pillow-stones', etc.), on the other, of the art of the Irish recumbent cross-slabs. Again, this is unlikely to be older than the middle of the eighth century, but can go, with the shrines, as a clue to Northumbrian ecclesiastical ideas in Shetland.

The second stone (*33*) is the so-called 'Burra' or 'Papil Stone', well known and often discussed.[2] It is a large, thin, upright slab of reddish sandstone with a rounded head. The face bears a cross with narrowed shaft, the head being patté, with knots of interlace in the angles of the arms, and in the two lower spandrels. Flanking the cross shaft are two panels, each with two inward-processing ecclesiastics, and a continuous oval knot marks the lower part of the shaft. Beneath this is a rectangular panel containing an animal which closely resembles the so-called 'animal symbols' of Pictish art, but whose only glyptic parallel[3] is not the Pictish wolf but a dog incised on the wall of Jonathan's Cave, Fife. This concludes the original schema, but on the lower part of the face, set a little obliquely and almost certainly added at a later stage, is a curious scene, where two spindly cloaked men with crane's heads, carrying Germanic T-axes, peck at an affronted human head.

There is no point in discussing whether or not this stone belongs to the seventh century. This is a sophisticated monument, at least as late as the Papil *A* shrine panel, with which it has clear affinities (e.g., the ecclesiastics, and the combination of pocking, incising, and low relief). Whatever the original of the 'dog', or 'lion', may be, it points to Pictland for its counterparts, whether as scroll-jointed beasts on Pictish Class II stones or as the related creatures in Hiberno-Northumbrian MSS. of the late seventh and eighth centuries. I would be inclined to see the Papil Stone as the grave of some notable, erected not before 750, but probably within the following generation. It gives

---

[1] Moar and Stewart (1943–4), 92–3, pl. v.
[2] Allen and Anderson (1903), iii. 10–15, figs. 5–9, with refs.; Stevenson (1955), 115.
[3] Cf. Thomas (1961), 23, fig. 6c; 48, fig. 11.

us a clear idea of what might have been done in Shetland, had Christian art and Christian ideas been permitted to expand and to develop.

St. Ninian's Isle—Christian Norse and medieval monuments

Six further stones from St. Ninian's Isle—one of them medieval, the others not obviously so—constitute the next phase. It is obviously impossible to be dogmatic as to whether or not surviving Shetland Christians continued to make, and to erect, cross-marked stones during the ninth and tenth centuries, and it is by no means certain precisely at what stage we can expect Christian Norsemen to have built, or rebuilt, local chapelries or to have reopened Early Christian graveyards. The five stones (*12–14, 16, 17*; pls. ix–xi) are, however, taken to be the work of Christian Norsemen, unlikely in Shetland to be before the mid-eleventh century. This assumption rests on three things: Firstly, as was shown earlier (p. 12), the chapel on St. Ninian's Isle was unquestionably rebuilt, but apparently not before the late eleventh or twelfth century A.D.; and no structural phase can be seen between this horizon and the eighth century. Secondly, all these five stones are made from steatite, which may be from the Cunningsburgh steatite quarries on the east side of the main island, may be from some slightly nearer source, but is not found on the Isle itself; and the quarrying of steatite is a well-documented Norse activity.[1] Thirdly, whether or not these stones are of Christian Norse date, they are typologically most unlikely to belong to the Early Christian (pre-Norse) age.

Stones *12, 13*, and *14*, which seem to be from three separate and broken slabs, are best regarded as forms of recumbent slabs. They are 2 to 3 in. thick, neatly chisel-dressed from steatite, of an odd shape, and outlined by a shallow chiselled groove about 1 in. from the edge. No. *12* is plain, and must be the lower end of a slab; the other two bear similar crosses, formed by shallow grooves about $1\frac{1}{2}$ in. across.

No immediate parallels come to mind, and the greatly simplified execution of these rustic slabs may conceal much more sophisticated models. For the border groove, one is inclined to look to the very late (tenth and eleventh century) recumbent slabs at major Irish sites (Glendalough, Clonmacnois, or Inis Cealtra) and perhaps at Iona; the groove represents the double-line rectangular frame surrounding the central cross.[2]

Stone *16* is, by contrast, the head of a small standing cross, with slightly expanded arms and a hint of circular depressions (hardly the semi-circular 'armpits') at the angles. The shaft is missing. What seem to be much earlier versions of such tiny crosses can be seen[3] from Ardwall Isle, where, however, direct Northumbrian inspiration and an eighth-century date could be argued. All that can be said here is that this is a tradition which could be long-lived (and, for that matter, has continued to the present day).

[1] Hamilton (1956), 206 ff.   [2] Lionard (1961), fig. 26.   [3] Thomas (1967b), 156, fig. 31.

Stone *17* (pl. xi) is a steatite hogback grave-cover, almost 4 ft. in length, neatly and regu-larly made. It is without parallel in Shetland and bears no ornament at all. The flattened cross-section may point to a late date in the hogback tomb series[1] and there is no reason why this should not be of the late eleventh or twelfth century.

The only slab which can be called medieval (*sensu* of the twelfth century or later) is no. *18*, found face downwards in 1956 within the nave (cf. fig. 8) and perhaps assignable to a burial within the (enlarged) church. It is a large flat slab, bearing the incised outline of a long-shafted, and long-headed, cross, and is now affixed to the wall of the vestibule in Bigton Established Church, on the mainland not far from the Isle. For this, one would compare the Galloway series,[2] but assume a date of at least the twelfth century, if not a little later.

Papil—Christian Norse and medieval monuments

Under this head comes a single object, stone *34*. This is a large reddish sandstone slab, over 5 ft. long, 2 in. thick, and 15 in. wide. It was noticed in 1877 lying in the kirkyard.[3] This again, despite the variation of a central circle and a stepped base, is essentially a slab in the tradition of no. *18* and must also be regarded as of the twelfth century, or later.

Miscellaneous objects

We need not discuss either the ogham-inscribed fragment[4] from St. Ninian's Isle (here, no. *19*), or a small rune-inscribed fragment[5] from Papil (here, no. *31*; pl. xv), save to notice, as Mr. Tom Henderson points out, that either or both could have started as fragments of shrine-panels or lids. There are, however, two further pieces, *21* and *22*, from St. Ninian's Isle, that merit passing comment.

No. *22* (pl. xi) is a (split) pillar of local stone, a foot high and originally 7 to 8 in. square. One end bears a shallow hollow, about 5 in. across and 1 in. deep. The stone is said to have been found within the chapel, and to have had 'traces of mortar on the back' (i.e. on the remaining long side). It is a small medieval cresset, the hollow being to receive oil for a floating lamp-wick. As a type, this falls within the range of medieval pillar cressets recently discussed, for the south of Britain, by Canon John Adams.[6]

No. *21* is a tiny fragment of marble, of *porfido verde antico* (mottled, but predomi-nantly in green hues), found within the centre of the nave. Although it was regarded by the excavators as the corner of a portable altar, this is not the explanation. There are indeed a few medieval portable altars or super-altars of this, or similar stone, employed

[1] Collingwood (1927), 164 ff.
[2] Thomas (1967*b*), fig. 30.
[3] Goudie (1880–1), 204, fig. 2; Allen and Anderson (1903), iii. 15.
[4] Allen and Anderson (1903), iii. 18, fig. 13, with refs.
[5] Moar (1951–2).
[6] Adams (1967).

as *cippi* to seal a central relic-cavity; but *21* has no consecration cross, and is furthermore not a corner, but a broken rectangle, $1\frac{1}{2}$ in. wide and 2 in. or more long, and about $\frac{5}{8}$ in. thick. The most likely function is as one of a series of inset panels in some kind of shrine, or portable reliquary. By a strange coincidence, the writer noticed another piece, of identical material, 1 in. wide and 2 in. or more long, but only $\frac{1}{4}$ in. thick, at Kilberry Castle, Argyll. Miss Campbell of Kilberry states[1] that this came from the remains of a medieval chapel just by the castle, and it affords confirmation that imported fragments of this kind were circulating in Scotland in the Middle Ages.

Summary

Despite the absence of any full excavation record, an aid to the understanding of these stones of which the excavator's untimely death has robbed us for ever, it can be seen that the various shrines and cross-slabs do fall into known categories, and in our increased knowledge of the archaeology of Early Christian Britain, it is possible to view them against a much wider selection of types. The most noteworthy aspect, to my mind, is the indication that (even if Christianity were first introduced to the Northern Isles from the western coast and by Irish or Irish-trained clerics) Shetland in the eighth century A.D. was looking to Pictland, and beyond Pictland to Northumbria, for artistic, and we may suppose ecclesiastical, ideas. Not hitherto mentioned, but certainly supporting this thesis, is of course the record of Class I (Pictish) symbol-stones, the pictographic memorials of deceased Picts, in the Northern Isles. There are quite a few in Orkney, and at least one is known[2] from Shetland; to this may be added depictions of symbols, or partial symbols, on stone and bone objects from Jarlshof and one or two other Shetland sites.[3] Further, the unusual portrayals of human figures on the Papil shrine-panel and the 'Papil stone' may be foreshadowed by the slightly earlier stone from Birsay, Orkney, with its three Pictish warriors and four Class I symbols.[4]

The St. Ninian's Isle and Papil stones thus add very materially to our knowledge. They also underline one urgent need—the recovery of one of these composite stone shrines (all known examples of which are represented by fragments from secondary positionings at the best), both *in situ* and by some skilled excavator cognizant with all the problems of Early Christian archaeology. As it is likely that a good many more shrines await discovery, this is not a forlorn hope. In the meantime, it is obvious that all worked stones on all such sites should be most carefully examined, since it is equally likely that parts of panels and of grooved posts have in the past been consigned to the

[1] Campbell and Sandeman (1962-3), 78, no. 488.

[2] From Sandness; Allen and Anderson (1903), iii. 4, fig. 2.

[3] Listed and shown in Thomas (1964), 44–8.

[4] Radford (1962), 168, pl. xi.

stone-dump through ignorance and inadvertence. At least we can now be aware of what we are looking for, and can examine all such finds with increased interest.

3. DESCRIPTIVE CATALOGUE OF THE STONES

1. St. Ninian's Isle; found 1957 in the 'Founder's Tomb' feature. Decorated corner-post, in light-coloured sandstone. Height 32 in.; dressed to a rectangular cross-section of 8 to 8½ in. by 6 to 6½ in. On the flattish top, a small round upstanding knob has been nearly chipped off.

All four faces are dressed roughly flat. Face *b* has a groove, 1½ in. wide, 1⅜ in. deep, 20 in. long, starting 5 in. below the top of the stone. On face *c* the corresponding measurements are 1½, 1½, and 20 in., also starting 5 in. below the top of the stone.

Faces *a* and *d* are framed by narrow pocked grooves which form continuous borders. Face *a* has a very worn design, showing two opposed S-dragons with interlaced limbs, above a triquetra; the design is partly in low relief and partly pocked out. On face *d*, the upper half of which is largely eroded, a series of continuous S-spirals executed in a broad pocked line.

Figs. 9 and 12, pl. iii. Part of St. Ninian's Isle, shrine 'A'.

2. St. Ninian's Isle; found 1957 in an inner corner of the 'Founder's Tomb' feature. Decorated three-grooved median-post, in light-coloured sandstone. Height 33½ in., with rounded irregular base; cross-sections roughly 8 by 5¾ in. On the flattish top is an upstanding decorated flat-topped knob or boss, 1 in. high, 5 in. diameter at the top tapering to 5½ in. diameter around its base.

All four faces are roughly dressed, face *a* noticeably so. Face *b* has a groove, 1½ in. wide, 1 in. deep, almost 15 in. long, commencing 5 in. below the shoulder. Corresponding measurements for face *c* are 1½, 1¼, 21, and 4 in.: for face *d*, 1⅜, 1⅜, 18, and 4½ in. On face *a*, there are four small pecked circular hollows arranged in diamond form, above three smaller hollows in an inverted triangle. The uppermost hollow is 4 in. below the shoulder, and face *a* is outlined in a continuous narrow pocked groove. The summit of the knob or boss is worn, but shows in rather clumsy relief a sort of triskele pattern.

Figs. 8, 9, and 12, pls. iii and iv. Part of St. Ninian's Isle, shrine 'A'.

3. St. Ninian's Isle; found 1957 in the 'Founder's Tomb' feature. Decorated corner-post, in light-coloured sandstone. Height 34 in., with irregular base; cross-section variable, 8 to 8½ in. by an average 6 in. On the flattish top is a small upstanding boss, rather worn, oval in plan, now 1¼ in. high.

Faces *c* and *d* bear grooves. On face *c* the groove is 1½ in. wide, 1⅛ in. deep, 20 in. long, and starts 8 in. below the shoulder. Corresponding measurements for face *d* are 1⅝, 1¼, 22, and 3¾ in.

Faces *a* and *b* are outlined by continuous narrow pocked grooves. On face *a* the design is a pair of opposed S-dragons, with double (two-tier) spiral tails, partly in relief and partly in pocked lines. On face *b*, the pocked design is a complex one, involving partly connected vertical S-spirals, finished rather uncertainly at the base.

Figs. 9 and 12, pl. iv. Part of St. Ninian's Isle, shrine 'A'.

Cf. also: *The Times*, 31 July 1958, p. 8 (photograph); *Illus. London News*, 23 August 1958, p. 301 (photograph).

4. St. Ninian's Isle; found 1957 in the 'Founder's Tomb' feature. Plain three-grooved median-post, in light-coloured sandstone. Height 32 in., with irregular base; cross-section is 8½ to 9 in. by 6 to 6½ in. On the flattish top is what remains of a small upstanding boss, now almost worn flat.

Faces *a*, *c*, and *d* are grooved. Face *a* has a groove 1½ in. wide, 1⅛ in. deep,. 14¾ in. long, commencing 10 in. below the shoulder. Corresponding measurements for face *c* are 1¼, 1⅜, almost 23, and 5 in.; for face *d*, 1½, 1⅜, 20, and 5 in.

The upper part of the plain face, *b*, is missing, a flake some 10 to 11 in. long, and up to 1 in. thick, having broken off here.

Fig. 9, pl. v. Part of St. Ninian's Isle, shrine 'A'.

5. St. Ninian's Isle; found 1957 in the 'Founder's Tomb' feature. Decorated corner-post, in light-coloured sandstone. Height 20 in. at least (the base of the stone is irregularly fractured); the cross-section varies from 8 in. by 5 in. (near the base) to 7 in. by 4 in. (near the top).

Faces *a* and *c* are decorated, face *a* being, in addition, grooved (as in face *d*). On face *a* the groove is 1½ in. wide, just over 1 in. deep, 15½ in. long, and commences 4½ in. below the shoulder; the corresponding measurements on face *d* are 1½, 1¼, 15½, and 4½ in. The stone is surmounted by a small plain knob or boss, 3 in. diameter and ½ in. high.

On face *a* the ornament occurs above the groove; an arc, terminating in two inward-turning spirals, is carried out in a pocked line, and enclosed in a narrow pocked groove. The same partial pocked-groove border encloses the upper part of face *b*, and also face *d* (above the main panel groove). On face *c* the ornament takes the form of a cross, in relief, with a raised pellet in each angle; this is much worn.

Figs. 8, 9, and 12, pl. v. Part of St. Ninian's Isle, shrine 'A'.

6. St. Ninian's Isle; found during the excavations. Fragment of a shrine panel, in fine white sandstone.

This is a small piece, 7 in. long, dressed roughly flat on the upper face, and about 2½ in. thick. It is cut away along the upper angle of this dressed face, to produce a tongue, 1¼ in. thick, and about 1½ in. out from the main part of the stone.

Fig. 10, pl. vi. Part of St. Ninian's Isle, shrine 'A'?

7. St. Ninian's Isle; found during the excavations. Fragment of a shrine panel, in fine white sandstone.

This is very similar to 6, but not apparently from the same side of the same panel. It is 7½ in. long, 2¼ in. thick, dressed more or less flat on both faces; and the tongue is less pronounced, being thinned to 1⅛ in. from one face only, and protruding for a little less than an inch.

Fig. 10, pl. vi. Part of St. Ninian's Isle, shrine 'A'?

8. St. Ninian's Isle; found 1957 in the 'Founder's Tomb' feature. Plain median-post, in light-coloured sandstone. The overall-height is 28 in., the cross-section being irregular, but generally 7 in. by 5 in.

This stone appears to have been shaped from a water-worn stone, the top being rounded; the heavy and irregular base is chipped, but only the upper 19 in. have been dressed to produce four faces. Three are grooved. On face *a*, the groove is 1½ in. wide, 1¾ in. deep, 12 in. long, and commences 7 in. below the top. The corresponding measurements for face *c* are ¾, ½, 11¼, and 7½ in.; and for face *d*, 1⅛, 1½, 10½, and 7 in.

Fig. 11, pl. vii. Part of St. Ninian's Isle, shrine 'B'.

9. St. Ninian's Isle; found 1957 in the 'Founder's Tomb' feature. Upper half of a plain corner-post, in light-coloured sandstone. This is broken, what remains being only 14½ in. high, with a cross-section of 9 in. by 4 in.

On face *a*, the groove is 1½ in. wide, 1 in. deep, and commences 4½ in. below the rounded top. The corresponding measurements on face *d* are 1½, 1⅛, and 9½ in.

Fig. 11, pl. vii. Part of St. Ninian's Isle, shrine 'B'.

10. St. Ninian's Isle; found in 1959, face downwards, in the south-west part of the nave of the medieval church. This is a small cross-incised slab of greyish sandstone.

The slab is an irregular rhomboid, measuring 14 in. by 8 in., and a little over an inch thick. The cross motif is lightly but clearly incised, and consists of a linear cross $2\frac{3}{4}$ by $2\frac{1}{4}$ in., with small barred terminals.

Fig. 8, pl. viii.

11. St. Ninian's Isle; found in 1959, outside the south wall of the medieval church, associated with the long cist graves. Tall thin slab of micaceous metaquartzite with pocked cross.

This is 25 in. long, the base narrowing to a 3-in. 'tang', and varies in thickness from $2\frac{1}{8}$ in. either end to $2\frac{3}{8}$ in. at the centre. The motif occurs near the upper end of one face, and consists of a simple, open-ended, outline cross, the lines being deeply and irregularly pocked out.

Fig. 8, pl. viii.

12. St. Ninian's Isle; found in 1956 (?), face upwards, in the south-west part of the nave of the medieval church, three feet from the inner face of the south wall. Broken slab of steatite.

The slab now measures 17 in. long, by $9\frac{1}{2}$ in. at the complete end to $15\frac{1}{2}$ in. across the break. It is $2\frac{1}{2}$ in. thick, and has been neatly dressed on both faces. A shallow pocked groove, $\frac{1}{2}$ in. to $\frac{3}{4}$ in. wide and of varying depth, runs around the unbroken sides, about an inch from the edge.

Fig. 8, pl. ix.

13. St. Ninian's Isle; found during the excavations, but exact context is not known. Broken cross-marked slab of steatite.

Only the thinner end (which must have resembled, but is not the same stone as, *12*) is missing. The slab is 21 in. along one side, $16\frac{3}{4}$ in. along the other, and a foot wide. It has been dressed flat, and averages 2 in. in thickness.

The cross is formed by two broad intersecting grooves, essentially pocked-out channels a half-inch deep, and $1\frac{1}{2}$ in. wide. They form a cross 7 in. by $11\frac{1}{2}$ in., its uppermost point $2\frac{1}{2}$ in. from the end of the slab. As with *12*, the slab is bordered by a shallow pocked groove, set not quite 1 in. in from the edge; this groove is roughly $\frac{3}{4}$ in. wide.

Pl. ix.

14. St. Ninian's Isle; found in 1956, face upwards, in the west end of the nave of the medieval church, 6 ft. east of the south jamb of the doorway. Broken cross-marked slab of steatite.

The slab is broken in such a way as to remove the lowest part of the cross. What remains measures 15 in. along one side, 9½ in. along the other, and 17 in. across the end; both faces are dressed flat, and the thickness varies from 2½ to 3 in.

The cross is 8½ in. by at least 10 in., and is formed by two broad intersecting pocked-out channels, not quite 1½ in. wide, and only ¼ in. deep. There is, as with *12* and *13*, a border of a shallow pocked groove, set 1 in. in from the edge; this is from a half to 1 in. wide.

Fig. 8, pl. ix.

15. St. Ninian's Isle; found in July 1958 in the area (fig. 8) of the nave of the medieval church, face downwards, covering the hoard or treasure of silver objects. Small broken cross-slab of grey sandstone.

This is an irregular flat slab, 5/16 in. thick all over, from 6 to 8 in. wide, and now 14 in. long. The cross is lightly incised and very regular; the shaft is 2¾ in. wide, 7½ in. from its base to the semi-circular openings (which are 1½ in. diameter); the arms are 2½ in. long.

Fig. 8, pls. viii, xvi.

16. St. Ninian's Isle; found during the excavations, but exact context is not known. Small broken shaped cross of steatite.

This curious little piece has been shaped from a flattened slab of steatite, averaging 1 in. in thickness. As it stands, it measures 7⅞ in. across the lower part of the arms, and 6¼ in. high. The arms expand slightly towards their terminals, and all their angles are slightly chamfered.

Pl. x.

17. St. Ninian's Isle; found in 1957, outside the west wall of the medieval church. Hogback stone of steatite.

The hogback is complete, well shaped, with a rough but regular finish. It measures 3 ft. 11 in. over-all length, is 11 in. wide across the centre, and 5½ in. at the ends. The flattened central summit is 3½ in. wide.

Fig. 8, pl. xi.

18. St. Ninian's Isle; found in 1956, face downwards, against the inner face of the south wall of the medieval church, 5 ft. west from the inner south-east angle of the nave. Cross-slab of greyish sandstone.

The foot of this slab is broken and missing. What remains is 13 in. wide at the top, 14 in. across the break, and 2 ft. 9 in. high. The slab is 3½ in. thick. The cross is lightly incised.
Fig. 8, pl. xii.

19. St. Ninian's Isle; found within the burial-area around the medieval church in 1876. Regularly shaped sandstone slab with an ogham inscription along one edge.

This well-known slab is 2 ft. 6½ in. long by 10½ in. wide, and 2 in. thick; it is of light-coloured sandstone. Along one edge, an ogham inscription reads *besmeqqnanammov-vez*; it is generally conjectured that if the word *meqq* represents the Primitive Irish word for 'son', the other two elements may be personal names. Mr. Tom Henderson has pointed out that there is no special reason for the shape assumed by this slab *vis-à-vis* the inscription, and wonders if it has not been cut down from a former shrine panel.
Allen and Anderson (1903), iii. 18, fig. 13, with references.

20. St. Ninian's Isle; found during the excavations, but exact context unknown. Small rounded fragment of soft sandstone.

This piece is part of a slab, 2¼ in. thick, dressed flat on both faces. It measures 9 in. along one side, 14 in. along another (broken) side, and is 5 in. wide across both broken ends. Clearly part of a much larger slab, the side which is now 9 in. long is neatly rounded off. It seems likely that this is a fragment of a lid, or a panel, from one or other of the shrines.
Fig. 10.

21. St. Ninian's Isle; found during the excavations, in the main cutting in the nave of the medieval church.

A small fragment of the variegated limestone or marble, known as *porfido verde antico*. It measures 19 mm. thick, and appears to be part of a rectangular piece 36 mm. wide by at least 48 mm. long. All unbroken edges, and both faces, have been ground smooth.

22. St. Ninian's Isle; found during the excavations, probably within the medieval church. Broken stone cresset-lamp.

This is a greyish gneiss, and began as a block, 11 to 12 in. high, and probably 7 to 8 in. square. At one end is a shallow hollow, tapering in diameter from 5¾ in. to 3½ in., the depth in the centre being exactly an inch.

Pl. xi.

23. Papil; found April 1943 during grave-digging in the kirkyard. It was encountered 20 in. below surface, upright, supported by two 'socket-stones' (= corner-posts), possibly, though not certainly, *26* and *27*—in any event, a secondary setting. Long-side panel of a corner-post shrine, in light-coloured sandstone. Dimensions are top, 40 in., bottom, 39 in.; (seen from decorated front) right side, 12⅛ in., left side, 13¼ in. The thickness is irregular, but nowhere more than 2½ in.

The sides of the stone have been trimmed away from the lower corners, upwards for a short distance, to form lateral tongues. The right side tongue is 13⅛ in. long, projecting to a half-inch; left side, 13½ in. long, projecting to 1 in. Both tongues are chamfered, from an outer edge ⅞ in. wide (right) and ⅝ in. wide (left).

The panel scene measures 34 in. horizontally, and about 13 in. vertically, is centred, and lies 1½ in. below the top edge. The ornament is partly in relief, with additional detail in a finely pocked or incised line.

Figs. 7 and 13. Part of Papil, shrine 'A'.

Cf. also: Moar and Stewart (1943–4), 92 ff. (their 'Papil Cross Slab'); Stevenson (1955), 115.

24. Papil; found at some unspecified time in the past, in the Papil kirkyard, and removed to Lerwick by Mr. Tom Henderson. Plain corner-post in a very light sandstone.

The top of the stone is broken, the present height being 21½ in. The cross-section is fairly regular, roughly 6 in. by 6 in., and all four angles are noticeably chamfered.

Faces *b* and *c* are plain. On face *a*, there is a groove, 1¼ in. wide and 1¼ in. deep, the top missing, 12½ in. long. The corresponding figures of the groove on face *d* are 1¼, 1, and 13 in. The base of the stone is irregular and perhaps split.

Fig. 13, pl. xiii. Part of Papil, shrine 'A'.

Cf. also: Moar and Stewart (1943–4), 94 (one of their 'other three socket-stones').

25. Papil; found at some unspecified time in the past, in Papil kirkyard, and removed to Lerwick by Mr. Tom Henderson. Plain three-grooved median-post, in light-coloured sandstone.

This appears to be, originally, an elongated water-worn stone, and the top and base are still rounded; one face (*d*) has been roughly dressed flat. Grooves occur on the other three faces. The total height is 22½ in., the cross-section being, at its least irregular central section, about 6½ by 7 in.—some attempt has been made to batter the faces flat.

On face *a*, the groove is 1½ in. wide, 1¼ in. deep, 11½ in. long, and commences 5 in. below the top of the stone. The corresponding measurements for face *b* are 1½, 1 (the face is partially split here), 11, and 5 in.; and for face *c*, 1, 1, 11, and 5 in.

Figs. 7 and 13, pl. xiv. Part of Papil, shrine 'B'?

Cf. also: Moar and Stewart (1943–4), 94 (one of their 'other three socket-stones').

26. Papil; found April 1943 during grave-digging in the kirkyard, possibly, though not certainly, supporting the panel *23*. Plain three-grooved median-post, in light-coloured sandstone.

This stone, according to Moar and Stewart's photograph, had the left-side tongue of *23* engaged in the groove in its face *b*. This is an impossible position for a median-post, and confirms that this must have been a secondary setting.

The stone is 24½ in. high, and a part of its top has been diagonally broken away. It tapers from a cross-section of 8 in. by 6 in. (base) to 4½ in. by 4 in. at the top.

On face *a*, the groove is 1¼ in. wide, 1 in. deep, almost 15 in. long, and commences 3¼ in. below the top. The corresponding measurements for face *b* are 1, 1, 17, and not more than 2 in. (top broken at this point); and for face *d*, the lower part of which has been flaked flat, 1, ½, 10¼, and 5½ in.

Figs. 7 and 13, pl. xiv. Part of Papil, shrine 'B'?

Cf. also: Moar and Stewart (1943–4), 93, pl. v, 2.

27. Papil; found April 1943 during grave-digging in the kirkyard, possibly, though not certainly, supporting panel *23*. Decorated corner-post, in a light-brownish sandstone.

This is also shown by Moar and Stewart with the right-side tongue of *23* engaged in the groove in its face *d*. In this position, the base of *27* would come some inches above the base of *23*, which suffices to show that this cannot be the correct placing.

Like *25*, this seems to have been a water-worn stone, and the base is still rounded. The total height is 25 in., the top having been dressed flat, though hardly to what could be called a boss or knob. The approximate cross-sections are 8 in. by 4 in., at the base, tapering to 5 in. by 4 in. near the top.

Face *a* bears a roughly and shallowly incised ornament, a long-stemmed cross being flanked above its arms by two S-shaped spiral motifs. On face *b*, the stone has been dressed flat, leaving a small upstanding boss, 2¼ in. diameter, which begins 4¼ in. below the top, and stands out about half an inch.

On face *c*, the groove is 1½ in. wide, 1½ in. deep, almost 14 in. long, and commences 7½ in. below the top. The corresponding measurements on face *d* are 1, 1¼, 12½, and 7¾ in.

Figs. 7, 12, and 13, pl. xiii. Part of Papil, shrine 'A'.

Cf. also: Moar and Stewart (1943–4), 93, fig. 1, pl. v, 2.

28. (*Lost*). Papil; apparently still in the kirkyard in 1943. Side panel, either a long-side half-panel from a double shrine, or a median-panel from the same; and was one of three (this one being fairly certain, the others rather less so) found still engaged in a three-grooved median-post, either *25*, or the (also now lost) *29*.

The dimensions, according to Moar and Stewart, were 14 in. high, 14 in. wide, and about 2 in. thick, with lateral tongues 12 in. high, formed by chipping away the bottom 2 in. on each side, the tongues being thinned to 1½ in.

Fig. 7.

Cf. also: Moar and Stewart (1943–4), 94.

29. (*Lost.*) Papil; apparently still in the kirkyard in 1943. Plain three-grooved median-post, either on its own, or the one found with *28* and two other panels engaged in it.

Moar and Stewart (1943–4), 94 (one of their 'other three socket-stones').

30. Papil; found near the now disused church in Papil kirkyard, and removed to Lerwick by Mr. Tom Henderson. Upper part of a corner-post, in coarse light-coloured sandstone.

The surviving fragment is 10½ in. high, and has a regular cross-section of 6 in. by 2¾ in. Sides, faces, and the rounded top are all well smoothed and dressed evenly. On one face there is decoration, incised in a broad shallow line, down to a point 6 in. below the top; it comprises a double arc, the inner arc terminating in two inward-curling spirals.

Despite its relative thinness, this seems as likely to be the top of a corner-post as anything else.

Figs. 12 and 13, pl. xv. Part of Papil, shrine 'C'?

31. Papil; found in the course of excavating a trench for a water-main, about 2 ft. down, and about 200 yd. south-east of the disused church (i.e. outside the kirkyard as shown in fig. 8). Small rune-inscribed piece of a brownish sandstone.

This measures 7½ by 6 by 4 in., being roughly a triangle. It is not quite 1½ in. thick; both faces are quite smooth, and the runes are marked on the longest edge, a flat face not quite at right angles to the main faces. The runes have been read as]R. REISTI . S[, a fact which strongly implies that this is part of a larger stone with a much longer inscription.

Pl. xv.

Moar (1951–2), 206, pl. xliii, 2; Shetelig (1954), 158–9.

32. Papil; found in the kirkyard in 1943, 'about four feet away' from the group consisting of *23*, *26*, and *27*. Part of a small cross-marked slab of brown sandstone.

Originally this had a rounded top, the left side of which is diagonally broken away. It is now 16¾ in. high, 13⅜ in. wide below the rounded top, and 12¾ in. wide at the break, with a thickness averaging 1 in. On one face, the ornament, executed in a narrow and shallow incised line, shows a simple cross in two-strand split interlace, having a central ring with a four-way junction, and expanded terminals with splayed points. This has been carried out with some uncertainty.

Pl. xv.

Moar and Stewart (1943–4), 92–3, and pl. v, 1.

33. Papil; the so-called 'Burra' or 'Papil Stone', first noticed in 1877 by Gilbert Goudie. It was then lying, presumably with the worked face upwards, over the grave of a Baptist missionary in Papil kirkyard, very approximately as shown on the plan, fig. 8. Shortly afterwards, the stone was removed to Edinburgh.

It is a rectangular slab of a reddish sandstone, 6 ft. 10 in. high, from 1½ to 2½ in. thick, and varying in width from 1 ft. 7½ in. (top) to 1 ft. 5½ in. (base). The top is rounded, with a slight break about 10 in. long. Ornament occurs on one face only, the details being reserved (in low relief) and additionally incised on a sunken background. The various elaborate motifs are described in the standard accounts (see below).

Fig. 7.

Cf. also: Allen and Anderson (1903), figs. 6–9, with full account; Curle (1939–40), pl. xxix. a, fig. 7. c; Stevenson (1955), 115 and 128; Radford (1962), 173, pl. xiii.

34. Papil; first noticed lying in the kirkyard at Papil.

This is another large reddish sandstone slab, the uppermost angles being slightly rounded. It is 5 ft. 4½ in. high, 1 ft. 4½ in. wide (tapering very slightly upwards), and from 2 to 2½ in. thick. The incised ornament shows a long-shafted cross occupying the

upper half of one face, a cross with a splayed-out base and below it a kind of near-rectangular 'tang'.
Fig. 7.
Cf. also: Royal Commission on Ancient Monuments, Scotland; *Orkney and Shetland Inventory*, vol. iii. 75 (no. 1266), fig. 577.

ADDENDA

The two stones below, *35* and *36*, were recovered in January 1971 during grave-digging in the new extension of Papil kirkyard—just visible at the top centre of fig. 7—and thus about 40 yards north of the church. I am indebted to Mr. Tom Henderson (*in litt.*, February 1972) for this information, and for the photographs (pl. lvii). The context suggests that these must be referred to yet another Papil shrine (provisionally labelled 'D' ?) and do not form part of any shrine described above.

35. Papil; found in grave-digging in the new north kirkyard, 1971. Plain corner-post from a single shrine in greyish sandstone, made from a water-worn stone.

The total height is $22\frac{5}{8}$ in. The stone is badly weathered. The cross-sections are $5\frac{1}{4}$ in. by $3\frac{1}{8}$ in. near the top, and $4\frac{3}{4}$ in. by $3\frac{5}{8}$ in. near the base. Two contiguous faces are grooved. On face *a*, the groove is $1\frac{1}{4}$ in. wide, $\frac{7}{8}$ in. deep narrowing slightly towards the base, and 14 in. long, commencing about $3\frac{1}{2}$ in. below the top. On face *b*, the groove is about 1 in. wide, but both sides are so abraded that the original depth is not ascertainable; the groove is $11\frac{1}{8}$ in. long, and starts about 5 in. from the top. Face *c* bears a curious lateral indentation, $\frac{1}{2}$ in. deep and $3\frac{1}{2}$ in. long, which is $1\frac{1}{4}$ in. on the angle between faces *c* and *d* and tapers to $\frac{3}{4}$ in. across; its bottom line is $6\frac{1}{8}$ in. below the top of the stone. Face *d* bears signs of dressing (pecking) and two eroded lines or grooves, which may just possibly be the remains of decoration.
Pl. lvii.

36. Papil; found with *35* above. Fragment of greyish sandstone slab, probably part of shrine (side ?) panel. This is $1\frac{1}{8}$ in. thick, and has a bead worked along the upper edge. The fragment is $13\frac{1}{4}$ in. wide, and 17 in. high. Both the top edge, and the right-hand side (in *pl. lvii*) for the 13 in. before the lower break, appear to have been worked straight, and there are signs of slight chamfer on the right-hand side.
Pl. lvii.

Mr. Henderson adds that local opinion confirms that the stone used for *35* and *36* is not native to the Papil area. He further states that there is still a very large pile of unsorted stone rubble in the old Papil church, and it is thus quite possible that the two lost stones (*28* and *29*) may yet be recovered.

Location

The Shetland County Museum, Lerwick, Shetland: 1, 2, 3, 4, 5, 6, 7, 8, 9, 10, 11, 12, 13, 14, 15, 16, 17, 20, 21, 22, 23, 24, 25, 26, 27, 30, 31, 32, 35, 36.

National Museum of Antiquities of Scotland, Edinburgh: 19, 33.

Bigton Established Church, Dunrossness, Shetland: 18.

Papil Kirkyard, Shetland: 34.

Lost, but probably still within Papil Kirkyard: 28, 29.

III–VII *The treasure*

DAVID M. WILSON

The St. Ninian's Isle hoard was found on 4 July 1958 (pl. xvi) close to the centre of the east end of the nave of the standing church ruins (fig. 8). It was covered by an irregular sandstone slab (no. 15, p. 37)—the fragment of an inscribed cross. The hoard, which consists of twenty-eight pieces of orna-mented silver and the jawbone of a porpoise, was enclosed in a box of larch-wood, of which only a few fragments (impregnated with metal salts) survived.

The intention of this portion of the book is to catalogue and discuss the hoard. The main conclusions concerning the hoard (outlined in Chapter VII) are that it is of secular Pictish origin and that it was deposited towards the end of the eighth, or at the beginning of the ninth, century, although some of the objects may have been of some age when they were buried. Appendices A and B should be considered in association with this section of the book.

III *Catalogue of the treasure*

THIS study of the hoard is arranged so that fact and theory are separated. To this end this chapter records the contents of the hoard by detailed description and omits—as far as is practicable—all theories, save only that when the identification of the use of an object is open to question the ultimate general identification revealed by my arguments is used for the reader's convenience. All entries in the catalogue are accompanied by limited bibliographical references to important discussion or publication; many short general articles and notes on the treasure have appeared and some of these are included only in the general bibliography.[1] The objects are illustrated in the accompanying volume, as far as possible at a scale of 1/1.

All the objects in the hoard, with the exception of the porpoise bone, are of silver alloy and, wherever practicable, this has been analysed by a colorimetric method by Dr. Hugh McKerrell of the National Museum of Antiquities of Scotland, whose results are published as Appendix B (pp. 174 f.). The significance of these figures, save only in so far as they reveal the very low silver content of the objects, is at the moment minimal. We can, however, trust that these figures may be used for comparative purposes by future students of the period. It was impossible to analyse the bowls.

The objects were treated immediately after discovery in the Research Laboratory of the British Museum, after which they were for some time displayed in the Marischal College Museum at Aberdeen. After certain legal actions (see Chapter VIII) they were declared treasure trove and deposited in the National Museum of Antiquities of Scotland in Edinburgh. The National Museum has donated copies of the objects to the County Museum at Lerwick, Shetland.

Catalogue

The objects are catalogued under the numbers given to them in the preliminary publication.[2] The inventory number recorded in the course of each entry refers to the register of the National Museum of Antiquities of Scotland. The weights recorded at the end of most entries are uncorrected for vacuum and include the weight of all preservative

---

[1] e.g. O'Dell (1959), Bruce Mitford (1960), and Wilson (1970).   [2] O'Dell *et al.* (1959).

and repair materials which in the case of nos. 2, 7, and 8 is quite considerable.[1] The pre-conservation state of most of the objects is published in O'Dell (1960).

1. SILVER BOWL in the form of a cone of a sphere. The centring point of the spinning process is visible both inside and outside. The bowl has a large dent and in this place the metal is slightly fractured. Otherwise the bowl is in good condition and shows no corrosion or concretions. It is ornamented externally with incised lines flanked by punched dots. The border of punched dots below the rim and the small groups of three, four, or five punched dots elsewhere in the design are executed with a heavier punch than that used for the dots which flank the incised line. The rim is plain and slightly thickened. The main body is about 0·7 mm. thick.

The design consists of a central circle, 8·6 cm. in diameter, round which are constructed four circles of slightly smaller diameter with centres equidistant along the circumference of the central circle, leaving a 3 mm. square in the centre of the field. In the space between the overlapping circles, chords of a circle (of 7 cm. radius) have been drawn to give a cruciform effect to the central portion of the bowl. The marks of the compass used to describe the five circles are clearly visible. In the middle of the remaining space of each of the flanking circles is a circular loop (2·3 cm. in diameter), from which are produced two curved lines which join on the opposite sides of the bowl in a similar loop; each line touches the circumference of the intervening circle. All the lines of construction are incised and are flanked by dotted lines (about eight punched dots per cm.). In the major spaces produced by this construction are groups of punched dots, set out in regular fashion (see pl. xvii).

Diameter: 15·1 cm.[2]

Height: 5·6 cm.

Weight: 90·0 g.   Inventory no. FC 268

Cf. pl. xvii, fig. 20a, and pp. 106, 134.

BIBLIOGRAPHY: O'Dell *et al.* (1959), 245, 257, pl. xxv *a* and *b*. O'Dell (1960), 6, 27, and 28. McRoberts (1960–1), 303–4. McRoberts (1965), 229–30.

2. SILVER BOWL with an omphalos; the centring point is clearly visible on the inside. The rim is plain, but perhaps slightly thickened. The bowl is ornamented with punched dots and the ornament is executed from the outside, from which position it is described.

---

[1] I am grateful to Dr. H. McKerrell for providing me with these figures.

[2] Note that this measurement (and that of the bowls described below) is the mean diameter: all the bowls are distorted and none of them retains its circular rim form.

Below the rim is a punched line which forms the border of a frieze of interlaced animals. The animals are defined by, and reserved against, a background of punched dots. The animals, all of which face in the same direction (with heads at top right), are described in the order in which they are illustrated in fig. 21. The outstretched head of the first animal is rounded, it has an open mouth, and a muzzle defined by a short line. The eye is comma-shaped and the pupil is indicated by a punched dot. The neck forms a single knot with itself and with one of the animal's front legs. This leg returns on itself, having passed through the looped neck, to expand into a paw with three toes (indicated by single lines), which rests on the contour of the other front leg. This has a shaped hip and stretches back from the body in a straight line to a three-element paw. The body forms an S-curve and terminates as a spiral. The legs emerge from the spiral at right angles to each other, having interlaced with the spiralled body. Their paws are similar to those just described. The hind leg is bent forward in a natural position, but the other paw is at a right angle to the leg.

The second animal has a more naturalistic stance. The mouth is open and from it emerges a tongue which loops round an outstretched foreleg to terminate in a bifoliate element. The eye is similar to that of the first animal. The bottom of the jaw is indicated by a short line on the neck. From the top of the head—lappet-like—emerges a ribbon which forms a rough triquetra knot between the neck and the hindquarters. The neck curves gently, the lower contour forming a line with the hindmost front leg. One front leg is extended forward and has a shaped hip and a three-toed paw; the other leg is bent backwards, the hip-line is indicated and part of the back of the foot forms and touches the border: it has a two-toed paw. The body has a slender waist and the hind legs an exaggerated length. They emerge from the hips with a slight bend at the knee, so that the front of each three-toed paw rests on the lower border—with which it has a common contour. The tail forms three loops—one interlacing with each leg and the other with itself. It terminates in a simple coil above the neck of the first animal.

The third animal has a head with a mouth opening towards the lower border; a line defines both the upper and lower jaws. The eye is similar to those of the first two animals. The tongue forms a loop with the foremost front leg and terminates in a roundel. The neck curves sharply, its lower contour forming an S-shaped curve with one of the front hips. One front leg has a shaped hip and stretches forward to form a three-toed foot, resting on the lower border. The second front leg has a shaped hip and bends to a three-toed foot below the chest of the animal. The body forms a spiral round the hindquarters of the animal. The hind legs emerge at right angles to each other; one to bend forward and form a three-toed foot with a common contour with lower border; the other to stretch backwards, above the snout of the second animal, to form a three-toed foot. The tail emerges above the hindquarters and makes a right-angle bend to terminate in a trefoil, behind the animal's neck and above a convex line which breaks the otherwise smooth curve of the back.

The fourth animal has a closed mouth and down-bent head on a gracefully curved head. The cheek and lower jaw-line are indicated as lines, there is a comma-shaped eye, a dot represents the pupil. The nose is indicated by a short, curved line. One front leg stretches forward to terminate in a three-toed paw; the other stretches backward from a hip indicated by two lines. It has an exaggerated length and the three-toed paw is upturned beneath the hind hip. The body of the animal is waisted. The bowl is somewhat damaged here, but the dotted lines of fig. 21 give some indication of the possible form of the hindquarters. One leg stretches backwards from the hip; the two-toed paw being upturned, its back forming a common line with the lower border. The other leg appears to interlace very uncomfortably with the body to form a three-toed paw behind the neck of the beast. The tail forms a loop round the outstretched hind leg and appears to terminate in another loop in front of the head of the third animal.

Below this band of animal ornament, above the plain footing of the bowl and defined by two punched lines, is a band of linear ornament consisting of interlocking Ls which is muddled at one point. The omphalos is defined by a line and the circle thus formed is divided into four quadrants. That to the top left in fig. 21 encloses a muddled linear interlace pattern with pointed terminals to the loops. The line ends arbitrarily at both ends and a single odd dot is enclosed within the ornament. The field to the top right has a similar confused interlace pattern, but the line seems to end more logically in a small, roughly defined loop. In two of the spaces left by the interlace are groups of three dots. The bottom-left field contains a logical, symmetrical linear interlace pattern. The bottom-right field also contains a logically symmetrical interlace based on a triquetra knot.

When found the bowl was badly damaged at the rim and it has been repaired by lining much of the rim with a strip of metal, patching a few holes with Fibrenyl, and lining the whole bowl with polystyrene.[1]

Mean diameter: 14·4 cm.
Weight: 101·3 g.   Inventory no. FC 269

Cf. pl. xviii, *figs.* 20*b*, 21, *and pp.* 106–7, 125–31.
BIBLIOGRAPHY: O'Dell *et al.* (1959), 245, 249, 257 ff. and pl. xxvi *b*. O'Dell (1960), 6, 16, and 17. Organ (1959), 43.

         [1] This technique is described in Organ (1959), 43.

3. SILVER BOWL, heavily encrusted with extruded copper and very much corroded on one side. The bowl has an omphalos, in the centre of which is a pointed feature which may be a repair to a hole accidentally made during spinning. The bowl is decorated and the patterns are designed to be seen from the outside (from which position they are described).

Immediately below the rolled rim is a line of punched dots (between seven and eight per cm.). The border below this consists of a zigzag line, heavily scribed with a blunt tool: each angle of the zigzag is heavily, but bluntly, punched. Bisecting each angle is a straight line which produces a pair of oblique offshoots—one on either side—forming lines parallel to the zigzag. The three terminals so produced are emphasized with a bluntly punched dot. The zigzag line is fairly regularly constructed, on average measuring about 1·7 cm. between each peak.

The rest of the body, between the border and the slight foot which forms the undecorated border of the omphalos, is decorated with a design of interlaced animals. They are outlined by, and reserved against, fine punched dots. One group of animals is badly damaged but the main design consists of four pairs of animals—the animals of each pair face in opposite directions and each pair is more or less symmetrical. The first pair consists of two animals whose C-shaped bodies interlace together. They have large heads and mouths with carefully defined heavy lips which emit ribbons. One ribbon joins the lappet, and the other terminates in a trefoil beneath the fourth pair of animals. The former animal has two lappets, the second disappears into the corroded portion of the bowl, having formed a simple knot between the two animals; the lappet of the second animal cannot be traced because of corrosion. The eye is formed of a heavily punched dot (probably made by the same punch used in border motif) and the pronounced socket is comma-shaped. The front hip is picked out as a spiral. One of the rather weak-looking forelegs is raised to the lower jaw and the other is pendant. The main part of the body is ribbon-like and curls round to the back hips which are picked out as a spiral. The two hind legs pass over and under the curled body. The tails are produced into interlace, one becoming the tongue of the first animal in the second pair, while the second becomes the tail of the second animal in the second pair.

The third group of animals is very similar in design to the first group, save only that the tongues, tails, and lappets are not disposed in exactly the same way.

The second pair of animals is entirely different. The fore part of each animal is similar to that of the first pair; the lappet of one animal becomes the lappet of the other forming a simple knot between the two heads. One tongue forms a loop and terminates in a trefoil, the other tongue becomes the tail of one of the first pair of animals. The two front legs are widely splayed. The animals' ribbon-shaped bodies form a loop and interlace the one with the other, the hindquarters appearing just below the head of the other animal. The legs are separated on either side of the body. One tail forms a single loop and ends in a closely curled spiral; the other, as shown, becomes the tail of one of the animals in the first pair.

The fourth pair of animals is much damaged by corrosion and the drawing of this portion of the ornament (fig. 22) must be treated as slightly tentative. Although the main details in this figure are correct, there is a possible tendency to error due to distortion. They are similar to the first pair of animals, save only that the bodies are adorsed and do not interlace with each other. The lappet of the surviving animal head becomes its tongue. The position of the right foreleg is rather doubtful.

The foot is plain, but the omphalos is decorated with six lentoid panels interspaced with sub-triangular panels in a debased marigold pattern, all reserved against the same fine dotted background.

Two gauges of punch appear to have been used in the decoration: a large blunt point for the eyes of the animals and the terminals of the border decoration, and a smaller point for the background of the ornament.

The bowl is much warped and corroded and in some cases the corrosion has pierced the bowl. The rim has been repaired in the laboratory with a modern metal strip for much of its diameter. Measurements are consequently difficult to determine.

Reconstructed diameter at mouth: 15·7 cm.

Weight: 76·7 g. Inventory no. FC 270

Cf. pl. xix, figs. 20c, 22, and pp. 106–7, 126–31.

BIBLIOGRAPHY: O'Dell et al. (1959), 245, 257, pl. xxvi c and fig. 3. O'Dell (1960), 6, 20, and 21. Henderson (1967), 213–14, pl. 21.

4. SILVER BOWL, very much corroded in a wavy manner for about two-thirds of its diameter; it is consequently much warped. The bowl has an omphalos which is pierced by a small hole in the centre—presumably the centring point for the spinning of the bowl. The rim is slightly flared and there is a slight peaning, which might be a cut-down rolled rim, for in the corroded portion the rim is rolled over. The bowl is decorated with designs executed entirely in punched dots. A single punch is used throughout. The foot remains plain. The ornament is described from the outside of the bowl.

Three zones of ornament, defined by dotted borders, decorate the body of the cup. The uppermost zone contains a complicated interlace pattern, consisting of pairs of loops placed alternately at the top and bottom of the zone—all executed as a single line of dots (nine punched dots per cm.).

The main zone of ornament consists of broad ribbons defined by dotted lines forming a pattern consisting of triple loops interlaced at either end with similar constructions. There are approximately nine punched dots per cm. in this band of ornament.

The lowermost zone bears a dotted zigzag line (between seven and nine punched dots per cm.).

The base flows smoothly into the omphalos with no real exaggeration at the foot. The main field formed by the omphalos is bordered by a single line of punched dots and divided by a cross reserved by further punched dots. The two arms of the cross were apparently meant to interlace with each other, but a mistake in the design has added a single line of dots across the arm which is meant to appear uppermost. In each of the fields defined by the cross is a crude triquetra knot, executed in the same technique as the ribbon pattern of the main zone of the bowl. The edge of the ribbon is often common with the border of the field. There are between nine and ten punched dots per cm. in this part of the design.

The bowl is in poor condition; part of the rim, for example, having been broken away in antiquity, is now corroded into position below the rim proper. There is a bad tear in the rim on the good side of the bowl. There is a good deal of extruded copper on the outer surface.

Approximate diameter: 14·5 cm.

Weight: 77·8 g.   Inventory no. FC 271

Cf. pl. xx, *figs.* 20d, 25, *and pp.* 106–7, 131 f., 134.
BIBLIOGRAPHY: O'Dell *et al.* (1959), 245, 258, and pl. xxvi *a*. O'Dell (1960), 6, 24, and 25.

5. SILVER BOWL, much corroded and warped for about one-third of its side. The ornament is executed in punched dots, a single, square-based, metal punch having been used throughout. The centring hole for the spinning process can be seen in the interior, it has apparently been plugged from the outside. The rim is plain and square-cut, being more than 1 mm. thick in places. The base has a slight omphalos. The ornament is designed to be seen from the outside and is so described.

The side of the bowl is divided into two main zones, defined by a single line of punched dots. The upper, narrower field is decorated with a series of interlocking T-shaped panels, the upper and lower borders of which are the borders of the main field. The lower and larger field is filled with a series of roughly oval panels, the long sides of which are in part common; the ovals tapering towards the base. The field continues into the slight omphalos. The centre of the omphalos contains, within a ring, four fields divided by straight lines at right angles to each other. From the edge of each of the dividing lines is produced a triangular, straight-line spiral, which fills the quadrant.

The punched dots, although producing a clumsy pattern, are applied with great uniformity at the rate of six or seven per cm.

The metal is badly fractured and has been repaired in the laboratory. It has, at the line of fracture and at a few other places, a coppery tinge.

Approximate diameter: 14·7 cm.

Weight: 127·3 g. Inventory no. FC 272

Cf. pl. xxi, fig. 20e, and pp. 106–7, 131 f., 134.
BIBLIOGRAPHY: O'Dell *et al.* (1959), 245 and pl. xxvii *a* and *b*. O'Dell (1960), 6, 18, and 19.

6. SILVER BOWL with internal mount. It is slightly warped. The bowl has an omphalos, on which the mount is set, and is decorated with patterns executed with punched dots. The patterns are punched from the outside and are described from that aspect.

At the rim, below an encircling line, are a series of pendant triangular fields made up of three triangles with their base on the encircling line. The outermost triangle normally has a side of between 9 and 13 dots (including those at the corners) and in one place the side has been redrawn, the artist having miscalculated four of the dots. There are between seven and nine dots per cm. in this zone of ornament. The second triangle has a side of six or seven dots; in one field an extra dot has been added at the apex. The innermost triangle has sides of three or four dots. The whole pattern is drawn in a clumsy fashion: sometimes there is a dot at the border between the two outermost triangles, but more often not; the lines are not straight and the punched dots are of uneven depth.

Below these pendant triangles is another encircling line of punched dots and below this is a zone of interlace ornament. For the most part it appears to consist of a single wavy band, interlaced with another band, which forms loops alternately at the top and bottom. At one point, however (arrowed in fig. 20*f*), the two bands join and change their role. There are three slight mis-punches. There are about six or seven dots per cm. in this zone.

This zone is bordered by another encircling line of punched dots and just above the slightly formed foot is another dotted line. These flank a pattern of interlocking rect-angles which have their base on the bordering lines. The long side of the rectangle is made up of between six and ten punched dots; the short side towards the centre of the bowl usually consists of six dots and measures between 6 and 7 mm.

A plain area forms the foot and the omphalos is decorated, within a dotted border, with a cruciform pattern. From, and between, each of the arms of the central cross is produced a straight-line, triangular spiral with one curved side. There are either six or seven dots per cm. in this field.

Fastened by two bronze rivets to the inside of the omphalos is a mount, which is in turn fastened to a circular silver plate by means of three globular-headed, silver rivets. The plate has a faceted edge, but is otherwise plain; it is 3·1 cm. in diameter. The mount is sub-triangular with convex sides (maximum over-all length: 2·8 cm.); it is framed by an undecorated hollow bar of semi-circular cross-section, pierced in the centre of each side by one of the three silver rivets heads. On two of the sides are bronze rivets with rather more flattened heads. At each corner is a modelled human mask, which is gilded (the gilding spilling over on to the border of the escutcheon, which is otherwise of plain silver). The masks have a pointed chin, a mouth with an emphasized upper lip (or moustache) and pear-shaped eyes. The hair line is indicated by an incised line, but on each of the masks the top of the head is much worn. Within the border, and held by it, is an openwork gilt mount overlaying a plain gilt back plate. This is bounded by a double-contoured border. Bisecting each angle is a plain rib which joins the corner of a triangular central field filled with red enamel and bordered by an incised, hatched line. The enamelled field is flat and at more or less the same level as the border of the mount. In each of the fields formed by this division is an openwork interlace pattern. In one field is a simple, single-band, ribbon interlace with pointed loops of reasonably symmetrical design. The single-band ribbon interlace in one of the other fields is much more complicated and irregular in character, but has the same pointed loops. In the third field is an interlaced zoomorphic ornament, consisting of a smoothly interlaced double figure-of-eight pattern terminating at either end in animal heads. The inner loops of the figure-of-eight are pointed. The animal heads have open mouths and a distinct cheek line. The ornament of the mount has been cast, drilled, and finished with hand tools.

The metal of the bowl is fractured on the outer surface, particularly at the foot, while the rim has been repaired in the laboratory in one section with two Fibrenyl patches, backed by a narrow strip of silver.

Approximate diameter at mouth: 14·3 cm.

Weight: 90·5 g. Inventory no. FC 273

Cf. pls. xxii, xxvi c, figs. 20f, 26, and pp. 106–7, 131 ff., 134.
BIBLIOGRAPHY: O'Dell *et al.* (1959), 245, pls. xxvii *b*, xxxii *d*, xxxix *a*. O'Dell (1960), 22, 23.

7. SILVER BOWL in fair condition. It has an omphalos, in the centre of which is the centring hole for the spinning. The rim has been slightly peaned, the ridge being only noticeable on the outside. The bowl has been decorated entirely with punched dots and the same punch has been used throughout: there are about six punched dots per cm. The decoration is executed on the outside of the bowl, from which aspect it is described.

The bowl is divided into two zones by means of three lines of punched dots each of which is filled with interlace ornament. The upper panel is filled with a ribbon interlace reserved against a background of punched dots. This consists of a ribbon forming a series of narrow loops at an angle of 45° to the rim interlacing with another ribbon which lies at 90° to it. The edge of the band is sometimes common with the dotted line of the border. The size of the loops varies considerably around the bowl. The lower zone contains a similar pattern executed in a single line of dots, save that at one place the two patterns join in a slightly muddled fashion.

There is a slight tendency to a ridge at the foot. The whole omphalos is filled with a whirl pattern composed of eight interlocking concentric spiral lines.

The bowl has been repaired in the laboratory at three places on the inside of the rim by the addition of thin silver strengthening strips. The body of the bowl has been patched with Fibrenyl in two places. Apart from these repairs the object is generally in good condition.

Diameter: 12·9 cm.
Weight: 68·6 g. Inventory no. FC 274

Cf. pl. xxiii, *figs.* 20g, 27, *and pp.* 106–7, 131 f., 134.
BIBLIOGRAPHY: O'Dell *et al.* (1959), 245 and pl. xxviii. O'Dell (1960), 33.

8. SILVER HANGING-BOWL with silver-gilt and plain silver mounts. It is much corroded on one side and consequently slightly warped. The bowl has a sharply defined omphalos and three ribs which form a hook at the rim to carry rings for suspension. Inside the bowl a circular gilt mount is riveted to the omphalos and a loose sheet of impressed silver was originally mounted outside the bowl, within the omphalos; the latter is now detached. At the rim the metal which forms the body of the bowl is folded over on itself; immediately below the rim is a deeply grooved neck.

Spaced equally round the bowl are three silver-gilt ribs, with straight sides. The ribs taper towards the base and take the form of displayed animals, the bodies of which are modelled in the round. The body of each animal is defined by a simple chip-carved interlace pattern. The interlace is angular and irregular. The animal's head is cast in the round and its chin lies on the top of the rim; the head and neck form the loop for the ring: the eyes, which are lightly engraved below modelled triangular ears, are lentoid. The snout is faceted and the mouth is indicated by a pair of engraved lines. The backbone of the animal, which appears below the ears, forms a billeted midrib to the mount; the tail forming an extension of the same line. Three sub-triangular fields, each filled with hatching and terminating in a volute—the whole design representing a mane—are engraved on either side of the backbone at the neck.

The front hips are represented by a pair of simply engraved lines, some of which take the form of the central element of a trumpet-spiral pattern. The rather weak legs stretch towards the corners of the plate. Four pairs of roughly quadrant-shaped fields on either side of the backbone are incised to represent hair. The hindquarters are covered with similar engraving, executed in slightly broken wavy bands round a series of interlocking spirals. The hind legs are pendant on either side of the tail, which terminates in a volute. The mount is hammered over into the angle of the omphalos and is firmly attached to the bowl by means of rivets inside each of the four feet. The rivets have slightly domed, gilt heads.

The internal mount is circular and is held in place by a silver-gilt collar, as indicated in fig. 23b. The collar is riveted into position by three silver rivets with rounded gilt heads, two of which pierce the base of the bowl. The collar has a flat top on which is an engraved beaded band. The ornament of the mount is chip-carved and is bordered by a band of herring-bone design. In the centre is a raised circular setting; this is now empty, but inside it can be seen the flat head of a bronze rivet which pierces the base of the bowl. The setting is encircled by three bands of beading, each of different gauge. Between these bands and the border is a zone decorated with three animals, all of practically the same design (fig. 23a). The back of each animal is towards the border. The head, which has a pear-shaped eye, is curved round beneath the neck. The mouth, with its square-cut jaws, bites across the foreleg. The neck curves round to the front hip and the foreleg passes through the mouth and across the neck to a plain foot, just in front of the neck. The body forms a gentle curve to a panelled back hip. The hind leg, which in one case terminates in three toes, bends forward to enclose the interlaced tail. With the exception of the head, hips, and legs, the body of the animal is hatched in basket-work fashion.

Attached to the base was a (now detached) circular mount of impressed thin silver sheet, the decoration of which consists of three contiguous trumpet spirals with a simple border. The sheet was attached to the base by the four rivets (one now missing) which fulfilled a similar function for the internal mount. There was almost certainly some support behind the plate as the top of the central rivet is nearly 3 mm. above the surface of the omphalos and is concreted solidly to that point. The escutcheon has been strengthened in the laboratory by the addition, in one quadrant, of a lint backing and modern solder.

The bowl is badly damaged at one place, but it has been reassembled in the laboratory and repaired with Fibrenyl. The whole bowl has been lined with Araldite. One of the animal heads had been broken off at the neck in antiquity and repaired with a billet of metal. This has had to be repaired again during laboratory treatment. A modern wire has been soldered, for strengthening purposes, inside the rim of the bowl.

Maximum diameter at rim: 14·0 cm.

Weight: 188·0 g.

Weight of *Pressblech* disc: 2·3 g.   Inventory no. FC 275

Cf. pl. xxiv, *figs.* 23, 38, *and pp.* 108–12, 134–7.

BIBLIOGRAPHY: O'Dell *et al.* (1959), 245, 248–9, 257 ff., frontispiece and pls. xxix *c* and xxx *a* and *b* and fig. 4. Organ (1959). O'Dell (1960), 6, 28–32. McRoberts (1960–1), 304–5. McRoberts (1965), 230–3.

9. SILVER SPOON, with long stem, the terminal of which turns upwards to become a loop. The bowl and stem are formed of the same piece of metal. The stem has irregularly spaced transverse cuts, which give it a baluster appearance. A groove down the back of the stem was presumably caused by the rounding process. There are slight traces of a similar feature at the front. The bowl rises to a point 2·9 cm. above the back of the base of its bowl. Attached by a rivet to the end of the stem, projecting into the bowl, is a carved animal head in full relief. From the open mouth a free-standing tongue extends to lick the bowl. The nostrils of the animal consist of small bored holes, and the eyes are of blue glass. The ears are formed of single elements of a trumpet spiral. A triangular field is reserved at the back of the head.

The spoon is much damaged:[1] it has been broken across the stem behind the animal head, and the tip of the bowl has been made up of five broken pieces.

Over-all length: 21·6 cm.

Weight: 21·5 g.   Inventory no. FC 276

Cf. pl. xxvi *a, fig.* 24, *and pp.* 113–15, 137.

BIBLIOGRAPHY: O'Dell *et al.* (1959), 246, 258–9, pl. xxxi *a–c*. O'Dell (1960), 7, 28, 34, and 35. McRoberts (1960–1), 307–8. McRoberts (1965), 237–8. Henderson (1967), 213, pl. 19.

10. SILVER STEMMED OBJECT. The stem is of square section and has a moulded baluster in the middle of its length. The terminal consists of a pierced cube

[1] The broken stem can be seen in the picture of the hanging-bowl, before conservation, in O'Dell (1960), pl. 28.

with a plain roll moulding below; it is crowned by a moulded baluster. A fragment of a silver ring remains in the hole. The other end of the object consists of a long claw-like projection (repaired in one place),[1] which springs from an expanded spur at the base of the stem. The spur is decorated with an interlace tendril pattern with curved ends; the space between the interlace being filled with billets. This motif is seen on both sides, but is badly worn on the face. At the point where the spur emerges from the stem is a rectangular band—on one side is a single row of hatched lines, on the other a double row of hatched lines, forming a herring-bone pattern.

Length: 16·9 cm.
Weight: 10·5 g.   Inventory no. FC 277

Cf. pl. xxvi *b, fig.* 28, *and pp.* 115–18, 137.
BIBLIOGRAPHY: O'Dell *et al.* (1959), 246, 258–60, pl. xxi *d* and fig. 5. O'Dell (1960), 7, 28, and 34. McRoberts (1960–1), 307. McRoberts (1965), 237–8. Henderson (1967), 214 and pl. 22.

11. SILVER-GILT POMMEL. It appears to have been hollow-cast in one piece as there is no sign of a seam on its plain ridge. It is fractured and slightly buckled at the ridge, at a point where it has been pierced by a bronze rivet. A random measurement of the thickness of the wall is 1·4 mm. Inside the pommel is a considerable concretion of corroded metal, of no recognizable form, but presumably part of an associated loose silver bar. One end of this bar has been hammered flat; the other, rather more slender, end has been turned in a slow curve at right angles to the main shaft (fig. 17a).

Each side of the pommel has an arched central field, which stands slightly proud of two flanking fields. The ornament is basically executed in simple chip-carving, but in places—particularly on the animal heads and at points of interlace—some slight surface relief is achieved.

The design in each of the central fields consists of two symmetrically interlaced animals, the bodies of which (where they are not of ribbon-like form) are speckled with triangular nicks executed with the point of a graver. The necks of the two animals are crossed in the centre of the field, as are the short tongues. The cheeks are slightly modelled and appear as a panel with bored eye in the corner. From the head of each animal springs a common lappet: this interlaces in a simple knot between the necks of the animals. The curved neck is roughly parallel to the base of the field and slender legs are produced from a hip-like swelling of the animal's body in each corner. The legs have a three-element foot and are bent at the knee-joint at right angles

---

[1] The pre-conservation state of the object can be seen in the picture of the hanging-bowl published by O'Dell (1960), 28.

to each other. From the hip the body tapers to a ribbon, which interlaces with itself and with the body of the other animal to produce, within a spiral, speckled hindquarters three-quarters of the way up the field. The hind hips are at the centre of a spiral formed from the body of the animal. The two hind legs pass in a straight line towards the border of the field, interlacing with the body so that the off leg appears initially to be the near leg. The feet have a three-element paw. From the hindquarters springs a long ribbon-like tail which forms a series of asymmetrical loops and knots along the side of the field to terminate above the snouts at the base of the field. The whole design is set within a plain border and is basically similar on both sides of the object.

The design in each of the lateral fields consists of two interlaced animals. In the lower corner is an animal head with a panelled, speckled cheek and circular eye. Its lappet forms an interlaced knot and terminates as the animal's tail. A ribbon-like tongue ends in a two-element knot in two of the fields and a triangle in the others. The front hips consist of a spiral within a speckled panel—the actual form varies from field to field. The straight legs extend towards the base, interlacing with the looped body of the other animal in the field; the feet have three-element paws. The body then becomes ribbon-like and forms a figure-of-eight loop completed by speckled hindquarters and hind legs, which interlace the ribbon-like element of the body of the other animal in the field. The legs have three-element paws. A portion of the loop of one of the animals is speckled with triangular nicks, and three further nicks appear behind the hip of another animal.

The second animal found in each of the lateral fields has a full-face head in the top of the panel. Two ribbons emerge from the top of the head to form a simple interlace pattern which joins the corresponding detail of the other lateral field on the same face of the pommel. The neck, shoulder, and hindquarters of the animal are speckled with triangular nicks. One of the forelegs rests along the border of the field and terminates in a three-element paw beneath the head of the animal; the other stretches downwards and the paws are emphasized by nicks. The body forms a great double loop to terminate in hindquarters and legs, which interlace with the body and with a loop formed by the body of the other animal in the field, to reach the bottom corner of the panel. The legs interlace so that the off leg comes first to the near side. The feet have three-element paws. Behind the neck of the animal is, in two cases, a triquetra knot and in the other two cases a simple triangle.

Length at base: 5·5 cm.
Height: 3·1 cm.
Length of rod: 2·9 cm.
Weight: 34·9 g.   Inventory no. FC 278

Cf. pls. xxvi *d,* xxviii *a, fig.* 17, *and pp.* 118–22, 137–40.
BIBLIOGRAPHY: O'Dell *et al.* (1959), 246, 260, pl. xxii *h* and fig. 6. O'Dell (1960), 6, 8, and 9. McRoberts (1960–1), 313 and fig. 6. McRoberts (1965), 243 and fig. 6.

12. SILVER-GILT OBJECT of truncated spheroid form. It is hollow and stands on a base-plate, the foot of the object being surrounded by a beaded wire ring. The base-plate is fractured and has, together with the ring, been stuck on to the base with glue in the Research Laboratory of the British Museum. It seems unlikely that it was replaced in the correct position. The wall of the object is pierced by circular drilled holes (4·3 mm. in diameter) in two places on opposite points of a diameter about a third of the way up. A silver tube joins the two holes. It is constructed of a single sheet of metal; the butted joint of which has sprung a little. The end of the tube is a little proud of the surface of the object at one of the holes.

The surface is decorated with eight animals in a complicated interlace pattern. The decoration is carried out by means of deep engraving, which is occasionally given a three-dimensional effect by moulding. The major lines of the design are formed of two pairs of back-to-back interlaced animals at the bottom of the field. Apart from minor details, such as the treatment of the paws, these four main animals are similar in design.

They each have a squared-off snout, a mouth formed of a zigzag line, a pear-shaped eye, a segmented cheek, and a narrow body which, save at the front hips where it forms a spiral, is filled with panels of herring-bone hatching. The front hip consists of a slight broadening of the body and is composed of two spirals interlocking to form a whorl. The front legs are stretched forward to interlace with the front legs of the other main pair of animals. The body narrows to form a spiral of two ribbons at the centre of which are two more or less naturalistic haunches, panelled in herring-bone. The legs are produced at about ninety degrees to each other but having interlaced with the coiled body, curve towards each other to form a two-element (in one case a three-element) paw. The off leg appears to cross the body above the near leg.

Between the necks of each of the two opposed groups of animals are the front legs, necks, and heads of two further animals. The design of this portion of the animal is similar to that of the creatures described above, save only that the panels within the body are filled with simple diagonal hatching and the spiral hip runs more effectively into the upper front leg. The body then tails off in the same way as that of the previously described animals to form five loops as it interlaces with the three other similar animals; it terminates in roughly lunate hindquarters within the curve of the neck and the front quarters of one of the main animals described above. The hip-joint is portrayed as three interlocking spirals. One leg is produced to interlace with the hind legs of the other animals, while the other is folded along the contour of its hip. The hips and a small portion of the body contiguous to them are decorated with panels of simple hatching. The animals are set in pairs and their heads are on the opposite side of the object from their hindquarters; the interlace differs slightly on each side.

The base-plate has been broken, but originally had two slots on either side of the centre—presumably like those of no. 14. The outer edges of these slots were chamfered externally and there is some indication that the inner edges were chamfered internally.

There is much wear below the pierced holes, and at two points on the edge of the base-plate (which must originally have been below the holes). The end of the tube and the edge of the hole are also very worn. The top of the object is also worn.

Height: 4·3 cm.
Diameter at base-ring: 3·7 cm.
Weight: 34·8 g. Inventory no. FC 279

Cf. pl. xxvii *a, figs.* 18*a,* 32, *and pp.* 122–3, 140–3.
BIBLIOGRAPHY: O'Dell *et al.* (1959), 246, 260–1, pls. xxxi *e* and *h,* xxxii *a* and *e,* fig. 7. O'Dell (1960), 6, 10, and 11. McRoberts (1960–1), 313 and fig. 6. McRoberts (1965), 243 and fig. 6.

13. SILVER-GILT OBJECT of truncated spheroid form. It is hollow cast and a plug filling a casting flaw can be seen internally at the top. It originally had a base-plate and a beaded wire ring, which are now detached, but stay soldered to each other. There is a considerable encrustation of solder inside the base-plate. The wall (on the chip-carved face) varies in thickness between 1·1 and 1·3 mm.: a random measurement of the thickness of the base-plate is 0·59 mm. The wall is pierced near the base, on a diameter, by circular holes (3 mm. in diameter), the internal burr caused by the drill can be seen from the inside. These holes were almost certainly drilled after the surface had been decorated, the apparent collar which appears on the exterior of the wall being achieved by skilful, but not perfect, manipulation of existing ornament.

The ornament is executed in two techniques—chip-carving and engraving. The main body of the object is divided up into four main arched fields by means of mouldings. There is a smaller field at the top, which is a quadrilateral with concave sides. Within this field, which is much worn, is a design consisting of four heavily incised spirals which do not, apparently, meet in the centre. In each corner of the field is a carved element which might be interpreted as an animal mask seen from above, but, due to wear, the details cannot be reconstructed.

The lateral mouldings of the borders of the four main fields are, alternately, an incised herring-bone pattern, and a faceted egg-and-tongue motif. The capitals of these latter borders rest on a double billet, but the herring-bone borders have no capitals; the two elements bifurcating to form a hatched hood to the arch.

Two opposing fields contain a ribbon-interlace ornament of four strands executed in chip-carving (pl. xxviii*b*). In the centre of the base of each of these fields is the pierced hole. The interlace is similar in each field, save within the head of the arch where the pattern differs slightly. The other two fields contain animal ornament. Each field has a pair of adorsed animals caught in an interlaced ribbon ornament, which springs from the body as a tail. The background interlace is chip-carved, but the main features of the animals are executed in deeply incised engraving. The designs are similar but differ in the disposition of the hindquarter and of the ribbon ornament. In both fields the bodies are of the same design, the snouts being in one case squared and in another slightly rounded. The mouths are closed, but the ribbon passes over the lower jaw and emerges as a knot between the snouts. The eyes are round and set in a pear-shaped socket. There is a curved cheek line. The backs of the straight necks of the animals are separated by a single incised line. The front hips consist of a three-element spiral whorl: the two legs of each animal bend one towards the top the other towards the bottom of the field. The feet vary slightly, but each seems to have a three-element paw. The thin ribbon-like bodies—which are hatched within a plain border—cross each other and form a slow spiral curve, one in each corner of the field. The splayed legs interlace with the body so that the lower leg appears to pass over the body and the upper leg under it. In one field the upper pear-shaped hip is hatched in a herring-bone pattern, within a plain border; the lower hip is left plain. In the other field both hips are plain. In the first case the body curves round so that the hips and legs are towards the side. The feet have two-element paws. The animal ornament is slightly faceted to give an appearance of relief; this is particularly noticeable on the plain surfaces.

The base-plate is pierced by two semi-circular slots on either side of the centre. The straight edge of the slot is chamfered on the inside, the curved lines on the outside. The portion of the plate between the two slots is slightly buckled. The beaded wire collar shows traces of internal gilding.

The object is much worn at the top and on the edge of the base-ring. The original position of the base-plate cannot now be determined.

Height: 3·8 cm.

Diameter at base: 3·1 cm.

Diameter of plate: 3·4 cm.

Weight: 33·2 g.   Inventory no. FC 280

Cf. pls. xxvii *b, d,* xxviii *b, fig.* 18*b, and pp.* 122–3, 140–3.

BIBLIOGRAPHY: O'Dell *et al.* (1959), 246, 260–1, pls. xxxi *f* and *i*, xxxii *c*, fig. 8*c*. O'Dell (1960), 6, 14, and 15. McRoberts (1960–1), 313 and fig. 6. McRoberts (1965), 243 and fig. 6.

14. SILVER-GILT OBJECT of truncated spheroid form. It is hollow and originally had a base-plate soldered to it; this is now detached but heavy encrustations of solder, both on the plate and as much as 6 or 7 mm. above the base on the inside of the wall, demonstrate that this was very effectively fastened. The base of the object is surrounded by a beaded wire ring, which protrudes beyond the contour of the object and forms a collar, resting on the base-plate but soldered to the wall of the object. The walls of the object vary between 0·75 mm. and 1·10 mm. in thickness and are pierced on opposite sides by circular holes, 3·9 mm. in diameter, which are secondary to the ornament. These holes were apparently drilled, as each has an internal burr.

The surface of the object is decorated with a continuous interlocking spiral design; unless otherwise stated this is engraved. The basic design (fig. 33) consists of six contorted trumpet-spiral patterns round the wall, which expand into a three-element trumpet-spiral at the apex. The centres of each series of spirals take varying forms. The lowermost row of large spirals have a sequence of (*a*) three two-lobed, leaf-like terminals carved in relief; (*b*) a triskele terminal carved in relief, followed by (*c*) an engraved triskele terminal—a system which is repeated twice. The zone of spirals above this consists of alternating large and small spiral patterns. The three smaller spirals of this zone have centres in which the three lines join to form a frame for three comma-shaped elements. The large spirals in this zone have a broken reversed curve at the centre, which almost joins to form a frame for groups of three lentoid incisions. The third row consists of groups of two spirals one made up of two lines the other of three. The two lines of the former are joined by a wavy line, while the latter join in the centre. The mouths of the trumpets and the semi-triangular spacing fields at the top of the zone are hatched and have a pear-shaped central element. The large spaces between the trumpets are filled with groups of three incised lentoid elements set as a rough trefoil, other spaces are filled with single incised, pear-shaped features, or, if not, faceted. The top of the object is decorated with three simple trumpet-spirals, which are produced out of the main zone of ornament.

The base-plate, which is not gilded, is heavily encrusted with salts internally: microscopic examination shows that there is no non-mineral substance present in this encrustation. The plate is pierced in the middle by a pair of rectangular slots, one on either side of the centre. A strengthening bar (fig. 18*c*) was originally fixed internally, this is now in fragments. The beaded ring round the base is semi-circular in cross-section and has a flat base. It is gilded only on the curved side. The whole mount is much worn, particularly at the top. The collar is badly worn below each of the holes, and there is perhaps more wear on the walls in this position. The mount is buckled towards the top, where there are two minor dents.

Height: 3·8 cm.
Maximum diameter at base ring: 3·5 cm.
Weight: 24·6 g.   Inventory no. FC 281

Cf. pl. xxvii c, e, fig. 18c, 33, and pp. 122 f., 140–3.
BIBLIOGRAPHY: O'Dell *et al.* (1959), 246, 260–1, pls. xxxi *g* and *j*, xxxii *b, f,* and *g*. O'Dell (1960), 6, 12, and 13. McRoberts (1960–1), 243 and fig. 6. McRoberts (1965), 243 and fig. 6.

15. SILVER GILT U-SHAPED CHAPE. Cast in three pieces: two side faces and a binding strip which caps the crest. The binding-strip terminates at either end in a crudely formed animal mask, consisting of a lozenge-shaped snout with a setting for two eyes, which originally held blue glass studs (only one of which survives). The strip, which is much worn, is decorated with alternating bands of opposed hatching; it is fixed at one end between the eyes of the animal head by a rivet and has then been carefully hammered over the joint and clasped in three places on one side, and four on the other by means of triangular projections. The mount has a narrow internal opening throughout its length; it is slightly buckled at one end and has been repaired on the back face at the terminal. There is also a slight fracture on the middle of the loop at the back. Where there is no buckling the average width of the opening is about 4 mm. The edge is chamfered into the opening. At each terminal a small rivet hole pierces both faces of the object.

Front face: At each end is an animal-head terminal executed in relief. The snout has a plain lower contour, defining a shape suggestive of a dewlap, and has a regularly corrugated pattern running transversely across the snout which is continued on the back face. The upper contour of each corrugation has a narrow channelled incision. The mouth is open, and two large pointed teeth bite a small fish contorted into a semi-circular position—the whole executed in openwork. The head of the fish and its eye are defined, the eye being formed of blue glass (one broken). The body is panelled and bears an incised rope-like pattern. The tail has an internal V-shaped incision, enclosing a straight central line. The eye socket of the animal-head terminal stands proud and is empty, but has a central depression at the base. The eye socket is drawn out from each side of the eye to a spiral terminal, the field so defined being filled by engraved concentric curved lines. The cheek is plain. Behind the animal head is a small panel of basket-work hatching. The crest below the binding strip is decorated by a series of equally spaced pairs of curved lines, backing towards the terminals, changing direction at the centre, where the triangular projections of the binding-strip are bordered by a double-contoured zigzag line. Behind each of the basket-work panels on the flat main panel of the face is a projection in the form of four spheres with a central sphere on top. This is repeated in the centre. Between the incised border of the field is an incised cursive minescules inscription: INNOMINEDS (*in nomine d. s.*), the inscription being broken after the second down stroke of the M.

A rivet occurs on the crest to one side just below the animal-head terminal of the binding-strip. This apparently has no function and may merely fill a flaw in the casting.

Back face: The animal-head terminals are simpler on this face. The snout is decorated in the same fashion as on the front but is narrower. The eye is similar but the socket is a simple incised triangle. The plain cheek terminates in an incised spiral. There are no free-standing teeth and the mouth is indicated by a zigzag line on the same plane as the snout. The main field bears, between an incised border, an inscription (the meaning of which is discussed below, pp. 167–73), in the same style as that on the front: RESAD-FILISPUSSCIO. The crest is decorated with a series of curvilinear animal heads facing towards the terminals, the series being divided in the centre by the single triangular extension of the binding-strip. There are seven heads on one side of the extension and six on the other. The heads have an open mouth, a bored dot for the eye, and an incised cheek-line. At the back of the head the curve swirls into a circle, which is placed within the open mouth of the head behind. The snout is slightly faceted to give a relief effect to the heads. Below the triangular extension of the binding-strips, towards the terminals, is a plain field with a circular extension like those at the back of the animal heads. The triangular fields towards the terminals are filled with pellets, triangles, and hatching.

Maximum width: 8·1 cm.

Weight: 62·9 g.   Inventory no. FC 282

Cf. pl. xxix, fig. 29, and pp. 118–22, 137–40, 167–73.

BIBLIOGRAPHY: O'Dell *et al.* (1959), 246, 261, pl. xxxii *k* and *l* and fig. 9. O'Dell (1960), 7 and 46. McRoberts (1960–1), 306–7. Jackson (1960). Wilson (1964), 15, 16, pl. iv *b*. McRoberts (1965), 236–7. Henderson (1967), 215, pl. 25.

16. SILVER U-SHAPED CHAPE, cast in two pieces and joined together by rivets at the terminals, the rivets being finished flush with the surface. The mount has a

narrow internal opening (*c.* 2 mm.) throughout its length. The object is in almost pristine condition, save that there is a possible trace of wear at the middle of the crest. Part of the crest is damaged on the front face, and traces of bad casting may be seen on the back.

Front face: Each terminal takes the form of an animal head executed in relief. The snout has slightly upturned nostrils and is corrugated. The mouth is open and the lower jaw terminates in a spiral scroll. Two teeth clasp a protruding tongue, which is decorated with a series of ovolos. The rest of the head is executed in a carved running spiral ornament, around a glass eye set in a plain collar. The eye on the left (the opening of the U being taken as the top) consists of a blue-glass dome with a red basal ring, while that to the right is of plain blue glass. Behind the eye a socket is indicated by means of transverse curved lines. Behind the head is a collar, consisting of a band of key-pattern ornament, defined by two incised lines. The main panel is of semi-circular cross-section and is decorated with chip-carved ornament. At points of interlace the carving is faceted to give the effect of 'under-and-over'. In the middle of the field is a cruciform panel defined by a plain border. It contains a series of inter-connected deeply incised spirals, consisting of a central spiral and a spiral in each arm. Carved interlace animal ornament fills the rest of the panel. The animals are speckled with minute triangular cuts, and signs of finishing with a graver can be seen. There are two animals in each of the two fields formed by the central cross. The design in each field is roughly similar: the animal heads are in the bottom corners; they have no eyes, the mouths gape, and the lips, which are separated by a deeply cut line from the cheek, terminate in slight curls. The animals have long necks, spiral front hips, and elaborate three-pawed feet. The animals in the left-hand field are asymmetrical, but form loops which terminate in more or less naturalistic hindquarters—the one pair to the left of the field, the other at the top: the legs interlacing with the limbs and bodies. The hindquarters of the animals in the other field are placed above the heads of the opposing animal.

The crest is decorated with a series of incised spirals, which make up a basic pattern of interlocking hooks. At each end of the crest, as it diminishes, the spirals are replaced by a key-pattern.

Back face: In most respects similar to the front face. The differences are that the eye of the left-hand terminal animal is blue and that of the right-hand animal is blue with red inclusions. The crest is completely filled with a key-pattern and the main panel is filled with triangular straight-sided spirals.

Maximum width: 8·2 cm.

Weight: 73·5 g.   Inventory no. FC 283

Cf. pl. xxx, *fig.* 30, *and pp.* 118–22, 137–40.

BIBLIOGRAPHY: O'Dell *et al.* (1959), 246, 261, pl. xxxii *i* and *j*, fig. 8 *a* and *b*. O'Dell (1960), 7 and 46. McRoberts (1960–1), 306–7. Wilson (1964), 15, 16, pl. iv *a*. McRoberts (1965), 236–7.

17. SILVER-GILT PENANNULAR BROOCH. The ornament is executed in chip-carving and engraving, within free-standing borders. The front of the brooch is gilded; the back is plain, but somewhat pitted with casting flaws. A few radial lines scored on the back of the hoop may have been caused by the smoothing process.

The hoop terminates in expanded sub-triangular fields. At the point where hoop and terminals join are large semi-circular cusps which rise 12·9 mm. above the back of the brooch (compared with an average 5·0 mm. for the other borders), and slope down to the normal border height. The corners of the terminal are cut off by raised borders; that nearest the hoop with a concave band, the others with convex bands. In the middle of each terminal is an empty setting with a central depression and inturned collar, which is surrounded at the base of the setting by a carved rope-like band. Below this band four zoomorphic extensions, set at right angles to each other, extend to the nearest border, further subdividing the field. They take the form of animal masks, have emphasized eyes, face outwards, and have a keeled slightly upturned snout. All the fields of the terminals are filled with chip-carved, ribbon-interlace ornament which, in each field, merges into a faceted border. The interlace pattern varies from field to field. In two of the fields (between the outermost arms of the central cross) the interlace terminates in a minute animal head, of which the eye and the open mouth are the only obvious features.

Opposite the terminals, on the hoop, is an elongated field with curved ends which rise like the cusps at the terminals. In the centre of this field is a square setting (now empty) which is surrounded by a double-hatched border. The field on either side of the setting is divided by a roughly faceted rib. The panels so formed are filled with interlace of the same type as that in the terminals. Each side of the rest of the hoop is divided into two sub-rhomboid fields by means of a bar, made up of animal masks placed back to back. They have long pointed ears, a moulded snout, and small bored eyes. The fields are filled with regular, double-strand, ribbon interlace. This is more or less similar in each field, save that the spaces between the ribbons are differently treated. One field has single, ribbon-interlace patterns in three places, another field has similar patterns in one place. Elsewhere the spaces are left plain, filled only with roughly shaped, faceted billets.

The pin is now in a number of pieces and has largely disintegrated towards the point. It has a plain back and had an out-turned hooked loop. It is made of a strip of silver and the only remaining decorated portion is the face of the pin, which bears a complicated series of chip-carved interlacing ribbon ornaments, enclosed within a slightly raised plain border. As on the main face of the brooch, the interlace joins with a faceted plain area, just inside the border. The interlace is broken up into irregular panels towards the expanded portion of the pin, where the ornament, due to the corrosion, is obscure. The pin is incomplete at the tip and most of the front of the head is missing. The remaining fragments were mounted on a Perspex reconstruction of its original shape in the Research Laboratory of the British Museum and the length of the pin given below is based on this reconstruction.

Diameter across the ring: 10·8 cm.
Reconstructed surviving length of pin: 19·0 cm.
Weight of hoop: 149·7 g.
Weight of surviving fragments of pin: 22·7 g.   Inventory no. FC 284

Cf. pl. xxxi, *fig.* 15, *and pp.* 81 ff.
BIBLIOGRAPHY: O'Dell *et al.* (1959), 246, pl. xxxiii *a.* O'Dell (1960), 7, 36, and 37.

18. SILVER PENANNULAR BROOCH, gilt on the front only. It is much worn and was originally mounted with ten glass studs, of which two (which are possibly secondary), survive; both are of brown glass. They are set in collars with slightly sloping sides. The ornament is executed in V-shaped incisions and the gilding only survives within the engraved portions. The back of the brooch is plain, save for a number of faults of casting, which give a pitted impression.

Each terminal has a sub-triangular shape and, where it joins the hoop, a roughly semi-circular cusped field (which rises 4·8 mm. above the back of the brooch compared with the normal 2·2 mm., at the terminal), which at the point where it touches the border of the terminal, forms an out-turned volute which stands free from the contour of the brooch (this is almost worn away on the outside edge). The cusp encloses a triquetra-knot pattern, executed so as to give an impression of under-and-over ribbon interlace. In the centre of each terminal is a triangular setting containing an amorphous brown glass stud with a domed top, which fits rather imperfectly into the field. From the corners of the triangle in each terminal is produced another setting, that towards the hoop being pear-shaped, the other two being lentoid. They are all empty, the base of the cell having a central circular indentation, surrounded in some cases by another circular indentation at a higher level. Between the settings are three rhomboid fields defined by beaded borders which are contiguous with, and (in places) common to, the borders round the settings (the beading is worn away in part). Within each of these fields is a roughly executed ribbon-interlace pattern.

Opposite the terminals the hoop is embellished with an elongated oval field with a heavy border which rises at either end to form cusps similar to those at the terminals. In the middle of the field is a rectangular setting with a central depression. This is surrounded by a hatched border and is flanked by beaded lines and fields enclosed within a beaded border. The fields contain ribbon-interlace patterns, which have an unfulfilled hint of zoomorphic character by the expansion of the terminals. The interlace is competently executed, giving the impression of under-and-over work. The 'tail' of the interlace (to the left in pl. xxxiii) is incised—giving the impression of a false start to a double ribbon interlace. The hoop has two incised bands of opposed hatched ornament, one on either side of a substantial midrib. The plain borders terminate in slight volutes outside the main contour at the field on the hoop. The volutes are practically worn away on the outside contour.

The pin is formed of a strip of metal, with a hoop at one end, behind an expanded, lentoid-shaped head. On the head is a panel containing a central circular setting. The setting is empty and has a deep central depression. It is surrounded by interlace which consists of a pair of triquetra-like knots joined, on either side of the setting, by a double twist of interlace. From the end of this field a groove is cut along the length of the pin; the groove expands a little, with the pin, where it crosses the hoop. The back of the pin is plain save for a groove which runs down its length; this feature cannot be seen at the point where the pin expands.

The wear on the brooch is heavy. The wear on the projecting volutes has already been noted, but it is particularly noticeable at the terminals, where part of the border is missing—on one side it has been partly torn away.

Diameter across ring: 7·0 cm.
Length of pin: 10·9 cm.
Weight: 48·0 g.   Inventory no. FC 285

Cf. pl. xxxiii, *fig.* 15, *and pp.* 81 ff.
BIBLIOGRAPHY: O'Dell *et al.* (1959), 246, 555, pl. xxiv f. O'Dell (1960), 7, 40, and 41.

19. SILVER-GILT PENANNULAR BROOCH with roughly square terminals. It is well worn and was originally mounted with five domed glass studs (of which a blue one survives in the centre of the left-hand terminal and a brown one in the centre of the right-hand terminal). Each stud is set within a collar of truncated conical form (the surviving studs are not as big as the settings and are very roughly cemented in). The ornament is executed in V-shaped engraving and the gilding only

survives within those portions protected by the raised borders and within the carving. The back is plain and was never gilded.

Where the terminal joins the hoop the corner of the field is extended into a cusp which rises to a height of 5·5 mm. above the back of the brooch (the normal height is approx. 3·5 mm.). The cusp encloses an empty circular setting (the base of which exhibits the central depression caused by the boring bit). Two lines extend from the cusp to the centre of the field and enclose a ribbon-interlace pattern executed in chip-carving (the actual pattern varies on each terminal). The whole element—cusp, setting, and lines—produce a formalized beaked head.

Between the central setting of each terminal and the three angled corners of the field is a dividing feature consisting of three elements of semi-zoomorphic aspect: from the centre, four parallel ribs extend to a much-worn amorphous blob, which produces a single rib. The fields formed by these divisions are filled with chip-carved ribbon-interlace patterns, based on a triquetra-knot pattern but varying in detail from field to field.

In the middle of the hoop is an elongated field within an upstanding border with ends of similar form to the cusps at the terminals. Within this field is an empty, central, circular setting, flanked by rather clumsy, asymmetrical, chip-carved ribbon interlace. The hoop is of plano-convex section and is defined by heavily incised, cable-patterned borders.

The pin has a lentoid head, which is produced to form a hook (fig. 15). The face of the pin is decorated within a plain border. In the centre of the head is a repoussé boss, which is divided into quadrants. The boss is much worn, but may originally have been decorated with a series of knots. On either side of the boss two animal heads face outwards. Each has a well-defined cheek line and a curled lower lip: from the mouth emerges a tongue which extends downwards to interlace with the first loop of the interlace pattern on the shaft of the pin. The neck falls away to a front hip, from which emerge two formalized legs which form a symmetrical interlace with the legs of the opposing animal. The uppermost 'foot' may coincide with the beginning of the interlaced ribbon round and above the boss. The pin is decorated for a third of its length with a simple single-element interlace, which finishes at the expanded point of the pin. Beyond this point the pin is plain between the two raised borders.

There is a groove along the back of the pin as far as the expanded portion: beyond this point it exhibits the wave-like pattern of hammering.

Diameter across ring: 7·5 cm.
Length of pin: 14·6 cm.
Weight: 69·6 g.   Inventory no. FC 286

Cf. pl. xxxii, fig. 15, and pp. 81 ff.
BIBLIOGRAPHY: O'Dell *et al.* (1959), 246, 255, pl. xxxiii *b*. O'Dell (1960), 7, 44, and 45.

20. SILVER-GILT PENANNULAR BROOCH, slightly worn. It was originally mounted with three glass studs (only one of which survives complete, one is broken). The back is plain and not gilt.

Each terminal has three projecting ears which more or less balance a similar field at the joints of the hoop and the terminals. Each field is of an elongated semi-circular form. The curve of the frame at the joint of hoop and terminal is cusped and slopes from a height of 5·8 mm. above the back of the brooch, to the height of the border of the central element of the terminal. Each field contains, within a single ribbon, a freestanding formalized animal mask, seen from above. Each mask consists of a pair of eyes, represented by bored holes, linked by a curved line; a stalk-like snout extends to the circular field in the middle of the terminal. On one of the terminals the border of the central feature consists of two ribbon-like lines which are broken where the heads occur. The main fields of the terminals are circular and contain a setting mounted with glass studs, the right-hand stud being of blue glass, the left-hand one of brown glass. Only the broken base of the latter remains. The setting is surrounded by a complicated ribbon-interlace pattern, executed in chip-carving. Attached to each of the terminal ears is a modelled animal head. It has a slight, bored eye, a curved cheek-line; the snout and lower jaw are emphasized as a continuous curved line.

In the middle of the hoop is an elongated oval field within an upstanding border with ends of similar form to the cusps at the terminals. In the centre of this field is an empty setting, the base of which has a depression made by the boring bit. It is flanked by pairs of straight lines and two bosses of rather angular contour, each of which is surrounded by a D-shaped ribbon border.

The rest of the hoop is decorated within a sunken field by an interlaced ribbon ornament, faceted to give an impression of true under-and-over plaiting. The interlace is bordered by a simple linear border.

The head of the pin loops round the hoop in the form of a hook. The panel at the head is lentoid in form and bears a complicated ribbon interlace, with included pellets, all executed in chip-carving. The interlace is extended on to the pin in the form of a squared cable pattern which broadens with the pin (where the latter crosses the ring) into a normal interlace pattern. The pattern ceases some 2 cm. from the tip, although the incised border round the whole ornament continues almost to the tip.

Diameter across the ring: 7·9 cm.

Length of pin: 14·4 cm.

Weight: 98·5 g.   Inventory no. FC 287

Cf. pl. xxxii, fig. 15, and pp. 81 ff.

BIBLIOGRAPHY: O'Dell *et al.* (1959), 246, 255, pl. xxxiii *c.* O'Dell (1960), 7, 44, and 45.

21. SILVER PENANNULAR BROOCH. The brooch, which is well worn, was originally mounted with three studs, none of which survives. The settings for the studs are of a truncated conical shape and those at the terminals have a central hole, with inward sloping sides which pierce the object. That in the panel on the hoop has a central depression which does not pierce the brooch. The back is plain.

The terminals are trilobate, each lobe backing on to the central circular field. Where the central field joins the hoop is an elongated semi-circular field defined by a cusp which rises from the border of the central element to a height of 4·3 mm. above the back of the brooch (compared with 2·2 mm. for the border of the central element). This cusp encloses a rather angular triquetra knot. The lobes comprise a degenerate animal mask constructed of two pairs of V-shaped incisions of varying depths. The snouts face inwards and each mask is enclosed on three sides by a U-shaped, double-contoured border, which links the three lobes. Each central field is defined by a plain border and has an empty setting in the middle, surrounded by two ribbon-like lines.

The elongated panel in the middle of the hoop follows the contours of the ring and terminates in curved ends which take the same form as the cusps at the terminals, but are not quite so high (4·1 mm. above the back). The panel is divided into three, roughly equal-sized, fields. The central field contains an empty round setting, which stands upon a rhomboid base. It is flanked by semi-circular fields containing triquetra knots. The border to this field is broken in one place by a casting flaw.

The hoop is of plano-convex section and is bordered by an engraved rope-like pattern, defined by two deeply engraved lines, the borders terminating in a small volute at the ends of the panel on the loop.

The pin is incomplete, it lacks its head and its loop. The process of rounding its sides has formed a longitudinal groove, back and front. On the face this has been emphasized by cutting the metal to form a hollow-based channel. The expanded portion is left plain. The break has been rubbed smooth.

Diameter across the ring: 7·2 cm.

Length of pin: 8·1 cm.

Weight: 39·7 g.   Inventory no. FC 288

Cf. pl. xxxiv, *fig.* 15, *and pp.* 81 ff.

BIBLIOGRAPHY: O'Dell *et al.* (1959), 246, 255, 256, pl. xxxiii *f*. O'Dell (1960), 7, 42, and 43.

22. SILVER-GILT PENANNULAR BROOCH, much worn, originally mounted with four circular dome-shaped studs, of which one (of blue glass) survives. They are set in truncated conical settings. The ornament is executed by V-shaped

incisions. The gilding only survives within the ornamented panels and the back is plain and not gilded.

Each terminal is trilobate, each of the lobes taking the form of a mask surrounded by a curved frame consisting of two ribbons with outward-turned, slightly scrolled ends. A fourth field of similar shape occurs on the hoop, where it joins the terminal; it has a cusped border which slopes downwards towards the central circular field of the terminal. The ornament in the field on the hoop is similar to that on the lobes save that the mask is surrounded by three plain lines. The central field on one of the terminals contains a cabochon of blue glass in its central setting; the setting in the other field is empty. Each setting is surrounded by three concentric rings. In the middle of the hoop is a long field defined at either end by free-standing semi-circular borders, like those at the terminals. These fields flank a central circular field, similar to (but smaller than) the circular fields of the terminals. The flanking fields are similar in design to those at the terminals. Here it can be seen that the masks are produced in a small extension over the border of the circle to form a beak—a feature which is present, but less clear, at the terminals. Each of these masks, and those at the terminals appear to be formed as a snout and a skull (the latter in every case being worn), the snout being decorated with pairs of oblique incised lines to give a hipped contour. The centring mark of the boring implement can be seen in the base of each empty setting.

The main portion of the hoop is decorated with two incised bands of rope-like ornament.

The pin has a lentoid head with a shallow, but empty, central setting (with a pierced central hole) surrounded by a complicated interlace pattern. Behind it is a hook (fig. 15). Within an elongated lentoid field, half-way along the front of the pin in a slightly flattened and expanded area, is a simple single-strand interlace pattern with pointed terminals.

Diameter across the ring: 6·6 cm.
Length of pin: 12·6 cm.
Weight: 55·0 g. Inventory no. FC 289

Cf. pl. xxxiv, *fig.* 15, *and pp.* 81 ff.
BIBLIOGRAPHY: O'Dell *et al.* (1959), 246, 255, pl. xxxiii *e*. O'Dell (1960), 7, 38, and 39.

23. SILVER-GILT PENNANULAR BROOCH, well worn, originally mounted with four circular dome-headed studs of which one (of brown glass) survives in the right-hand terminal. They are set in collars with slightly sloping sides. The

ornament is executed by means of V-shaped incisions and the gilding only survives within the ornament. The back is plain and not gilded.

Each terminal is composed of a circular roundel from which spring three ears, each with a border enclosing an amorphous free-standing element (reminiscent of an animal's head seen from above) which terminates on the border of the central disc, but with no features remaining. This is surrounded by a ribbon. A fourth field of related shape occurs at the join of the terminal of the hoop. It has a raised border (0·44 cm. above the base of the brooch), which slopes down to the border of the edge of the terminal. Within this field is a band of interlaced ribbon, which on one side of the right-hand terminal continues as the frame of the 'head' in the right-hand ear. The central roundel comprises a central setting surrounded by three concentric circles, broken opposite each head by three radially placed short lines. A fourth circle forms an unbroken immediate frame to the setting.

In the middle of the hoop is an elongated field with curved top and curved ends. The latter rise slightly in the manner of the similar feature at the terminals. Within the field is a central empty setting, flanked by triquetra knots—the whole bordered by a single line. The hoop is decorated near either edge with an incised band of rope-like ornament.

The pin is formed of a strip of metal, the lentoid head of which is produced to form a hook, with an out-turned terminal (fig. 16). The lentoid head has a central setting (with a circular depression at the bottom) flanked by triquetra knots. From a fork below one of the knots is produced the single median ridge of ornament of the pin, which expands into a simple twist pattern where the pin broadens to cross the loop.

Diameter across the ring: 7·2 cm.
Length of pin: 13·3 cm.   Inventory no. FC 290

Cf. pl. xxxiii, *fig.* 16, *and pp.* 81 ff.
BIBLIOGRAPHY: O'Dell *et al.* (1959), 246, 248, 255, 256, pl. xxxiv *d.* O'Dell (1960), 7, 38, and 39.

24. SILVER-GILT PENANNULAR BROOCH, the pin is particularly worn. Much of the gilding has gone. Originally mounted with four circular studs of which only the truncated conical settings survive. The back is plain and not gilded. The back of the pin has a slight groove for about three-quarters of its length, which is missing where the pin expands to cross the ring.

Each terminal has three projecting ears, each of which contains a pear-shaped feature with the point towards the centre of the terminal. These apparently have no zoo-morphic attributes, and are framed by a pair of comma-like features with a common internal line and heavily scrolled terminals. The tip of the ear to the left has been broken away in antiquity and has been worn smooth. Where the hoop joins the terminals is an elongated semi-circular field bordered by a curved upstanding frame (the right-hand one rises 5·5 mm. above the back of the brooch) which slopes down to the height of the central element of the terminal to form two out-turned scrolls. The contour of this frame is allowed for by a slight angle on the inside of the hoop. The frame encloses a single line of conjoined lentoid loops of ribbon-like form around a pear-shaped projection like those on the ears (that on the right is, however, much less prominent and more ovolo shaped). The central field of each terminal is circular; each has a raised border and a central setting, with a central bored depression. The settings are enclosed by two plain flat-topped bands, defined by grooves of V-shaped section.

In the middle of the hoop is an elongated field with curved ends which rise, like the cusps at the terminal, to a height of 5 mm. The field has a central circular setting and this is flanked asymmetrically by interlace ribbon ornament. The centre of the setting is now pierced. The hoop has been broken just to the right of the setting, having been repaired with solder. The border is deeply carved in imitation of a cable pattern.

The lentoid head of the pin hides the hook at the back (fig. 16). The head has an empty setting with a low collar flanked by triquetra knots which join on either side of the setting. From the point of the lowermost element of this design is produced a rib which forms the spine of the pin. The rib widens slightly at the point where the pin broadens and a row of fine dots flank it through its length.

At the top of the hoop two flaws in the casting on the back of the brooch have been carefully plugged and polished.

Diameter across the ring: 6·6 cm.
Length of pin: 10·8 cm.
Weight: 43·8 g.   Inventory no. FC 291

Cf. pl. xxxiii, *fig.* 16, *and pp.* 81 ff.
BIBLIOGRAPHY: O'Dell *et al.* (1959), 248, 255, pl. xxiv e. O'Dell (1960), 7, 42, and 43.

25. SILVER-GILT PENANNULAR BROOCH, worn. Much of the gilding has gone from the proud surfaces. Most of the ornament is chip-carved and the brooch was originally embellished with ten studs, set in truncated conical settings, all of which are now missing. The back is plain and not gilt; it shows traces of pouring during the casting process. The back of the pin has a slight groove for about three-quarters of its length: the groove is not present under the expanded portion of the pin.

Each terminal has three projecting ears containing a (now empty) circular cell, with a plain rim and a slight central depression. The settings are crowned by two comma-like features with a common internal line and scrolled terminals. At each end of the hoop, at the point at which it joins the terminal, is an elongated semi-circular field. This is bordered by an upstanding frame (the right-hand one rises 6·1 mm. above the back of the brooch) which slopes down to the height of the border of the central element of the terminal to form two out-turned scrolls. The frame forms an angle with the inside contour of the hoop and encloses a symmetrical, but angular, ribbon-interlace pattern. The central panel of each terminal is circular and had central circular settings, which are now both broken. That on the right seems to have been broken off in antiquity and replaced by a loose stud, as a rough seating has been made for such a stud on the face of the brooch and a central hole in this position has been plugged with bronze— perhaps the remains of a rivet. Round each of the central settings is a ribbon interlace, consisting of a series of loops, which seem to represent in their execution an 'under-and-over' technique.

In the middle of the hoop is a roundel with a high free-standing border flanked by two semi-circular fields, the borders of which rise a little towards the ends. The flanking fields and the circle are defined by slightly faceted moulding on the edges of the hoop. In the circular field is an empty setting surrounded by a beaded border. In the flanking fields are symmetrical ribbon-interlace patterns, framed by a single ribbon. The hoop has a beaded border towards either edge. The beads are conically shaped.

The head of the pin is lentoid and hides the hook behind it (fig. 16). In the centre of the lentoid field is an empty setting flanked by triquetra knots which join on either side of the setting. From the lowermost portion of this design a rib runs down the spine of the pin. On the top of the rib and on the left-hand side are lines of very fine, saltire-shaped dots. At the expanded central portion of the pin the single line develops into an angular interlace pattern, consisting of a simple twist pattern with rings round the central portion. Towards the tip the median line is rather broader and flanked by dotted lines. It finishes 9 mm. from the tip, although one of the contours continues almost to the tip itself.

Diameter of the ring: 7·1 cm.
Length of pin: 12·2 cm.
Weight: 54·5 g.   Inventory no. FC 292

Cf. pl. xxxv, *fig.* 16, *and pp.* 81 ff.
BIBLIOGRAPHY: O'Dell *et al.* (1959), 248, 255 and pl. xxxiv *c.* O'Dell (1960), 7, 40, and 41.

26. SILVER-GILT PENANNULAR BROOCH, well worn (much of the gilding has gone), originally mounted with ten dome-shaped glass studs (of which seven of brown glass and one of green glass survive). They are set in truncated conical settings. The ornament is deeply engraved in a chip-carving technique. The back, which is not gilded, is much pitted and a small hole pierces one of the terminals.

Each terminal has three projecting ears, each containing a central setting with a glass stud (that to the right being of green glass). The setting is framed by a curved hood which has scrolled terminals and two segmental lobes, a feature which is much worn and only survives complete on the internal ears. At the point of junction of hoop and terminals is an elongated semi-circular field, bordered by a semi-circular cusp which slopes down towards the terminal, where it turns outwards to form scrolled ends. Within the field so formed is a triquetra knot of single ribbon interlace within a plain ribbon border. The central circular panel of each terminal is defined by a plain, free-standing border. In the centre of the field is a glass stud in a plain setting (the stud on the left-hand terminal is missing and reveals the centring point of the boring-bit at the base of the socket). Surrounding the stud is a skilfully carved interlace pattern, executed three-dimensionally so that the strands appear to go under and over each other.

In the middle of the hoop is an elongated field consisting of a central circular field, surrounding a single ribbon, which in turn surrounds a glass stud. It is flanked by free-standing cusps like those at the terminals. The cusps enclose triquetra knots within a plain ribbon border. The hoop is plain, save for two deep grooves with a median ridge.

The pin consists of a single piece of metal bent round to form a loop at the head. The head has a lentoid shape which bears a central setting (now empty) flanked by deeply carved triquetra knots. The pin is panelled and the panel encloses a ribbon-interlace pattern consisting of a simple twist at the top of the pin and a double twist at the broader portion. Towards the tip the interlace degenerates into plain hatching.

On the back of each terminal are some slight scratches which seem to be unintentional.

Diameter across ring: 7·1 cm.
Length of pin: 11·2 cm.
Weight: 57·9 g.   Inventory no. FC 293

Cf. pl. xxxv, *fig.* 16, *and pp.* 81 ff.
BIBLIOGRAPHY: O'Dell *et al.* (1959), 248, 255, pl. xxxiv *b*. O'Dell (1960), 7, 42, and 43.

27. SILVER-GILT PENANNULAR BROOCH, much worn (much of the gilding has gone from the proud surfaces). It was originally mounted with nine dome-shaped glass studs, of which six—four brown and two blue—survive. They were set

in truncated conical settings. The pin was mounted with a cabochon jewel (now missing) set in an applied cell. The back is plain and not gilded. The edge is slightly damaged above the central field of the hoop.

Each terminal has three projecting ears, each of which contains a circular cell with a plain rim; at the base of the empty cells can be seen a central bored hole. Two cells on the left-hand terminal, and one on the right, carry ill-fitting glass studs. The settings are placed towards the apex of each ear and from them emerge, on either side, gently curved ribbons which rise slightly from the setting and curve downwards to form a slight scroll towards the base of the field. Enclosed by these two lines, and by the setting, is a ribbon-interlace pattern consisting of two triquetra knots conjoined below the setting and continuing, by way of a small triangular protrusion, to join the interlace in the next field. The external ears are much worn—indeed in one case almost half of one cell is worn away. At each end of the hoop, conjoined with the terminal, is an elongated semi-circular field, bordered by a cusped frame which slopes down to the height of the circular border of the central element of the terminal. This contains a symmetrical ribbon-interlace pattern. The central panel of the terminal is circular and is defined by a plain, free-standing border. In the centre is a glass stud (blue to left, brown to right) surrounded by a carved ribbon-interlace pattern.

In the middle of the hoop is an elongated field. The curved ends are cusped like those at the terminals. In the centre of the field is a blue glass stud set in a circular mount and surrounded by a symmetrical interlace ribbon. The hoop is plain, save for two deep bordering grooves which are cross-hatched across the base.

The pin consists of a single piece of metal bent to form a hook at the head. The head is of lentoid form and of rectangular cross-section. The pin is of roughly circular cross-section, save at the tip, where it becomes oval. The head of the pin has a broadened face which is mounted with an empty oval setting. The setting, which is soldered to the pin, consists of a silver collar, slightly inturned at the top, surrounded at the base by a worn beaded wire. The wire collar is broken towards the point of the pin. This break is perhaps intentional, as two moulded, wire-like lines run off the edge of the pin at this point. At the head of the pin two pairs of incised lines pass obliquely from the edge of the setting to the edge of the pin. The setting is empty and the collar much damaged.

Diameter across ring: 7·1 cm.

Length of pin: 11·1 cm.

Weight: 65·9 g. Inventory no. FC 294

Cf. pl. xxxv, *fig.* 16, *and pp.* 81 ff.

BIBLIOGRAPHY: O'Dell *et al.* (1959), 248, 255, pl. xxiv *a*. O'Dell (1960), 7, 38, and 39.

28. SILVER-GILT PENANNULAR BROOCH, well worn, originally mounted with three studs of which the truncated cone-shaped settings are all that remain. The marks of the boring tool used in making the settings are clearly seen under the microscope: there is a central depression at the base of each setting. The ornament is executed within prominent borders with V-shaped cuts of the chisel. The back is plain, save for a slight groove down that part of the pin which is not expanded where it crosses the hoop. The brooch is gilded only on the face.

Each terminal takes the form of an animal head with a completely straight snout and curled lips. The ear stands out as a backward-curved projection, and both it and the lower lip (which might be interpreted as a beard) are panelled with hatching. Behind the ear is a coiled lappet. The eye is formed of a collar-type setting with slightly sloping sides (the bored centring holes being clearly visible at the base). The mouth is crudely drawn with serrated teeth on either side of a straight band. The rest of the space is filled with interlace ribbon patterns, which extend in the top corner to form a spiral hook inside the lip. Behind each head at the end of the ring is a D-shaped field with a border which diminishes in height towards the terminal (its maximum height above the back of the brooch on the right-hand terminal is 5·2 mm.). The border encloses more interlace ribbon, that on the left-hand terminal being most carelessly executed.

In the middle of the hoop is a long field with a curved top and ends. The latter rise very slightly in imitation of the lugs at the terminals. From each corner of the field, both inside and outside the hoop, emerges a small tightly curled volute. The field is filled with crude interlaced ribbon ornament, which surrounds a central setting. The hoop itself has two V-shaped lines cut into it, following each contour, to give the impression of a single faceted ribbon at each border.

The pin, which is much pitted with corrosion, forms a hook beneath the head with a spatulate, out-turned terminal. The lentoid-shaped head of the pin has a central repoussé boss (now much worn), surrounded by an interlaced ribbon pattern. The interlace is produced to form a simple single-looped interlace down the pin to the expanded portion where the pin crosses the ring, here the interlace doubles up, but returns to a single-loop pattern towards the tip; some 2·3 cm. from this point only the bordering incised lines remain, crossed at intervals by four pairs of slightly incised lines.

Diameter across the ring: 7·1 cm.

Length of pin: 12·0 cm.

Weight: 68·3 g.   Inventory no. FC 295

Cf. pl. xxxiv, fig. 16, and pp. 81 ff.

BIBLIOGRAPHY: O'Dell *et al.* (1959), 248, 256, 257, pl. xxxiii *d* and frontispiece. O'Dell (1960), 7, 40, and 41,

29. RIGHT HALF OF LOWER JAW-BONE of a mature porpoise (*Phocaena communis*), much stained with copper oxides. It is intact save for the teeth and a slight crack in the thinnest part of the bone.

Length: 20·8 cm.   Inventory no. FC 296

See pp. 123–4.
BIBLIOGRAPHY: O'Dell *et al.* (1959), 248, 262, 266. O'Dell (1960), 7 and 47.

IV *The brooches*

THE importance of the St. Ninian's Isle hoard in the study of one of the most ubiqui-tous antiquities of the early Christian period in Scotland—the brooch—is hard to under-estimate. In this chapter I shall attempt to discuss the brooches in detail within their general cultural context and within the context of the hoard.[1]

It is my contention that the St. Ninian's Isle brooches are of Pictish origin and were manufactured in the late eighth century. I shall attempt to distinguish between Pictish and Irish brooches and try to demonstrate a different origin for the two groups, the Pictish being influenced by the true penannular brooch and the Irish by the ring-headed pin.

The Pictish brooch of the eighth century

The Revd. J. M. Joass, minister of Golspie, founder of the Duke of Sutherland's private museum and a considerable Scottish antiquary, wrote to the Secretary of the Society of Antiquaries of Scotland on New Year's Day, 1870, as follows:

. . . in /68 a Railway workman in Rogart, blasting boulders for building, found 11 brooches under one of them. The largest, about 5½ in diamr is of white bronze, gilt. The next largest, about 2½ inches, of silver, another about the same size of Bronze silver gilt. The last I received for our Museum but the first Vale the rest had been taken away by a relative of the finder & sold. I could only trace the two first which were purchased by Cadboll . . .[2]

The Rogart brooches, which can now be seen as part of a more considerable find,[3] have for a long time comprised the principal find of penannular brooches in Scotland. Only three brooches are definitely known to survive from this hoard; two (pls. xxxvi, xxxvii *d*), in the National Museum of Antiquities of Scotland (and originally belonging

[1] I must particularly acknowledge the help I have received from Mr. R. B. K. Stevenson while writing this chapter. Mr. Stevenson's knowledge of Celtic brooches is unequalled and he has unhesitatingly and with his usual generosity placed his knowledge at my disposal. Although I must accept responsibility for the opinions expressed here, some of which differ from those of Mr. Stevenson, it would have been almost impossible for me to have undertaken this study without his aid.

[2] Letter in National Museum of Antiquities of Scot-land, MS. 379 (23). The 'Cadboll' referred to was R. B. Æ. Macleod of Cadboll.

[3] In the proceedings of the Society, 14 Feb. 1870 (*Proceedings of the Society of Antiquaries of Scotland*, viii (1868–70), 309), we get our only printed hint of the size of the find: 'these three brooches were found with a number of others (which cannot now be traced), on blasting an earth-fast boulder in the course of the forma-tion of the Sutherland Railway in the parish of Rogart . . .'.

to R. B. Æ. Macleod of Cadboll), and a third, now in the possession of the Countess of Sutherland, which apparently consists of the ring of one brooch and the pin of another. It seems likely, however, that two brooches (one a fragment) acquired by Sir John Evans in 1881 from Thomas Mackenzie of Tain, now in the Ashmolean Museum, Oxford (pl. xxxvii *a, b*), may have come from Rogart. When they came to the museum they were labelled 'found in Sutherland, 1873' and were associated with two Anglo-Saxon ninth-century strap-ends of similar provenance.[1] The letter to Mr. Joass and these slender clues in the Ashmolean Museum may indicate a lost hoard of a size which approaches that of the St. Ninian's Isle treasure. The twelve St. Ninian's Isle brooches can, therefore, nearly be matched in quantity by the Rogart find.

Another Scottish hoard contains at least three penannular brooches (two merely fragments)—the hoard from Croy, Inverness (pl. xxxviii), which came to the National Museum of Antiquities of Scotland in two parcels.[2] This hoard may have included a fourth brooch of rather peculiar form which cannot now be traced.[3] The Croy hoard also included a number of other objects, including a balance-beam and two English coins, one of which dates from the middle of the ninth century—the coins are pierced for suspension, a factor which must be considered in evaluating the date of deposition of the hoard. Mr. C. E. Blunt, who has published the coins,[4] has kindly confirmed his identification of these coins as follows: an early coin of Coenwulf (dated 796–805) and a coin of Æthelwulf (dated 843–8). The hoard is an oddity, perhaps to be interpreted as part of the stock-in-trade of a jeweller, and the dates of the coins are of little significance in providing an accurate date for the objects.

It is, however, interesting that these three hoards—St. Ninian's Isle, Rogart, and Croy —should all be found in the north-east of Scotland and that they should all contain a number of true penannular brooches. If we consider the distribution of penannular brooches of the St. Ninian's Isle type (listed pp. 89 ff.), this north-easterly bias is emphasized to an even greater extent (fig. 14) and their presence in Norway is also explained.

What then are the chief characteristics of brooches of the St. Ninian's Isle type? First, and most important, they are all penannular in the proper sense of the word; the one exception is the brooch from Ballynaglough, Co. Antrim (pl. xxxix *b*) which has had a secondary strengthening bar added in recent times, when the hoop was repaired.[5] Secondly, all such brooches have a panel with curved ends on the hoop. Cusps almost always occur behind the terminal, functioning as a stop to prevent the pin sliding over

[1] Listed, Wilson (1964), 113.

[2] Anderson (1874–6) and Ross (1885–6).

[3] See photograph taken in Perth before 1885 (National Museum of Antiquities of Scotland, MS. 307. 19).

[4] Blunt (1949–50). Coins illustrated by Stevenson (1966), pl. II, 59 and 82.

[5] This fact was originally pointed out to me by Mr. R. B. K. Stevenson.

the terminals; a similar feature often occurs at the end of the fields on the hoop. There are two basic types of terminal: *a*, the lobed terminal (e.g. pl. xli), and *b*, the plate terminal which can take a variety of forms (cf. pls. xl, xlix *d*). The pin usually has a lentoid head, is made in one piece from a sheet of metal, and expands at the point where it crosses the ring (where it would be seen when the brooch was in use). The head curves round to form a hook behind the panel—a feature which made it comparatively easy to remove the pin from the ring. While it is easy to recognize a pin from such a brooch in isolation,[1] the pin may sometimes have been replaced, as, for example, on the brooch from Loch Fyne (pl. xli *c*),[2] which is the only surviving brooch of St. Ninian's Isle type with an Irish form of pin-head. Again it has already been pointed out that the brooch from Rogart,[3] which does not fall into the main St. Ninian's series, has a pin from a St. Ninian's Isle type of brooch, which has obviously been added to the hoop since the hoard was found. In this case the pin probably came from one of the other brooches in the hoard. In the case of the Breadalbane brooch (pl. xlvi *a*) the St. Ninian's Isle type of pin was added in antiquity, when the brooch was converted from an Irish type (p. 85). This fact perhaps demonstrates the importance of the removable pin in the Scottish area. Some elaborate brooches in the series are decorated with inlaid gold plates,[4] whilst others differ in detail from the rest of the series (particularly in the treatment of the terminals), but a glance at the examples illustrated (pls. xxxvi–xlii) will quickly show the common and binding features listed above.

The size of the brooch can vary considerably, from large examples like that from Rogart (which is 11·9 cm. in diameter) (pl. xxxvi) or no. 17 from St. Ninian's Isle (pl. xxxi) (which is 10·8 cm. in diameter), to minute examples like that from Freswick (pl. xl *b*), the original diameter of which cannot have been more than about 2·5 cm.

The number of Irish brooches surviving within their country of origin is small, but their characteristics are clearly distinguishable. The typical Irish brooch has terminals joined either by a series of short bars or by a solid panel of the same length as the terminals:[5] thus the Irish brooches, which have an annular hoop, should be properly labelled 'pseudo-penannular'—a term I intend to use in this study. Only one elaborate truly penannular brooch from Ireland can definitely be said to be of Irish manufacture; it comes from Kilmainham, Co. Dublin.[6] The lobed terminals and the curved-ended panel on the hoop I believe to be of Scottish or Pictish influence, otherwise details—

---

[1] e.g. the secondarily adapted pin from the Viking cemetery site at Valtos on the Isle of Lewis, Gibson (1933–4), 430.

[2] Collection of the Duke of Argyll.

[3] Smith (1914), fig. 9, 3.

[4] e.g. the brooch from Perth, pl. xlii *d*.

[5] e.g. Henry (1965), pls. 44 and 45; Mahr (1932), pls. 20, 1 and 3 and 23, 4 and 6.

[6] Its only parallel is a fragment from Eia, Sogndal, Rogaland, Norway (pl. xlvii *c*).

such as the pin, the stitching of the gold inlay, and the curved new-moon shaped cells
are convincingly Irish. Otherwise penannular brooches of this elaborate form do not
occur in Ireland (with the exceptions listed on p. 90, which belong to the St. Ninian's
Isle series). While it is possible that some simple penannular brooches were produced
in Ireland in the eighth century,[1] following on from the forms of the previous centuries
discussed by Kilbride-Jones[2] and Elizabeth Fowler,[3] the true penannular brooch of
elaborate form found in Irish contexts[4] seems to be of much later date than the Irish
forms cognate to those from St. Ninian's Isle. Where there is a panel on the ring of an
Irish brooch it often, but not universally,[5] has squared ends. The pin of an Irish brooch
usually has a flat sub-triangular or rectangular head and is normally attached to the hoop
by means of a cast loop welded or riveted to the back of the head. The pin is often, but
not always, longer than that usually found in the St. Ninian's Isle series and is often,
though not universally, made separately from a rod of circular cross-section, socketed
into the pin-head.

Some brooches are at first sight difficult to fit into either of the former categories.
The Kilmainham (p. 83) and Ervey brooches have already been mentioned, while the
'Londesborough' brooch could also be used to illustrate this uncertainty. The latter[6]
brooch has the cusps and panel of the hoop of the St. Ninian's Isle series, but it also has
the joined terminals and pin-head of the Irish group. The cusps and the panels on the
hoop are surely derived from a prototype common to both series and the fashion
presumably grew due to the constant contact between the various Celtic areas. The
Londesborough brooch is certainly made outside the area influenced by the St. Ninian's
Isle series.

A similar fusion of forms can be seen on the brooch from Skryne, Co. Meath,[7]
which has lobes and cusping similar to those on the St. Ninian's Isle type, but has
joined terminals and a square panel on the hoop (the pin may be secondary). This is

---

[1] A penannular brooch was found in a crannog at
Ervey, Co. Meath (*Journal of the Royal Society of Antiquaries
of Ireland*, xc (1960), 35). The only feature which dis-
tinguishes it from the St. Ninian's Isle series is the square
panel on the hoop. I would see this as being produced
under very strong Scottish influence (pl. xlii *e*).

[2] Kilbride-Jones (1935–7).

[3] Fowler (1963).

[4] I refer here to such brooches as Mahr (1932), pl. 48, 4,
Smith (1914), pl. xxviii, and Wilson (1958). I have always
had doubts about the date of the 'Dalriada' brooch (Mahr,
op. cit., pl. 21, 3), which was found near Coleraine in
Co. Londonderry. It has a detail of brambling, later

found in ninth- and tenth-century thistle brooches, but
best paralleled on such ninth-century pseudo-penannular
brooches as that from Killamery (ibid., pl. 40, 3) and a
pin which is very close in style to the Scottish series of
pins. The brooch is the only penannular brooch of gold
and it therefore must be considered *sui generis*. I would
tend to place it in a ninth-century context along with the
poorer brooches mentioned below, p. 88.

[5] Such exceptions occur especially on the richer
brooches, cf. the Kilmainham brooch (pl. xlvii *a*).

[6] Mahr (1932), pl. xxiii, 2.

[7] Smith (1914), pl. xxvi, 3.

probably an object of Irish manufacture and physical examination shows it to be an insubstantial piece of casting, much lighter than the average brooch of either Irish or Pictish type. I should imagine that both this brooch and other similar brooches (as that from Longhill,[1] from Co. Antrim in the British Museum,[2] or a brooch without provenance in the National Museum of Antiquities of Scotland,[3] and even that from Mull),[4] may well be products of a fusion of forms of brooches of the Irish and St. Ninian's Isle series, perhaps initiated in the Western Isles and north Ireland. In the case of some Scottish finds (e.g. pl. xlvi a) the bar has been removed in antiquity;[5] perhaps because the true penannular type of brooch was the fashion in Scotland. The richest example of a brooch with this feature is the 'Breadalbane' brooch (pl. xlvi a)—an object which is presumed to have been found in Scotland. The bar between the terminals of this brooch has been cut away and, as has already been noted (p. 83), a St. Ninian's Isle type of pin has been added to the brooch in antiquity. These brooches and certain others of Scottish provenance are almost certainly of Irish·manufacture; there are not many of them, however, and they are usually found in purely Viking contexts or areas,[6] where they are likely to have been brought from their original homeland.

Other brooches, much richer than the rest, are not so easy to locate in the same way. Some indeed may belong to the seventh century. Chief amongst these[7] are the Tara brooch,[8] the Hunterston brooch,[9] and the brooch from Westness in Orkney.[10]

The problem of the place of manufacture of these objects has been much discussed of late.[11] It could be argued that all three were made in Ireland; the Tara brooch because of its Irish provenance (it was found at Betaghstown, Co. Meath), and the other two because they are known to have been at one time in Viking hands (the Hunterston brooch because of a secondary inscription in Scandinavian runes on the back, the Westness brooch because it was found in a Viking grave). On the other hand, the ornament on these brooches is closely comparable with that found in the Northumbrian insular manuscripts, and particularly with that of the Lindisfarne Gospels, implying a Northumbrian origin for the style. The problem is, in the present climate of discussion, incapable of solution and need not concern us here. It does, however, appear that all

---

[1] Ibid., pl. xxvi, 6.

[2] Reg. no. 1924, 10–25, 2.

[3] Mahr (1932), pl. 37, 7.

[4] Smith (1914), pl. xxvi, 8.

[5] Cf. Anderson (1881), fig. 11. Note also the atypical brooch from between Abergeldie and Birkhall, Aberdeenshire (pl. xliv c).

[6] Cf., for example, the brooches from Mull, pl. xlviii and ibid., fig. 9, or the brooch from Smulan, Sparbu, Nord Tröndelag, Norway, Shetelig (1940), v, fig. 166.

[7] An example not discussed here is the fragment of a brooch from Acharole, Dunbeath, Caithness, which seems to belong to this series—Anderson (1881), fig. 11.

[8] Henry (1965), pls. 38 and 40–2.

[9] Shetelig (1940), ii, fig. 88.

[10] *Brooches in Scotland*, National Museum of Antiquities of Scotland, 2nd ed., Edinburgh, 1966, pl. 9. Cf. also Stevenson (1968).

[11] Cf. Bruce Mitford in Kendrick *et al.* (1960), 251 f., and *contra*, Henry (1965) 108 ff.; cf. also Stevenson (1968), 30.

these brooches are earlier than the St. Ninian's Isle series and that they influenced the design of this series. Particularly noticeable, for example, is the curved-ended panel on the hoop of the Tara brooch, the semi-circular settings on the hoop of the Westness brooch, the curved cusps on the Tara brooch, and a semi-circular setting at the heel of the terminals of the Westness example. The Hunterston brooch has a stop formed in a slightly less sophisticated manner. It might be wiser in this context to beg the question of the origin of these three brooches, and of the pieces closely allied to them, and see them as the product of an Irish Sea cultural zone—a thesis which reflects the well-documented seventh- and early eighth-century contact between Ireland, Iona, and Lindisfarne.[1]

The penannular brooch has a long history which has been detailed by Mrs. Fowler.[2] It developed in Britain during the La Tène period and the earliest examples appear to date from the third century B.C. It survived through the Roman period into the 'Dark Ages' and Mrs. Fowler has taken the story down to the ninth century—ignoring, quite properly, the rich brooches of the seventh and eighth centuries which concern us here. The penannular brooch continued to be used in the ninth and tenth centuries, when it took the form of the Hiberno-Saxon series[3] and of the thistle-headed brooches,[4] the production of which appears to have ceased in the second half of the tenth century. After this date the large decorated penannular brooch is not encountered in the British Isles.

The St. Ninian's Isle series falls naturally into this sequence, the form of the animal-head terminal on such brooches as that from Ardagh[5] providing the stop for the pin which is the prototype of the curved cusp of the St. Ninian's Isle brooches. This process of development can be seen in the published side-views of such brooches in a sequence which could be taken, for example, from the brooch from Bloomfield, Co. Roscommon,[6] to the St. Ninian's Isle series, by way of the Luce Sands, Wigtownshire, brooch,[7] with tentatively cusped terminals (pl. xliv a). This brooch, however, which is only 2·5 cm. in diameter, is very closely related to the series discussed here. In size it approximates to the example from Freswick (pl. xl b) and must, on grounds of form and decoration,[8] be dated only very slightly before the St. Ninian's Isle series, and not as Rynne suggests to the fifth or sixth century.

[1] I would suggest a similar origin for the unique penannular brooch from Bergøy, Rogaland, Norway—pl. xxxix a and Shetelig (1940), v, fig. 43, a and b.

[2] Fowler (1960) and (1963).

[3] Wilson (1958).

[4] e.g. those from the Skaill hoard: Shetelig (1940), ii, fig. 60.

[5] e.g. Fowler (1963), fig. 3, 3.

[6] *The Journal of the Royal Society of Antiquaries of Ireland*, lxxxviii (1958), 129 and fig. 6, 1; or on many of the brooches illustrated by Kilbride-Jones (1935–7).

[7] Rynne (1965).

[8] For a brooch with a similar hoop decoration, cf. Mahr (1932), pl. 23, 8.

The long pin and fixed position of the head of the Westness brooch[1] demonstrates its descent from the ring-headed pin—an object which functioned as a pin (often fastened in place on the cloak by a thread or cord) and not as a brooch. It can be compared, for example, with the less-richly decorated pin from Dunipace, Stirlingshire,[2] which is of roughly the same form. The pseudo-penannular brooch probably derives from the ring-headed pin, which has a long history.[3] Initially the ring was cast as one with the pin—the free ring developing only during the late Roman period. But, even at the late stage of development exhibited by the Westness example, the ring continued to function simply as a stop and as a decorative adjunct, and not as a locking device. The Tara brooch,[4] with its long pin, presumably demonstrates an early stage in the evolution of the elaborate Irish pseudo-penannular brooch out of the ring-head pin series. A result of the Irish series is demonstrated by the large brooch from the Ardagh hoard,[5] which has very little room for cloth within the hoop. The brooch could only have functioned as a pin with an elaborate head, locked by a thread of cord, such a brooch being depicted worn in this manner on one of the White Island figures.[6]

On the other hand, the St. Ninian's Isle series developed, I would suggest, directly out of the true penannular brooch series. Such a form would need a stop to prevent the pin from slipping off the hoop, the hoop itself acting as a locking device. The distinction between the St. Ninian's Isle brooch and the Irish pseudo-penannular brooch is, then, clear. At all times, however, there was a close relationship between the two series (as demonstrated by the Skryne and Longhill brooches mentioned above, pp. 84, 85).

It has already been pointed out, and emphasized by a distribution map (fig. 14), that the St. Ninian's Isle parallels are most commonly found in north-east Scotland and the northern isles. One find, however, might be seen to disturb the argument. Scratched on a piece of slate (pl. 1 b) from the excavations of the fort at Dunadd in Argyll (in the west of Scotland) is a representation of a brooch which is in many ways similar to the St. Ninian's Isle type. It is of incidental interest in that it shows the method of construction of the design, based on the use of two compass-drawn circles—such indications of construction are rarely found in relation to metalwork, but are quite common in manuscripts.[7] It is more important to note, however, that the drawing portrays a truly penannular brooch, which has expanded terminals and the round-ended panel with a

---

[1] Stevenson (1968).

[2] *Stirlingshire, an inventory of the ancient monuments*, RCHMS, i (1963), pl. 10.

[3] The most recent discussions of this class are those by Stevenson (1955a) and Fowler (1963).

[4] Henry (1965), pl. 38.

[5] Mahr (1932), pl. 54.

[6] Lowry-Corry (1959), pl. vi, 4.

[7] e.g. the Lindisfarne Gospels, Kendrick *et al.* (1960), 221 ff.

central circular setting which is almost an universal feature on the hoops of brooches of the St. Ninian's Isle series. The terminals are not, however, completely typical of this series (but to this I shall return below). It seems reasonable to suppose, particularly because of the ease and economy of line of the sketch and because of its association with clay moulds for metal objects, that this was a jeweller's design. An examination of the clay moulds from Dunadd,[1] however, shows that, although there are fragments of moulds for penannular brooches amongst them, both these fragments, and those from the similar site (also in the west of Scotland) at the Mote of Mark,[2] appear to bear no relation to the St. Ninian's Isle series and include some forms which might be later in date.

Returning, therefore to the design on the terminals of the brooch depicted on the Dunadd stone, it can be seen that it bears a series of circles and linking lines which are strongly reminiscent of the ninth- and early tenth-century series of Hiberno-Saxon brooches, the terminals of which are divided by billeted lines with bosses at the intersections.[3] The design seen on the Dunadd stone is, however, more closely related to a (now lost) brooch from the Isle of Coll,[4] which apparently had almost exactly similar terminals.[5] The Dunadd drawing is possibly a missing link in the typological sequence which runs from the St. Ninian's Isle brooches to the Hiberno-Saxon brooches of the late ninth- and early tenth-century. The Dunadd stone must be seen to be later than the St. Ninian's Isle series and its geographical position need not weigh too heavily against the north-easterly distribution of the St. Ninian's Isle type.

While it is impossible to base any firm conclusions on the statistical sample available in the appended list of brooches of this type, there is a strong temptation to point to the decided similarity in distribution of these objects (fig. 14) to that of the Pictish Symbol stones and objects decorated with Pictish symbols.[6] I propose to fall to this temptation and label these brooches as Pictish in the discussion which follows.

[1] Craw (1929–30), fig. 7.

[2] Curle (1913–14), figs. 13–16.   [3] Wilson (1958).

[4] *Proceedings of the Society of Antiquaries of Scotland*, xv (1880–1), 79 f. and fig. 1.

[5] Another example is illustrated by Fairholt (1848), pl. 5, 3.

[6] Cf. Stevenson (1955), 100, map 3.

PENANNULAR BROOCHES OF THE ST. NINIAN'S ISLE TYPE

(BM = British Museum; NMAS = National Museum of Antiquities of Scotland, Edinburgh; NMD = National Museum, Dublin. The numbers refer to the map, fig. 14).

Find place	Museum or collection	Details	Primary publication
Scotland			
1. Banchory, Kincardine-shire (pl. xl *a*)	Unknown (electrotype in NMAS)	Square terminals	Stuart (1867), pl. 13
2. Birsay, Orkney, (pl. xlv *a*)	NMAS (HR 922)	Fragmentary	Unpublished
3. Clachan, Loch Fyne, Argyll (pl. xli *c*)	Duke of Argyll (cast in NMAS)	Triangular pin-head	Unpublished
4. Croy, Inverness-shire (pl. xxxviii *a*)	NMAS (FC 12)	In two pieces	Fraser and Anderson (1874–6)
5. Croy, Inverness-shire (pl. xxxviii *b*)	NMAS (FC 13)	Fragment	Ross (1885–6)
6. Croy, Inverness-shire (pl. xxxviii *c*)	NMAS (FC 14)	Fragment	Ross (1885–6)
7. Freswick, Caithness (pl. xlix *d*)	NMAS (IL 559)	Fragment	Curle (1938–9), 100–2
8. Freswick, Caithness (pl. xl *b*)	NMAS (IL 654)	Fragment	Edwards (1939–40)
9. Jarlshof, Shetland[1] (pl. xlii *b*)	NMAS (HSA 4163A)	Fragment; only possibly of this class	Unpublished
10. Loch Glashan (pl. l *e*)	Glasgow: City Museum and Art Gallery	Small brooch	Unpublished
11. Machrins, Colonsay (pl. xlvi *b*)	NMAS (FC 189)		Anderson (1906–7), 441, fig. 5
12. Perth, Perthshire (pl. xlii *d*)[2]	NMAS (FC 177)	Rich brooch	Anderson (1879–80), 449–52
13. Pierowall, Westray, Orkney (pl. xlv *c*)	NMAS (IL 198)		*Catalogue of the National Museum of Antiquities of Scotland,* Edinburgh, 1892, 276
14. Rogart, Sutherland (pl. xxxvi)	NMAS (FC 1)		*Proceedings of the Society of Antiquaries of Scotland,* viii (1868–70), 304–8 and pl. XVI, 2
15. Rogart, Sutherland (pl. xxxvii *d*)	NMAS (FC 2)		Ibid., loc. cit., and pl. XVI, 1 and 4
16. Rogart, Sutherland	Countess of Sutherland	Pin only (on another brooch from the same find)	Ibid., loc. cit., and pl. XVI, 3
17. Stromness, Orkney	Glasgow: Hunterian Museum	Terminal only	Cursiter (1886–7), 346
18. Sutherland (pl. xxxvii *a*) (? Rogart, see p. 82)	Oxford: Ashmolean Museum (1927, 126)	Pin missing	Unpublished

[1] This was not found during the excavations, but during tidying-up operations, 'on the cemetery above the Viking houses'. This is presumably the late cemetery recorded by Hamilton (1956), 196.

[2] Cf. a unique brooch of similar provenance (pl. xliii) which has not been included in this list.

Find place	Museum or collection	Details	Primary publication
19. Sutherland (pl. xxxvii *b*) (? Rogart, see p. 82)	Oxford: Ashmolean Museum (1927, 127)	Terminal only	Unpublished
20. Urquhart Castle, Inverness-shire (pl. xliv *b*)	Inverness Museum	Terminal only	Unpublished
21. Valtos, Lewis	Stornoway, Nicholson Inst	Pin only	Gibson (1933–4), 430
22. Scotland? No provenance (pl. xlvi *a*)	BM (1919, 12–18, 1)	The Breadalbane brooch—pin only (see p. 83)	*Proceedings of the Society of Anti-quaries of London,* xxxii (1919–20), 63–6
Ireland			
23. Ballinderry, Offaly (pl. xli *a*)	NMD (E6: 423)		Hencken (1942), fig. 15
24. Ballynagloch, Antrim (pl. xxxix *b*)	NMD (27.9.30)	Modern addition of bar between terminals	Mahr (1932), pl. 20, 2
25. Galway (pl. xxxvii *c*)	Lost		*The Gentleman's Magazine,* 1854, 147
England			
26. Canterbury, Kent, (pl. xliv *d*)	BM (1942, 10–8, 73)	Pin missing	Smith (1914), fig. 6
Norway			
27. Frigstad, Slidre, Opland (pl. xlii *c*)	Oslo, Universitetets Oldsaksamling (C. 11468)	Terminal only	Shetelig (1940), v. 16 and fig. 6
28. Hålen, Leikanger, Sogn og Fjordane (pl. xl *c*)	Bergen, Historisk Museum (B. 5854b)	Square terminal (fragment)	*Bergens Museums Årbog,* 1903, no. 14, 43 and fig. 13
29. Helgheim u. Nes, Sogndal (pl. xli *b*)	Bergen, Historisk Museum (B. 9065)		Fett (1939–40), 15 and fig. 4
30. Veøy prestegaarden Møre og Romsdal (pl. xl *d*)	Bergen, Historisk Museum (B. 1471)	Fragmentary	Shetelig (1940), v. 60 and fig. 64
31. No provenance, Valdres Norway (pl. xlv *b*)	Valdres Museum (1413)		Shetelig (1940), v. 22 and fig. 10

The St. Ninian's Isle brooches—detailed consideration

I shall examine here the various features and detailed parallels of the individual brooches from St. Ninian's Isle. In the immediately subsequent section of this chapter more general considerations will be taken into account.

No. 17 (pl. xxxi) is the largest and heaviest brooch in the hoard. It is in good condition, but the pin has been badly corroded. The pin was clearly made in the same workshop as the hoop, for the treatment of the interlace at the edges of the decorated panels of both elements is similar. In form its large triangular terminals can be compared very closely, within the Pictish series, to that drawn on the Dunadd stone (pl. 1 *b*), to the brooch from Canterbury in the British Museum (pl. xliv *d*), to one of the brooches from Sutherland in the Ashmolean Museum (pl. xxxvii *a*), to the Pierowall brooch (pl. xlv *c*), and outside this series to the Hunterston/Dunbeath series.[1] The strange and unique brooch from near Perth (pl. xliii) also has triangular terminals, as has brooch no. 18 (pl. xxxiii *c*) from St. Ninian's Isle. In size (10·8 cm. in diameter) brooch no. 17 is closest to the large Rogart brooch (pl. xxxvi) (11·9 cm. in diameter)—the largest brooch in the Pictish series.

Unlike all the other brooches from St. Ninian's Isle, save no. 20 (pl. xxxii *b*), the hoop of this brooch is panelled and the panels are filled with interlace. This feature is encountered on a number of other Pictish brooches and particularly on the large Rogart brooch (pl. xxxvi), the hoop of which is transversely divided in the same way as no. 17. It is rather more common in the Irish series; as for example on a brooch of no provenance in the National Museum, Dublin,[2] and on the Dunshaughlin brooch.[3] The main dividing lines on both the hoop and the terminals of the St. Ninian's Isle brooch consist of formalized animal masks of bar-like form. Although this cannot be accurately paralleled in the corpus of Celtic brooches, the idea of animal masks as dividing elements in the terminal fields of brooches is to be seen in only a slightly more developed form on nos. 19 (pl. xxxii *a*) and 20 (pl. xxxii *b*)[4] and on objects like the mount from Seim, Røldal, Hordaland, Norway.[5] Whilst not exactly common, double-strand interlace does occur occasionally in Celtic metalwork,[6] as on the pin of a brooch from near Perth (pl. xliii) or, in Ireland, on an unprovenanced bell-shrine crest[7] and on the 'Athlone' plaque from St. John's, Rinnagan, Co. Roscommon.[8] An unparalleled feature of the ornament, however, is the single-strand interlace filler, executed in a rather clumsy fashion, which forms a background to some of the double contoured interlacing.

The most interesting stylistic features of this brooch are the small animal heads which terminate the interlace in two of the panels in the terminals of the brooch. Similar heads occur as a projection of the terminals on brooch no. 20 (pl. xxxii *b*) and the pin of brooch no. 19 (pl. xxxii *a*), on the interlace of the internal mount of the small bowl (no. 6, pl. xxvi *c*), and on a number of other objects in the hoard, as, for example, the inscribed chape (no. 15, pl. xxix). This widespread occurrence helps to link the hoard together as an entity (see below, p. 133).

---

[1] For references see above, pp. 85 f.
[2] Reg. no. 1859: 88 (23). Mahr (1932), pl. 62, 3.
[3] Ibid., pl. 20, 3.
[4] See below, pp. 92 f.
[5] Shetelig (1940), iv, fig. 45.

[6] e.g. ibid. v, figs. 25 and 27 a.
[7] Mahr (1932), pl. 36, 1*a* (top left-hand field of right-hand roundel).
[8] Ibid., pl. 28.

It is perhaps not without interest that the square setting in the main panel of the hoop of the brooch is paralleled elsewhere in the hoard on the only other brooch with triangular terminals (no. 18, pl. xxxiii *c*). This feature occurs in one other place within the Pictish brooch series (on the Croy brooch, pl. xxxviii *c*), but is common in various positions on brooches of the Irish series[1] and occurs on the Hunterston brooch.[2]

No. 18 (pl. xxxiii *c*) is much worn, particularly at the bottom of the right-hand terminal. The brooch is a poor piece of work; some, but not all, of the interlace patterns being very crudely executed. I am not clear whether the pin belongs to this brooch or is a secondary addition; it is of practically the same design as the pin of brooch no. 24 (pl. xxxiii *b*) and its head is very similar in design to that of most of the other brooches in the hoard. A technical detail, seen here, occurs on most of the pins in the hoard: the groove down the back and front show how the pin has been formed from a flat sheet of metal by rounding the edges. This feature is emphasized and becomes a decorative element on the front of the pin.

The terminals are paralleled in form by those of the large brooch, no. 17 (pl. xxxi), and by the parallels quoted in the discussion of that object (see p. 91). The hoop, however, is of the type found on all the brooches in the hoard, save nos. 17 and 20. The treatment is slightly different in each case, but basically it consists of a plain central band of convex section flanked by a beaded border (in other cases the borders are billeted or the billets are set in an oblique fashion). In the middle of the hoop is a panel with curved, cusped ends. The hoop of no. 18 has volutes which stand free of the contour at the terminals and at the panel on the hoop, a feature which is paralleled only on nos. 21 and 28, although it occurs on the terminals of nos. 24, 25, and 26.

The square setting on the hoop has already been mentioned as a parallel in the discussion of the similar feature on no. 17 (pl. xxxi). The brooch is unique within the hoard in having lentoid and triangular glass settings at the terminals. The settings were originally prepared in the same way as the circular settings on the other brooches, by boring a hole with a bit; but in this case the circular holes have been enlarged. A similar triangular setting occurs on the brooch fragment from Croy (pl. xxxviii *b*) where it is filled with crude cloisonné garnets. Settings of similar shape also occur on another Croy brooch, where they are to be interpreted as the eyes of a stylized animal head (pl. xxxviii *a*).

An interesting feature of the brooch is the skilful use of interlace in the panels of the hoop. While not given actual zoomorphic form, there can be no doubt that these patterns are based on an interlaced snake pattern which is practically impossible to parallel in Celtic sources.

[1] Cf. Smith (1914), pl. xxvi, 6, 7.   [2] Anderson (1881), fig. 1.

The square terminals of brooch no. 19 (pl. xxxii *a*) are paralleled at Veøy, Møre og Romsdal (pl. xl *d*), and Hålen, Leikanger (pl. xl *c*) in Norway; in Scotland they are known on the lost brooch from Banchory (pl. xl *a*) and the minute brooch from Freswick (pl. xl *b*); in Ireland they occur on the brooch from Ballynaglogh, Co. Antrim (pl. xxxix *b*). The stylized animal heads seen from above, which are seen on the terminals of no. 19, occur on many of the examples quoted, and in all these cases the heads are surrounded by interlace ornament and spring from a central circular setting. The Veøy and Freswick examples apart, all the others could have come from the same workshop, so similar are the details; they vary in size by little more than a centimetre. The St. Ninian's Isle example differs from the others, however, in having a beaked animal head emerging from each terminal, the cusp forming the back of the head. This is probably dimly reminiscent of the animal heads on the earlier enamelled penannular brooches[1] and is a trait which continues through into the late ninth and tenth century when the gaping mouth appears on the Hiberno-Saxon silver brooches.[2] In the Pictish series it occurs only on the Canterbury brooch (pl. xliv *d*) and, in a different form, on one of the Croy brooches (pl. xxxviii *a*). A brooch of Irish type from Dunshaughlin, Co. Meath,[3] has a similar feature, and this is a brooch which may be related to the Pictish series, as it has degenerate animal heads on the terminals.

The hoop is unremarkable. The pin, however, is of an entirely different—and much finer—quality than that of the main body of the brooch: it is almost certainly a later replacement. It is decorated with animal ornament which is discussed below (p. 133). The brooch has both brown and blue glass. The use of different coloured studs occurs on no. 20 (pl. xxxii *b*) and other brooches in the hoard and is rarely symmetrical.

No. 20 (pl. xxxii *b*) introduces a group of seven brooches with lobed terminals. The unique feature of this brooch is the presence of the small projecting animal heads at each terminal. Such a feature is unparalleled in the whole corpus of Celtic penannular brooches. The form of the heads themselves is similar to that found on the crest of chape no. 15 (pl. xxix) and is closely related to the heads in the interlace of brooch no. 17 (pl. xxxi) and the internal mount of bowl no. 6 (pl. xxvi *c*).

The moulded animal masks in the lobes and in the panel on the hoop are degenerate versions of the complete detailed heads which bite from the lobes into the central panel of the terminal of the Rogart brooch (pl. xxxvi). In the St. Ninian's Isle treasure it is possible to see various forms of this motif on brooches nos. 21–4 (pls. xxxiii–xxxv) and, in a slightly different fashion, on nos. 17 and 19 (pls. xxxi, xxxii). The heads in the terminals of this brooch, with their detail of eyes and snout, are perhaps closer to the original

---

[1] e.g. Kilbride-Jones (1935–7), fig. 17.   [2] Cf. Wilson (1958).   [3] Mahr (1932), pl. 20, 3.

form than those which occur in the field on the hoop or on the other brooches, where the head tends to degenerate into a pear-shaped blob. But it is at the same time a further degree of degeneration away from the heads on the brooch found near Perth (pl. xlii *d*), which have much more easily recognizable zoomorphic traits. It is an odd fact that this pear-shaped form of head is found only in the Pictish brooch series. Animal masks on other objects[1] are of quite different form and the only occurrence of a pear-shaped animal head in Ireland, on a brooch found near Galway (pl. xxxvii *c*), is on an object likely to be of Pictish origin.

The hoop of this brooch, as was pointed out when discussing the similar feature on no. 17 (p. 91), is panelled. Such panels are rare in the Pictish series. The Rogart parallel cited above (p. 91) and brooch no. 17 are two of the very few examples of such a detail. Apart from these and the Dunbeath fragment,[2] all other truly penannular brooches are without this feature, save for the controversial Luce Sands brooch.[3] It seems to derive from the Hunterston/Tara brooch series and became very popular on the Irish pseudo-penannular brooches.[4]

Various minor points should be mentioned in relation to this brooch. The use of different coloured glass studs, with no apparent symmetry, is worthy of comment; it is a feature seen elsewhere in the hoard—e.g. no. 19 (pl. xxxii *a*). The quality of the gilding on the pin is different from that on the hoop—indicating that the pin may have been regilded or is a replacement. The marks of the engraving tool, which are most clearly to be seen on the pin, are more obtrusive on this brooch than on any other in the hoard.

No. 21 (pl. xxxiv *c*) is the only brooch in the hoard which has not been gilded. It exhibits considerable signs of wear, however, which show that it was not unfinished. It is interesting to note that the fractured portion of the pin is much worn and was obviously used in this state for a long period serving more as a lock than as an attachment, for the hoop. The general poverty of the brooch is emphasized by its rather crude design and by the fact that a casting flaw in the field on the hoop has not been filled.

Two technical features should be noted. First, the marks of an engraving tool can be seen in the carving of the field on the hoop. Secondly, the settings have an inverted conical section (which is entirely different from that of other brooches), and at the terminals they pierce the brooch.

In form this brooch belongs to a group where the animal masks appear within prominent horns, or where the horns themselves form the lobes of the terminals. The most remarkable example of the former detail is the lost brooch from Galway, Ireland

---

[1] e.g. Shetelig (1940), v, fig. 45.
[2] Kendrick *et al.* (1960), pl. 51 *f*.
[3] Rynne (1965), see above, p. 86.
[4] *Vide* Mahr (1932), pls. *passim.*

(pl. xxxvii *c*), which is closely paralleled by the brooch from Helgheim u. Nes, Sogndal, Norway (pl. xli *b*). Related examples occur at Birsay, Orkney (pl. xlv *a*), Urquhart Castle (pl. xliv *b*), and Clachan, Argyll (pl. xli *c*). Although not so well developed as these parallels, brooch no. 21 shows a step in the typological development from the brooch in which the lobes contain an animal head, to the brooches where the lobes have become horns and which are probably chronologically later, as two examples (the Birsay and Machrins Colonsay brooches, pls. xlv *a*, xlvi *b*) appear in Viking contexts.

It is perhaps interesting to note that the volutes at the ends of the panel on the hoop of this brooch are only paralleled elsewhere on brooches without semi-circular lobes, e.g. nos. 18 and 28 (pls. xxxiii, xxxiv). This feature might well be derived from the more elaborate scrolled animal heads which appear at the borders of the terminals of the richer brooches, e.g. that from Kilmainham,[1] or the earlier Tara brooch.[2]

No. 22 (pl. xxxiv) has animal masks which are very closely related to those on no. 20. The design of the panel on the hoop is very similar to that of the more elaborate Rogart brooch (pl. xxxvi). In fact, no. 22 must be seen as a scaled-down version of this large example. It differs in one major detail in that the lobes are bordered by a frame with curled ends, a feature which is encountered, in a rather more elaborate form, on no. 24 (pl. xxxiii) and (surrounding a simple setting and not a mask) on nos. 25 and 26 (pls. xxxiii, xxxv). Outside the hoard there is no accurate parallel for this detail, although the fragment of a brooch from Sutherlandshire in the Ashmolean Museum (pl. xxxvii *b*), which may be from Rogart,[3] has a very similar terminal design. No. 23 (pl. xxxiii) is in fact a simplified version of no. 20 (pl. xxxii). The three radial lines on the terminals may possibly be interpreted as the snouts of animals, but this is open to question. The pin is very similar in design and quality to those on nos. 18, 24, and 25 (pls. xxxiii, xxxv). A minor technical point worthy of comment is that the base of the setting exhibits a less definitely defined centring hole of the boring-bit.

No. 24 (pl. xxxiii *b*) is a more elaborate version of no. 22 (pl. xxxiv *b*) and is close in design to nos. 25 and 26 (pl. xxxv). The masks in the lobes have no real zoomorphic features and can only be so designated in view of their closeness in form to more easily recognizable masks elsewhere. The lobed frame round the masks on this example, however, is more closely related to the frames for the settings on nos. 25 and 26 (pl. xxxv). It can be seen in a similar context on the more elaborate brooch found near Perth (pl. xlii *d*).

The pin, although much more worn, is similar in design and in detail to that of no. 25. On both examples the midrib is speckled—a feature which does not occur elsewhere in the hoard.

[1] Mahr (1932), pl. 22, 2.   [2] Henry (1965), pl. 42.   [3] See p. 82.

No. 25 (pl. xxxv) is almost exactly similar in design to no. 26 (pl. xxxv) and the two brooches must be discussed together. They differ chiefly in that the centre of the panel on the hoop of no. 25 is a circular field which extends beyond the confines of the panel in the manner encountered on the Canterbury brooch (pl. xliv *d*) and on the large brooch from Rogart (pl. xxxvi), although in a less emphasized fashion. The decoration of the hoops and of the pins also differs. Otherwise the brooches are strikingly similar: there is also a close parallel in form to no. 24, save that the animal masks on the lobes have been replaced by glass studs. The fourth field of each terminal is filled with interlace.

No. 25 is in slightly better condition than no. 26. It shows distinct marks of casting on the back of the hoop. The speckling on the pin is similar to that on no. 24. The pin of no. 26 is rather heavier than the others in the hoard.

No. 27 (pl. xxxv) is another version of the two preceding brooches. It is very much worn, one of the cells at the terminal having been almost worn away. The general flatness of the terminals is not dissimilar to that encountered on the terminal found at Frigstad, Slidre, Oppland, Norway (pl. xlii *c*). The pin differs in form from all the other examples in the hoard—it is perhaps a replacement. It is of circular cross-section—like many of the Irish ones—and is mounted with a separate setting, perhaps for a cabochon glass stud. The setting was apparently made for the pin and is not a later addition as the moulded lines on the head are obviously designed to imitate the beaded wire at the base of the cell. The only other Pictish brooch with a separate setting on the head of the pin is that found near Perth (pl. xlii *d*). Oval settings of this form are rare in Celtic contexts of the eighth century, but are known in the Germanic area.[1] Unusually the setting is not riveted, but soldered to the base.

No. 28 (pl. xxxiv) has terminals in the form of animal heads and only has a single parallel in the corpus of penannular brooches—from Freswick, Caithness (pl. xlix *d*)—although this is a much slighter example with an open-mouthed animal. The idea of animal-head terminals was of course endemic to the earlier series of penannular brooches.[2] The beaks on no. 19 (pl. xxxii *a*) are presumably a survival of this feature and a pseudo-penannular brooch without provenance in the National Museum of Ireland[3] has an exaggerated animal head biting the lobed terminals. Ferocious masks occur occasionally in the Celtic metalwork corpus—two examples in the St. Ninian's Isle hoard can be seen on nos. 15 and 16 (pls. xxix, xxx). The ridge pole of the Emly shrine[4] provides another example, and in a similar position but greatly stylized they can be seen on the Loch Erne shrine.[5]

---

[1] e.g. Holmqvist (1955), pl. XIV.

[2] Cf. Kilbride-Jones (1935–7). It was also occasionally adapted in Scandinavia in the ninth century, cf. Petersen (1928), 186 and fig. 230.

[3] Mahr (1932), pl. 62, 3.

[4] Swarzenski (1954), fig. 10.

[5] Mahr (1932), pl. 9.

The grotesque biting head becomes very popular in the ninth century at the joint between hoop and terminal of the Hiberno-Saxon group of brooches.[1]

A noteworthy feature of no. 28 is the extraordinary mixture of competently and incompetently executed interlace in the various panels.

The St. Ninian's Isle brooches—general considerations

All the St. Ninian's Isle brooches are made from a rather debased silver. They were cast and then finished by hand tooling, of which a few traces can be seen (e.g. no. 21). The settings were bored by means of a bit with a centring point, as is demonstrated by traces of a small depression in the centre of the base of the setting in practically every example. More than one type of bit was apparently used, for on brooch no. 21 the holes take the form of an inverted cone. On no. 23 there is slightly less definition to the setting.

The pins were all hammered out of a single flat strip of metal. Many of them exhibit a lateral groove at the back, showing that the edges of the pin have been rounded from a flat sheet. This feature can be seen on both Pictish and Irish pins; both the Rogart brooches in the National Museum of Antiquities of Scotland (pls. xxxvi, xxxvii *d*) exhibit this feature, whilst amongst the many Irish examples that from Longhill, Co. Antrim, is the most convenient to quote.[2] The pins are all fastened to the hoop by means of a hook which could be quite elaborate in form (e.g. figs. 15, 16). The hook enabled the pin and hoop to be separated quite easily. The pins expand at the point where they cross the hoop and there is a curve in the profile at this point (e.g. fig. 15) which allows the pin to sit comfortably on the hoop. All the complete pins (save no. 27) have been ornamented with chip-carved patterns after the pin had been beaten into its final form. This would seem to suggest that all the chip-carving and detailed ornament of the brooches was executed after casting, a theory which is supported by the size of the brooches. Nos. 18, 21, 23, 25, 26, 27, and 28 all have a maximum diameter within 1 mm. of 7·1 cm.[3]—a coincidence too great to be ignored. It would seem likely that a rough penannular hoop was first cast and that this was then treated individually by the jeweller, for among these brooches of substantially the same diameter is one with triangular terminals and one with terminals in the form of animal masks. It is possible that nos. 22 (6·6 cm. diam.) and 24 (6·7 cm. diam.) came from a different mould, but the 4 mm. or so could readily have been consumed in the finishing process or in a decade of use. Similarly the hoop of no. 19 (7·5 cm. diam.) could have been distorted by the craftsman. The other two brooches, nos. 17 and 20, both have panelled hoops

---

[1] Wilson (1958).
[2] The detail can be seen in Smith (1914), pl. XXVI, 6.
[3] The actual figures are: no. 18: 7·0 cm.; nos. 25–8: 7·1 cm.; and nos. 21 and 23: 7·2 cm.

and fall outside this series. Apart from these brooches, the terminals of the other brooches are of roughly the same size and could be made in any of the forms in the series from blanks from a single mould.[1]

All the surviving studs are of glass, which are variously blue, brown, or green in colour; the elaborate multi-coloured glass of the chape (no. 16) is not seen in the brooch series. The studs were cemented into place and often fill the setting only in the roughest fashion. Only on brooches nos. 17 and 18 are the settings for the glass not circular.

All the brooches, save no. 21, are gilded on the face. The colour of the gilding varies considerably from brooch to brooch, but it is difficult to judge this colour change in view of the amount of wear which the various objects exhibit.

The gilding is possibly a clue in some cases to the fact that the pins may not have been original. This is particularly the case with regard to no. 20, where the quality of the gilding is entirely different, although this may merely be the result of regilding. A pin which is obviously a replacement is that on brooch no. 27, which is completely out of series. The replacement of the pin is known on other brooches, the most remarkable example being the Breadalbane brooch (pl. xlvi *a*), which has been turned from an Irish into a Pictish brooch by the addition of a different type of pin and the removal of the bar between the terminals.

Typologically the main features of the St. Ninian's Isle brooches are their true pen-annular form, the panel on the hoop with its curved ends, the cusping at the ends of major fields, the ribbed hoop and the form of the pin, with its lentoid head, hooked method of attachment, and point of expansion where it bends to cross the hoop. There are two main forms within the St. Ninian's find; forms, in fact, which are typical of the series as a whole. The first is the brooch with the plate terminal, the second is the brooch with the lobed terminal. There are two varieties of hoop: (*a*) two examples with sunken panels, which are closely related to the Irish series,[2] and (*b*) the others with their ribbed decoration. These latter are typically Pictish and are paralleled on one of the brooches found near Perth (pl. xlii *d*), on the fragment from Urquhart Castle (pl. xliv *b*), on one of the Sutherlandshire fragments in the Ashmolean Museum (pl. xxxvii *b*), on the lost Banchory brooch (pl. xl *a*), on the Clachan brooch (pl. xli *c*), and on the series of brooches with square terminals (pls. xxxix *b*, xl). Not all brooches of the Pictish type fall within these two types; some have plain, plano-convex hoops (pls. xxxvii *d*, xlv *b*), but this type is not represented at St. Ninian's Isle.

---

[1] Although it is more normal to find moulds of clay for the *cire perdu* method in Dark Age contexts, moulds for blanks of brooches are not unknown, cf. Hougen (1936),

fig. 37. See addendum below, p. 105.
[2] Cf., for example, Mahr (1932), pls. 14; 20, 3; 23, 1, 2, and 6; 54.

The ornament is basically very simple, the main decoration consisting of more or less competently executed interlace ornament of a type which is found on many of the other brooches in the group. The only really significant stylistic features are the formalized animal masks executed in relief on nos. 19, 20, 21, 22, 23, and 24, and the animal heads seen in profile on nos. 17, 19, and 20 which clearly relate the brooches to the finer objects in the hoard, e.g. to the inscribed chape (no. 15) and to the escutcheon of bowl no. 6. The stylized masks only seem to occur on brooches and not on other objects. Parallels have been cited from near Galway (pl. xxxvii c), Ballynagloch (pl. xxxix b), Banchory (pl. xl a), Hålen (pl. xl c), and Veøy (pl. xl d). The occurrence of rather more elaborate examples of masks can be seen on the brooch from near Perth (pl. xlii d), where they are applied. The most elaborate applied animals are those on the large Rogart brooch (pl. xxxvi). One might tentatively assume that the Perth and Rogart examples are, because of their less degenerate form, nearer to the source of the motif. The large brooch from the Irish Ardagh hoard exhibits complete three-dimensional birds which are obviously closely related to the Rogart series,[1] but this is apparently the only occurrence of any beaked mask on a brooch made in the western Celtic area. Masks of not dissimilar form occur in Anglo-Saxon contexts;[2] although the paucity of the material makes it difficult to find any adequate chronological parallels. It is possible that this particular form of ornament has Anglo-Saxon origins.

Whether this is the origin of the masks or not, there can be little doubt concerning the close relationship of the combined interlace and zoomorphic elements of the St. Ninian's Isle brooches with Northumbrian and Anglian metalwork of the eighth century. The animal heads in profile are closely paralleled in the Anglo-Saxon corpus. Isolated heads as a terminal to interlace, like that which occurs on brooch no. 17, can be seen, for example, on the metal mounts of the Gandersheim Casket (a feature nowhere adequately illustrated) on a plaque from Lunde, Hordaland, Norway,[3] a plaque from Bjørke, Norway,[4] and on a cross from Kaupang, Norway.[5] A close parallel to the heads on brooch no. 29 from St. Ninian's Isle is to be found on a plaque from Whitby Abbey, Yorkshire,[6] or on a sculptured slab from Brixworth, Northamptonshire.[7] Heads of this form and particularly heads in combination with interlaced ribbons are rare in Celtic metalwork and must be derived from the area where they are commonest—Northumbria and Mercia. Although zoomorphic interlace is to be seen in Celtic filigree ornament—as on the Hunterston[8] brooch—the parallels are not convincing when compared with the English examples.

---

[1] Ibid., pl. 54.
[2] e.g. Wilson (1956), fig. 1.
[3] Wilson (1964), pl. IId.
[4] Ibid., pl. Ic.
[5] Bakka (1963), fig. 12.
[6] Wilson (1964), pl. XXXVIII, 105.
[7] Ibid., pl. IIb.
[8] Shetelig (1940), ii, fig. 88.

The origin of the interlace ornament itself is more problematic. It could be derived from either Ireland or England. It is noticeable, for example, that there is a great technical similarity between the interlace on the Irish and Pictish brooches.[1] They were obviously much influenced by each other and it would be hard to pinpoint differences in the ornamental grammar of the two groups. On balance, however, in view of the technique, in view of the association with zoomorphic details, and in view of the general connections between eighth-century art in Pictland, Northumbria, and Mercia it seems more probable that the interlace on the brooches originates in Northumbria or Mercia. This is, however, a very tenuous argument and a dual origin in both England and Ireland could just as easily be postulated.

On the basis of the comparisons cited in this chapter it is clear that little can be said about the chronological position of the St. Ninian's Isle brooches. The only clue to absolute dating is provided by the Croy hoard, which contained the fragmentary remains of three, and possibly four, brooches as well as two coins, one dated 796–805 and the other 843–8.[2] I have already pointed out that this hoard is an oddity—perhaps the stock-in-trade of a jeweller. The Croy brooches were old when they were buried, and while it is certain that they cannot have been buried much earlier than the middle of the ninth century they could quite well have been made more than fifty years earlier.

Turning to the relative chronological position of the Pictish brooch series it is clear that typological and stylistic judgements provide a hopelessly inadequate yardstick. Of the two, the stylistic evidence is perhaps most tractable and should be examined first. The Pictish brooch series, as I have outlined it here, bears no decorative resemblance to the art of Pictland in the period in which the symbol stones were produced. It is therefore not necessary to enter into the vexed problem of the chronology of the Pictish symbols.[3] The inspiration for the art of this series of brooches must be sought elsewhere— undoubtedly in Northumbria and, possibly, in Ireland. There is no exclusively Style II ornament on any of the Pictish brooches, so one must assume that none of them were produced before the middle of the seventh century. There is, however, no convincing parallel with the stylistic development of the golden age of Northumbrian art and this is more puzzling in view of the parallels found elsewhere in the hoard with this stylistic group (see pp. 129 f.). The parallels which do exist are all to be associated with the Northumbrian/Mercian school of chip-carved metalwork, which is dated on the evidence of the Anglo-Carolingian art executed in the same technique and based on the same stylistic principles. The fixed point in the dating of this school is the Tassilo Chalice,

[1] Cf. Mahr (1932), pl. 23.
[2] See above, p. 82.

[3] Cf. Thomas (1963), and, *per contra*, Stevenson (1955).

which can be dated by inscription to between 777 and 778.[1] The art of the Tassilo Chalice and of the Pictish brooches stand in the same relationship to the English chip-carved ornament which must have developed towards the middle of the eighth century. The rich finds of these chip-carved English objects occur in Viking Age graves in Norway[2] which must have been buried in the early ninth century. It would not be un-reasonable therefore to see the *floruit* of the English style as somewhere between 700 and 800. I believe that the small animal heads included in this chip-carved series are more likely to be dated towards the end of the century, as they first emerge associated with foliage, as degenerate vine scrolls in the manuscripts of the Canterbury school which can be dated with some degree of certainty to between 750 and 825.[3]

One further chronological point related to style is illustrated in the Rogart find: the small brooch in the Countess of Sutherland's collection[4] has terminals decorated with bosses surrounded by beaded wire. Despite the fact that this brooch is of bronze, and not silver, it might well be seen with the stone design from Dunadd (pl. 1 *b*), discussed above,[5] as an initial stage in the development of the Hiberno-Saxon brooch of the late ninth century;[6] and the suggestion of a similar relationship, already made above in my discussion of the Dunadd stone, would imply that the Rogart hoard was buried in the late eighth or early ninth century.

The cumulative effect of the stylistic evidence suggests that the Pictish brooches were in fashion towards the end of the eighth century.

Typology has little to offer to this chronological discussion. The classic typology of Smith[7] which presumes that the lobed rosette at the terminal first appears on a triangular back-plate, which later disappeared, cannot be easily applied to the Pictish series, as fully developed lobed terminals seem to have no predecessor in this area; and, if we are to follow Smith's criterion, we must assume that the Pictish lobed type developed out of an Irish prototype. This is a fair assumption, but is slightly called into question by the logical supposition that the triangular terminal came first. That triangular terminals are known in Scotland at an early date is demonstrated by the penannular brooches from Tummel Bridge, Perthshire,[8] which I believe to be of seventh-century date, but which many scholars would place much earlier—in the early fifth century in some cases.[9] If we are to assume that the lobed brooch came from Ireland, we must also assume that

[1] Haseloff (1951).

[2] Cf. Bakka (1963).

[3] Cf., e.g., Kendrick (1938), pl. lxix, 2.

[4] *Proceedings of the Society of Antiquaries of Scotland*, viii (1868–70), pl. xvi, 3.

[5] p. 88.

[6] Wilson (1958).

[7] Smith (1914).

[8] Leeds (1933), fig. 37.

[9] e.g. Fowler (1963), 142 f. It is strange that Mrs. Fowler should date these brooches to the early fifth century when she dates the so-called 'brooches' from

the triangular terminal brooch was introduced into Ireland from Scotland, developed the lobes on the triangular terminal in that country, and then returned to Scotland as a lobed brooch. This is not an impossible sequence of events and the probability is strengthened by the fact that the only lobed penannular brooch that was not made in Scotland is that from Kilmainham, Co. Dublin (pl. xlvii *a*).[1] Irish pseudo-penannular brooches with lobes and without triangular terminals are rare. Examples like those from Skryne, Co. Meath,[2] and Longhill, Co. Antrim,[3] are, as has been pointed out,[4] rather flimsy and must be late in the Irish series of pseudo-penannular brooches, the half-hearted panels on the hoops with square ends seemingly being degenerate versions of the curved-ended examples of the Pictish and early Irish series. It is perhaps not without interest to note that both these brooches have pins of Scottish form, a feature probably indicative of a Scottish origin for this degenerate type.

The collection of brooches from St. Ninian's Isle is, as we have seen, technically remarkably homogeneous. On this basis it might be reasonable to say that, with the possible exception of the two brooches with panelled hoops (nos. 17 and 20), they all came from the same workshop and were made within a generation of each other. It is probably true, as has been pointed out by Stevenson, that the brooch with disc terminals and strong zoomorphic characteristics from the Croy hoard (pl. xxxviii *a*) is perhaps a later typological development than any encountered at St. Ninian's Isle.[5] Similarly it might well be said, as I have done,[6] that the bronze brooch from Rogart is slightly later in date than any found in the St. Ninian's Isle hoard. There seems a slight weight of evidence on typological grounds, therefore, that the St. Ninian's Isle hoard is in its deposition the earliest of the three hoards containing Pictish brooches.

Norrie's Law, Fife, *Proceedings of the Society of Antiquaries of Scotland*, vi (1864–6), fig. 3, to the seventh century. These objects have terminals which are almost exactly similar in form to those of the Tummel Bridge brooches and the context also seems to be similar. I would accept Mr. Stevenson's seventh-century date for the Tummel Bridge brooches and suggest at the same time that the Norrie's Law objects are neck ornaments and not brooches. No other brooch with a twisted loop is known to exist, but necklets are traditionally described as 'torques', a word which implies twisting.

The dating of the Tummel Bridge brooches I realize to be partially dependent on a typological comparison with such objects as the Pant-y-Saer brooch (Fowler, op. cit., 110 f.), but I feel that the evidence for the early date of such objects is of doubtful validity. (Alcock (1963), 284, while dating the Pant-y-Saer brooch to the fifth century on the analogies of the Scottish series, points out that 'the

soil conditions of the site were such that there was no true stratification to relate the brooch to the structures or other finds', and quotes Stevenson as dating it after 700.) The dating of the Tummel Bridge hoard to the fifth century, on the basis of the associated hanging-bowl (adumbrated by Leeds (1933), 145), is difficult to support. A hoard can only be dated by its latest component: why should not this be the brooches which are so close in form to those of seventh/eighth-century date? This is not the place to enter into a discussion of this complicated problem which is of only marginal importance to my argument.

[1] And probably the fragment from Norway (pl. xlvii *c*).
[2] Smith (1914), pl. xxvi, 3.
[3] Ibid., pl. xxvi, 6.
[4] See pp. 84 f.
[5] Most recently expressed in Stevenson (1968), 30.
[6] See above, p. 101.

Therefore, when we draw all these conclusions together—technical, associational, stylistic, and typological—it would seem at least probable that the brooches in the hoard are to be dated to the second half of the eighth century.

The use and significance of the brooches

One of the more interesting minor features of the St. Ninian's Isle brooches are the indications of use shown by the traces of wear. The loop and the pin make different marks on the body of the brooch and a study of these marks of wear demonstrates which way the pin would point (fig. 19). The pin was pushed through the material, which must have been of fairly loose weave (probably wool), and then passed through the opening in the head. The head was then twisted and the pin was thus locked into place by the pressure of the material. It was even possible, with perfect safety, to use the broken pin of brooch no. 21 in the same way. This method was obviously more satisfactory than the rather complicated motions necessary to adjust an Irish brooch with its annular head. On an annular brooch the cloth must first be pulled through the hoop, the pin must then be forced through precisely the right amount of cloth, and the cloth then pulled back so that the pin lies flat on the hoop.

There is no indication of the position in which the hoop was worn, but experiment has shown that a brooch, particularly if it had a long pin, would be most comfortably worn with the opening of the hoop to the top, or (as seems most likely) to the bottom, as portrayed on the stones from Monifieth[1] and Hilton of Cadboll.[2] A representation of Christ on the Cross of Muiredach, from the Irish monastery of Monasterboice, shows the pin in a horizontal position,[3] while on a panel of the West Cross at Kells, the pin is also more or less horizontal.[4] Although archaeologists[5] are perfectly happy to regard the St. Ninian's Isle brooches as secular objects, Monsignor McRoberts has tried to stress their ecclesiastical significance.[6] He has produced two Celtic texts referring to brooches in the possession of clerics. The first is the brooch, the *Delg Aidechta*, which by tradition had belonged to Gregory the Great and was preserved at Iona as a relic of Columcille. The second refers to a *torquis—Praeterea de torque quam Sancti Kanauci dicunt tacendum non censui*—which was said by Giraldus Cambrensis to have belonged to St. Cynawg. The word *torquis* is usually translated as a necklet or armlet of twisted wire, and Monsignor McRoberts may be stretching the evidence in translating it as

---

[1] Anderson (1881), fig. 78.
[2] Best seen in Stevenson (1958–9), pl. V, I.
[3] McRoberts (1960–1), pl. xxv, I. Drawing in Allen (1894), 164.

[4] Roe (1959), pl. xiv.
[5] With the possible exception of Dr. Henry, cf. Henry (1965), 92.
[6] McRoberts (1960–1), 305 f.

'brooch'. Other references to brooches occur, however, in ecclesiastical contexts—for example in the rather morbid story from the Monastery of Tallaght of the abbess Samthann who pierced her cheek with the pin of her brooch to demonstrate a point of chastity.[1] There is no reason to suppose that brooches were not worn by clerics and other references to brooches and pins could be quoted, although we cannot be sure of their relative value. It has also been suggested to me[2] that in a society without a monetary economy, where exchange of precious objects would form a means of trade, there would seem to be no reason why churches should not keep a hoard of precious objects for economic purposes, and brooches would certainly be included in such a hoard.

Monsignor McRoberts also considers the pictorial representations of brooches, as for example the scene of the arrest of Christ on the Cross of Muiredach at Monasterboice,[3] where he claims Christ is represented in ecclesiastical dress. There is no real evidence that Christ is dressed as an Irish cleric; he simply wears a cloak. Another case of a brooch portrayed on a cross occurs on the West Cross at Kells, where the spectators of Our Lord's baptism wear brooches as cloak fasteners;[4] but there is no suggestion that the spectators are clerics.

The manuscript representations used by McRoberts to support his arguments[5] refer to angels (not clerics) and seem to be purely ornamental motifs, normal terminals of the decoration. They certainly do not demonstrate any of the features of the penannular brooch series and cannot help in a discussion of the ecclesiastical significance of the St. Ninian's Isle brooches. A detail of the *Corp Naomh* (also quoted by McRoberts) where a circle encloses a cross on either shoulder of a figure,[6] could well represent brooches; but, whatever they are, they are not penannular in form.

On purely archaeological grounds it is only fair to McRoberts's arguments to note that two hoards containing objects of definite ecclesiastical significance did in fact include brooches. The hoard from Trewhiddle in Cornwall, buried *c.* 872–5,[7] included a chalice and a scourge, but also included such definitely secular objects as drinking-horn mounts, a buckle, belt-slides, and strap-ends which almost certainly came from spurs,[8] as well as finger-rings which appear to be purely secular in origin. The other hoard is from Ireland and contained the well-known Ardagh chalice,[9] as well as a bronze cup and two brooches (one of which is a ninth-century thistle-headed brooch). The

[1] Quoted by Hughes (1966), 177.
[2] I am grateful to Miss K. Hughes for allowing me to discuss this point with her.
[3] McRoberts (1960–1), pl. xxv, 1, and McRoberts (1965), pl. 3.
[4] Roe (1959), pl. xiv; drawing in Allen (1894), 165.

[5] McRoberts (1960–1), pl. xxv, 2, and McRoberts (1965), pl. 4.
[6] Mahr (1932), pl. 68.
[7] Wilson and Blunt (1961).
[8] Cf. Bersu and Wilson (1966), 38.
[9] Mahr (1932), pls. 51–6.

Trewhiddle hoard is certainly not exclusively ecclesiastical in character, while the Ardagh hoard could, in the light of Monsignor McRoberts's arguments, be purely ecclesiastical. While I am not convinced that these brooches are ecclesiastical in function, I would prefer to leave this matter open until I come to discuss the whole content of the St. Ninian's Isle hoard in relation to this problem.[1]

That brooches were primarily secular objects is demonstrated by the Irish Brehon Laws. Both men and women are exempted from liability to fine for injury from the pin of their brooch if they have the pin on their shoulder, or, in the case of women, on their breast.[2] In the same laws a precious silver brooch is enumerated among the customary insignia of a chief.[3]

It seems unlikely that a community of Celtic monks living in isolation would so far forget the ideals of poverty as to adorn themselves with rich personal jewellery. A Scottish religious foundation may well have been given secular wealth, as was certainly the case elsewhere in the British Isles, but they need not have used this wealth for personal display. It could be argued that there are too many brooches in the hoard for a single family, but if it is accepted that both men and women wore brooches this should not appear too strange among, say, two generations of a wealthy family. Furthermore, the Rogart hoard[4] has only one less brooch than that from St. Ninian's Isle and there is no suggestion that this contained any specifically Christian object.

Addendum

A recent discovery has enabled us to understand the Pictish brooch series more clearly. Amongst the material excavated at the Broch of Birsay, now being prepared for publication by Mrs. C. Curle, are a series of clay moulds for brooches of true penannular form, similar in every respect, save that they are rather smaller, to the examples found at St. Ninian's Isle. This Orkney find strongly supports my arguments as to the Pictish form of these brooches as well as providing further evidence for the method of their manufacture. I am grateful to Mrs. Curle for allowing me to mention this find prior to publication.

[1] See pp. 145 f.

[2] Brehon Laws, iii. 291, quoted by Allen (1894), 175.

[3] iv. 323, quoted ibid., loc. cit. Cf. also the *Senchus Mór* as quoted by Henry (1965), 102.

[4] See above, p. 81.

V *The bowls and miscellaneous silver: form and function*

I n this chapter all the silver objects, with the exception of the brooches, are discussed typologically and in relation to their function; a note on the porpoise bone (no. 29) is also appended. The stylistic implications of the ornament of all the objects in the hoard are discussed in the penultimate chapter of this section. As far as possible the objects are dealt with in the order of their inventory numbers. In the discussion which follows the conclusion that this is a Pictish treasure deposited in the late eighth or early ninth century should be borne in mind.

The bowls (nos. 1–7)
The seven bowls are unique in Scotland. Monsignor McRoberts has suggested that the six examples (nos. 2–7) with an omphalos are chalices and that the bowl in the form of the cone of a sphere (no. 1) is a bowl 'intended for use in the liturgy' as a hand-basin, 'used in conjunction with a ewer (perhaps of earthenware)'.[1] He has, however, been unable to produce any concrete evidence in support of his statement and I have been unable to find any material support for his theoretical observations. Chalices are of relatively frequent occurrence in western Europe at this period[2] and, although they vary in form, in all cases they have feet. This holds for both England[3] and Ireland.[4] There seems to be no evidence to suppose that any Celtic church after the synod of Whitby would have been so eccentric as to have six silver chalices of unparalleled form in a single church, together with a hand-basin of no liturgical parallel whatsoever.

Shallow silver bowls are known from a number of contexts in western Europe. In the great burial of Sutton Hoo were ten bowls of eastern Mediterranean origin,[5] which, with their rounded bases, may be related to no. 1. Another seventh-century find, from Kuczurmare in the U.S.S.R., produced seven shallow bowls with rounded bases, a

---

[1] McRoberts (1960–1), 303.
[2] Elbern (1964).
[3] Wilson and Blunt (1961), pls. xxv and xxviii *a*.
[4] Henry (1965), pl. D.
[5] Bruce Mitford (1968), 58.

beaker-shaped bowl, and a straight-sided silver vessel bearing control-stamps of the Emperor Heraklios (610–41).[1] These bowls are small and compare more closely with such eighth- and ninth-century examples as those from Fejø, Ribe, Terslev, and Lejre in Denmark.[2] The Lejre example was found in association with an insular hanging-bowl,[3] as were the St. Ninian's Isle examples. The Fejø bowls were found together with a cup decorated with Anglo-Carolingian ornament[4] and the Ribe example with a Carolingian cup of similar form.[5] Most of these small bowls have curved bases and some of them have necks. Only one—from Ribe—has a kick in the base.[6]

The only eighth-century object of comparable form from England is the Ormside bowl;[7] it is more elaborate—being decorated with an eighth-century vine-scroll in an impressed technique—but it is of similar size and form. A series of much larger silver bowls of similar size, some with fluted bodies, occur in eleventh- and twelfth-century contexts in Sweden.[8]

Silver bowls were obviously known and used throughout Europe from the seventh century onwards and it may be fortuitous that no example has hitherto been found in Scotland. It is often assumed that certain bronze bowls found in Norwegian Viking graves are of insular origin[9] and, if Petersen was right in this identification, some, at least, may come from Scotland.[10] Few of these bowls, however, approximate in form to the St. Ninian's Isle objects although the bowl from Flakstad, Vang, Hedemark,[11] is close in form to no. 1, which is of course the simplest form amongst those found at St. Ninian's Isle. Equally the bowls found in pagan Anglo-Saxon graves, with one exception known to me,[12] are equally dissimilar.[13]

The St. Ninian's Isle bowls can only be seen as table-ware; they may well have been drinking-bowls as, almost certainly, were the smaller Danish examples listed above.

[1] Noll (1958), pls. 47 and 48.

[2] Wilson (1960a), figs. 7, 21, 22, 23.

[3] Wilson (1960b).

[4] Wilson (1960a).

[5] Ibid., fig. 11.

[6] Ibid., fig. 21.

[7] Kendrick (1938), pl. lx.

[8] e.g. Wilson and Klindt-Jensen (1966), pls. lxii a and lxxx. Holmqvist (1963), figs. 38–43.

[9] Cf. Shetelig (1940), v. 8 ff. and fig. 91.

[10] There seems to be no good reason why some of these Norwegian bowls should not have been manufactured in Scandinavia. There was a perfectly good bronze industry there at the time, as is evidenced in the manufacture of jewellery, why should there not be a local bronze bowl industry? Certainly the presence of bronze bowls in Swedish Viking Age graves would suggest such a possibility; cf. a bowl from grave IX at Birka which is decorated in a very non-British manner—see Selling (1945), fig. 25. Few parallels in form and size have been found in early Viking Age contexts in Sweden, but in no case is there a suggestion that any of the bowls (of whatever size) found in that country came from Britain, although Germany has sometimes been suggested as the country of origin.

[11] Shetelig (1940), v, fig. 92 c.

[12] Unpublished, from Dover grave 137 (British Museum). It is in the form of the cone of a sphere and is 19·3 cm. in diameter. I am grateful to Miss V. I. Evison for allowing me to mention this object in advance of her publication of it.

[13] Baldwin Brown (1903–37), iv, pl. cxvi, 3.

The hanging-bowl (no. 8)

Out of about 150 recorded hanging-bowls[1] only three silver examples are known. One of these is lost (that from the River Witham, pls. li, lii *a*),[2] another is from Lejre in Denmark[3] and has lost its escutcheons, while the third comes from St. Ninian's Isle (no. 8, pl. xxiv). Hanging-bowls as a class have been the cause of much dispute and the dust of the arguments of more than thirty years—most of it unnecessary—has not settled to this day. A survey of all the material is now being conducted by the British Museum and may enable archaeologists to reach some agreement as to the function and origin of the series.[4] In this context it is impossible to consider the whole series of bronze hanging-bowls, which span a period from the fifth to the ninth centuries. The basic problem of the series is expressed by the fact that the vast majority of these objects are found in pagan Anglo-Saxon or in Norwegian Viking graves. Most scholars agree that they were not manufactured in southern England or Norway, although Françoise Henry has postulated the idea that some hanging-bowls were produced in the Irish monastery at Burgh Castle, near Yarmouth in Suffolk,[5] and the opinion has more than once been verbally expressed to me that some of the Norwegian hanging-bowls were made in Scandinavia. Henry[6] has listed eleven finds of hanging-bowls and similar objects from Ireland, of which five are bowls and four are hook escutcheons. Of the five bowls only one (from Derreen), which is of the Viking period, bears traces of escutcheons.[7] Two further triangular bowls bearing escutcheons are also listed. These are presumed to be lamps, although I see no reason to believe that they were not used for a more simple domestic purpose; the strainers which are present in both examples could be used in pouring liquid from a bowl ideally shaped for such a purpose.[8] Despite the very sparse material from Ireland there is ample evidence for the pre-conditions necessary for the manufacture of such objects in Ireland, based on the presence of raw materials for the manufacture of millefiori enamel on various Irish sites.[9]

Recently, however, the discovery in controlled excavations by Miss Cramp of a fragment of glass rod (the main raw material of millefiori enamel on many hanging-

---

[1] This figure is based on the index compiled in the British Museum by Mrs. G. Keiller.

[2] Kendrick (1941).

[3] Wilson (1960*b*).

[4] The main course of argument in this matter is to be traced in the following: Kendrick (1932), Leeds (1933), Clapham (1934), Henry (1936), Kilbride-Jones (1936–7), Kendrick (1938), 49–60, Peers and Radford (1943), 47 ff., Liestöl (1953), Stevenson (1955), Henry (1956), 79–83, Haseloff (1958), Henry (1965), *passim*, and Fowler (1968).

[5] Henry (1956), 82.

[6] Ibid. 80.

[7] Most conveniently published by Raftery (1966) and Henry (1936), fig. 14.

[8] The wooden example from Cuillard (Raftery, 1966) adds point to such an interpretation. As a lamp it would be a considerable fire hazard and it shows no sign of charring. But see below, p. 110.

[9] This evidence is cited with full references by Haseloff (1958), 99–100.

bowl mounts) at the Anglo-Saxon monastery of Jarrow[1] has demonstrated the possibility that enamel mounts could have been made in the Anglo-Saxon area, where hanging-bowls were obviously a popular type of vessel. Although this rod might itself have been imported into the area, and although there is no evidence that it was used in the manufacture of hanging-bowls, its presence at Jarrow is just as significant as the presence of a rod, say, at Garranes in Ireland.[2] It begins to seem reasonable to suppose that hanging-bowls were made in both Ireland and Northumbria and that the great demand for these articles in Anglo-Saxon England was fed from centres of production in both the north and west of Britain. Whether in fact they were produced in the Pictish area we cannot for the moment say.[3] Only one example, other than that from St. Ninian's Isle, has been found in Pictland—it comes from Tummel Bridge, Perthshire,[4] although another example has been found in the Highlands, at Castle Tioram (or *Tirrim*) in south-west Inverness-shire.[5]

It is reasonable to suppose that, whatever the origin of the Anglo-Saxon hanging-bowls, they were being produced by the second half of the seventh century on both sides of the Irish Sea, in the area influenced by the Celtic church. It is an undoubted fact that pieces of millefiori were being used in East Anglia—where it appears in a modified form on the Sutton Hoo jewellery[6]—and in Kent.[7] We have seen that it was almost certainly being manufactured at Jarrow, and there is sufficient dated material to show that bronze hanging-bowls, for which such millefiori could have been used, were being made in the late seventh century.[8] Henry's suggestion that hanging-bowls were produced in East Anglia[9] is interesting, but is not at the moment capable of proof; indeed as Mrs. Fowler has very cogently pointed out, the new date for Sutton Hoo (*c.* 625) would rule out the view that Fursa's monks who arrived at Burgh Castle *c.* 635 had very much to do with the Sutton Hoo bowls.[10] Whatever the case, there was a demand in Anglo-Saxon England for such objects as there was, by implication, in the Celtic area as well. When we move on to the eighth-century series this background should be borne in mind.

---

[1] Wilson and Hurst (1964), 232; illustrated by Bruce Mitford (1969), pl. xix, 2.

[2] O'Ríordáin (1942), fig. 15.

[3] Mr. R. B. K. Stevenson informs me that a piece of millefiori rod was found at Glenluce in Scotland. This is as yet unpublished and is in the National Museum of Antiquities of Scotland.

[4] Henry (1936), pl. xxiii, 2. Kilbride-Jones (1936–7), fig. 2, 2, implies and Fowler (1968), 309, states that there is a second hanging-bowl from Tummel Bridge. This statement rests on two rim fragments of a bronze bowl (originally about 15·5 cm. in diameter at its mouth), which survive from the hoard. There is no convincing evidence that they are fragments of a hanging-bowl, or otherwise.

[5] Kilbride-Jones (1936–7).

[6] e.g. Jessup (1950), pl. D.

[7] e.g. Fausset (1856), pl. iv, 7.

[8] The evidence is cited in Haseloff (1958).

[9] Henry (1956), 81 f.   [10] Fowler (1968), 299.

Before turning to a discussion of the St. Ninian's Isle hanging-bowl in its typological context, the vexed problem of the use of such objects must be considered. It seems incredible that hanging-bowls should be regarded as lamps, and even more incredible that they should be regarded as ecclesiastical lamps. Haseloff[1] and Liestöl[2] have both argued convincingly for their use as bowls for containing water. While there is no doubt that hanging lamps were used in churches,[3] we have no guarantee that all or any of the bowls which are seen suspended in arches in early medieval manuscripts are indeed lamps.[4] Radford has quoted a number of references to pendant vessels of precious metal in churches in Italy[5] and the idea of suspending objects in churches for display purposes is testified in the material remains by the well-known Visigothic 'crowns'.[6] Objects were certainly hung up in profane and domestic contexts and, in a period when cupboards were practically unknown, this would be the most convenient way of storing and displaying them. Mr. Vierck has recently made the interesting suggestion that the hanging-bowls might have been suspended by three hooks at the top of a tripod frame.[7] Mrs. Fowler, who quotes this theory, also points out that in many cases it would be mechanically impossible to hang a hanging-bowl by means of three chains from the roof: 'the upward pull . . . would result in a considerable pressure on the weakest part, the junction of the animal mouth and the rim'.[8] This very sensible suggestion is perhaps capable of extension, for it would also seem mechanically unsafe to hang a full hanging-bowl up at all, even in Mr. Vierck's frame. I would suggest that they were hung up after use to act as decorative objects.

It seems odd that, if these were indeed objects from Christian churches, so many of them should be found in pagan Anglo-Saxon graves. The interiors of many of the hanging-bowls were elaborately decorated and it is highly unlikely that they would be filled with oil—or with water and oil—and hung permanently so that the decorated internal features could not be seen. While it could be argued that the fish in the Sutton Hoo hanging-bowl[9] is a Christian symbol, it could equally well be argued that it would be in its natural element if the bowl were filled with water. The fact that the bowl from Kaupang, Norway, bears a runic inscription, I MUNTLAUKU (in the hand-basin)[2] lends credence to this view. These objects must be seen as the equivalent of the modern finger-bowl, containing the Dark Age equivalent of rose-water—they would be very

[1] Haseloff (1958), 75.

[2] Liestöl (1953).

[3] Dr. R. I. Page draws my attention, for example, to the passage in Æthelwulf's *De abbatibus* (Campbell (1967), 50): 'Many men wished to hang up numerous bowls, which would give soft light in the rectangular church.'

[4] e.g. Zimmermann (1916), pl. 298.

[5] Peers and Radford (1943), 47 f.

[6] Baldwin Brown (1903–37), iv, pl. cxliii, 1.

[7] Fowler (1968), 288 and fig. 69 b.

[8] Ibid. 288.

[9] Bruce Mitford (1968), pl. 10.

much needed in the days before forks! When not in use they would be hung up and would form splendid ornaments in the murky hall.

Even if the theory that the bowls were used to hold water cannot be accepted, the fact that they may have been used for non-religious purposes is illustrated by the statement that the recently excavated hanging-bowl from Ford, Wiltshire, contained vegetable matter—crab apples, onions, and lengths of fine string.[1] In my opinion, therefore, the hanging-bowl must be considered as a domestic vessel, used at table, and I would deny the ecclesiastical interpretation put on the St. Ninian's Isle example by Monsignor McRoberts.[2]

The general form of the St. Ninian's Isle bowl corresponds approximately to group B of Henry's second class of bronze hanging-bowls.[3] It has 'a deep circular depression' in the base and 'a deep groove under a folded over rim'. Dr. Henry's classification is no longer completely valid but the bowls she listed are all related by their rim form and the shape of their base to the St. Ninian's Isle example. In this class Dr. Henry included examples from Kingston, Kent; Lullingstone, Kent; Hawnby, Yorkshire; Lowbury Hill, Berkshire; York, and Winchester.[4] To these can probably be added the bowl from Ipswich,[5] two of the bowls from Sutton Hoo,[6] the bowls from Capheaton, Northumberland;[7] Wilton, Wiltshire;[8] Loveden Hill and Barton, Lincs;[9] and possibly the examples of the lost hanging-bowl from the River Witham (pls. li and lii *a*) and Lejre in Denmark.[10] With the exception of the two latter bowls a consensus of opinion would date the majority of these to the seventh century. The St. Ninian's Isle bowl is undoubtedly a direct descendant of this group and need not be very much later in date than them; in form it agrees completely, but it differs in metal, size, and elaboration, being closer to the examples from the Witham and Lejre.

These three bowls are all smaller than those of the bronze series. They are made of silver and have, or had, more elaborate mounts. The example from Lejre has lost its escutcheons, which must have been rather elaborate, and now survives with a circular mount of gold filigree on both the interior and exterior of the base. The Witham hanging-bowl (pls. li, lii *a*) was the most elaborate of the whole series. It had four escutcheons riveted to the bowl, the rivets being covered internally by blue glass studs in elaborate settings. Four of the rivets, which take the form of human heads on the outside

---

[1] Wilson and Hurst (1965), 176. Bowl illustrated by Fowler (1968), pl. xiii.

[2] McRoberts (1960–1), 304 f.

[3] Henry (1936), 231.

[4] Most Norwegian finds are listed in Shetelig (1940), v. 83 ff.

[5] Ozanne (1962), pls. xxi and xxii.

[6] Bruce Mitford (1968), pl. 11 *a*.

[7] Kilbride-Jones (1936–7), fig. 4, 10.

[8] Ibid., fig. 4, 8.

[9] Unpublished.

[10] Wilson (1960*b*).

of the bowl, form a stand. The escutcheons are inlaid with blue and white millefiori panels, are embellished with granulation and beaded wire, and have a hook formed of an animal head. Both inside and outside the base of the bowl are circular mounts decorated with filigree interlace and plant patterns. Standing in the centre of the internal mount is a naturalistic animal of cast silver. Kendrick's judgement that it was of late ninth-century Anglian or Mercian origin needs modification[1] in the light of modern knowledge of the period. Most scholars would, I believe, agree that it is of eighth-century date and of Mercian or Northumbrian origin.

The St. Ninian's Isle example is less elaborate than the Witham bowl and, apart from its general form and the material from which it is made, has little in common with it. The zoomorphic ribs are unique, although it is possible to see the beginning of this elaboration in the form of the escutcheons of the Witham hanging-bowl, where the square escutcheon (first encountered as a simple mount on the body of the large Sutton Hoo hanging-bowl)[2] is developed to form an elaborate mount which reaches into the omphalos. The only other features which could closely relate the two bowls are, first, the use of rivets to attach the mounts; and, secondly, the possibility that the St. Ninian's Isle example was originally embellished with a domed glass setting, a feature which occurs in a number of places on the Witham hanging-bowl.

The *Pressblech* plaque on the outside of the base appears to be original and a similar technique is used on the base mounts of the York hanging-bowl (pl. xlix *a*), but with an interlace pattern. Cast and chip-carved ornament on a mount like that on the internal base occurs rarely in the corpus of bronze hanging-bowls, but on the Ipswich hanging-bowl (which must date from late in the seventh-century) there is a partly enamelled, partly carved, base-mount, fastened to the bowl by a collar attached by three rivets (pl. xlix *c*). The use of rivets to attach the mounts and escutcheons to the bowl is a rare feature before the late seventh century. Usually they were soldered to the body of the bowl. The St. Ninian's Isle and the other silver hanging-bowls all have this feature as have the Ipswich and York hanging-bowls and many of the Norwegian series.[3]

Generally speaking, therefore, the bowl cannot be dated earlier than the middle of the seventh century and, in view of the stylistic considerations discussed below,[4] a date towards the end of the seventh century or at the beginning of the eighth century would seem reasonable.

[1] Kendrick (1941).
[2] Bruce Mitford (1968), pl. 10*a*.
[3] e.g. Shetelig (1940), v, figs. 95, 102, 104, 105, 112, 113*c*.
[4] pp. 134-7.

The spoon

The spoon (no. 9) is without parallel. It is only distantly related to the normal form of late Roman spoons found in Britain[1] and this only in so far as the animal head at the junction of the stem and the bowl is a feature found two-dimensionally on Roman spoons from the end of the third century.[2] No contemporary spoon of insular origin exists, the nearest datable example being the spatula-like, Anglo-Saxon objects from Sevington, Wiltshire,[3] which are dated by coins to before 850.

Strangely enough one of the nearest typological parallels comes from under the floor of the medieval nunnery at Iona, Argyll. (fig. 40),[4] in a hoard of late twelfth- or thirteenth-century spoons. The bowls of these objects are very obviously related to that of the St. Ninian's Isle spoon, having practically the same profile: similarly, the spoon from Pevensey Castle,[5] which I have dated, rather insecurely, to the eleventh century, has a profile like that of the St. Ninian's Isle object. The St. Ninian's Isle spoon must be considered as a precursor of the later medieval form and by the time the hoard was buried the rather clumsy Roman-type spoon, which last occurs in Britain in the early seventh century at Sutton Hoo,[6] may have completely disappeared; the St. Ninian's Isle object can be regarded as a harbinger of medieval taste. Possible links in the chain of development of the spoon are provided by a spoon from Basset Down, Wiltshire, which has a bowl of roughly the same form as the St. Ninian's Isle example,[7] and a unique spoon from Barnham, Kent,[8] which has a displayed animal beneath the bowl at the joint of the bowl and the stem. This latter should almost certainly be dated to the pagan Anglo-Saxon period; the former cannot, however, be dated, although it is said to have come from an Anglo-Saxon cemetery.

The animal head of the St. Ninian's Isle spoon must be seen as a survival of that so commonly placed in late Roman contexts at the junction of the stem and the bowl,[9] presumably having some functional significance as a strengthening element.[10] Bruce Mitford has pointed out that the bowl 'does not develop, as is normal in medieval spoons out of the mouth of a flattened animal head modelled at its junction with the stem'. The placing of the animal head in this position, does, however suggest that the continuous tradition from the period of the Roman Empire to the medieval period is not really being broken at St. Ninian's Isle.[11]

[1] e.g. Painter (1965), *passim*.   [2] Strong (1966), 178.
[3] Wilson (1964), pl. xxix, 67 and 68.
[4] Curle (1923–4).
[5] Wilson (1964), pl. xxvii, 59.
[6] Bruce Mitford (1968), pl. 22a.
[7] Baldwin Brown (1903–37), iv, pl. xcv, 4.
[8] Ibid., pl. xcv, 1–3.   [9] e.g. Painter (1965), pl. iv.

[10] Strong (1966), 178, points out that they first appear in the late third century.

[11] An imported spoon from Italy, with an animal head based on that of the Roman series was found in the rich sixth-century prince's grave from Krefeld-Gellep on the Rhine (Doppelfeld and Pirling (1966), pls. 118 and 119) and supports this statement.

The animal head is a splendid and individual piece of casting. It cannot be accurately paralleled,[1] but its composition is typical of the period: plastic animal heads occur in English,[2] Scottish, and Irish[3] contexts. The small beaded glass eyes are a common feature which occur elsewhere in the hoard (e.g. pl. xxx). The head itself, while quite naturalistic, can be easily paralleled in its detail in the St. Ninian's Isle treasure itself. The panelling of the cheek and the emphatic line of break between the cheek and the snout are seen in two-dimensional or low relief on the brooches (e.g. no. 20, pl. xxxii) and the chapes (e.g. the crest of no. 16, pl. xxx).

The spoon, then, can be seen to fit well with the general composition of the hoard. There is no reason to suppose that it was not made in the main area of the St. Ninian's Isle hoard's homeland.

The use of the spoon has been the subject of considerable theorizing. Monsignor McRoberts, in his discussion of this subject says:

> No other examples survive of such . . . spoons from the Celtic liturgy but, even without such comparative material, the identification [as a communion spoon] seems reasonable because a spoon for the administration of the intincted host would be a normal part of the church plate of any church which administered communion under both species in pre-medieval times.[4]

There is, in fact, no evidence for such an assertion. In all the illustrations of early medieval altars published by de Fleury,[5] not a single example of a spoon is shown. Both Leclercq[6] and Braun,[7] the two leading experts in such matters, deny the use of the eucharistic spoon in the western mass. Braun points out that the spoon was used for such a purpose in the eastern Church, but states that it probably came into use in the late eighth century.[8] De Fleury states that a spoon is mentioned in a eucharistic context in an eleventh-century French source, but gives no reference;[9] Braun, however, does not allow its use in such a context until the late thirteenth century, when a spoon was used to add a few drops of water to the chalice.[10] The only spoon regularly used in an ecclesiastical context is that used for incense, but this was much smaller. Unless therefore there was much more Eastern influence in the Celtic church than most scholars are willing to accept, I think we must deny the use of the St. Ninian's Isle spoon in a eucharistic context.[11]

[1] The treatment of the animal heads on the head of the stone from Nigg, Ross-shire, is very similar; cf. Stevenson (1955), pl. 9.

[2] e.g. Wilson (1964), pl. xvii, 18.

[3] Henry (1965), pl. 44.

[4] McRoberts (1960–1), 307.

[5] de Fleury (1883), pls. *passim.*

[6] Cabrol and Leclercq (1907–53), iii. 3174.

[7] Braun (1932), 265.

[8] Ibid. 272–3.

[9] de Fleury (1883), 43.

[10] Braun (1932), 44 ff.

[11] Ryan (1931), 349, states: 'An examination of the different elements in the Stowe Missal shows that its affinities are with the church in Gaul, but that it has been influenced by the liturgies of Spain, Milan and (above all) Rome.' This statement would seem to deny all Eastern influence.

The idea of the spoon as a Christian object dies hard. The strongest claimants to Christian significance are the spoons from the great seventh-century Anglo-Saxon cenotaph at Sutton Hoo, quoted above. Here the spoons bear inscriptions—one reading SAULOS, one PAULOS—which seem to refer to the conversion of St. Paul on the Damascus road.[1] Kitzinger in the original discussion of the Sutton Hoo silver was also under the impression that spoons were of liturgical significance, and pointed to other spoons inscribed with saints' names.[2] A large number of late Roman spoons are decorated with a *chi-rho* symbol,[3] but this need not necessarily imply anything more than the owner's confession of his own faith. The spoon itself provides no evidence of ecclesiastical usage. Monsignor McRoberts seeks to find symbolic significance in the animal head at the junction of the stem and the bowl:

. . . The origin and significance of the symbol are easily guessed; the symbol surely derives from the gospel incident, where the Syrophoenician woman claims that 'the dogs under the table eat of the children's crumbs' and it suggests the humility with which the Christian should approach the Holy Eucharist. While this is evident it has to be stated further that this particular eucharistic symbol is quite unknown in the rest of Christendom and, that being so, it is of great interest to find that this extremely unusual eucharistic symbol occurs in yet another instance in the iconography of Dark Age Scotland.[4]

Such an argument hardly holds water and, unless we can produce adequate inconographic parallels, it must surely fall. The parallel McRoberts quotes with the Nigg slab is false, for the animals here can have no eucharistic symbolism at all.[5] The scene on the Nigg slab can only represent the widely used Celtic scene of Paul and Antony in the desert and not the celebration of the mass; as the chalice is missing, and the animals could be lions, dogs, wolves, or whatever.[6]

The spoon has a loop for suspension at its tip and we must presume that it hung, with the claw-like object (no. 10), from a girdle in the manner of the pierced spoons of the pagan Anglo-Saxon period.[7] It should be seen as an adjunct to dress and not as a ritual object.

The claw-like object
The use of the claw-like object (no. 10, pl. xxvi *b*) has not been satisfactorily explained. It is best paralleled by a group of Roman objects which were used at table. Two objects of similar form from Kaiseraugst, Switzerland (figs. 34 *c–d*), occur in a completely

---

[1] Kaske (1967) questions the reading of the Sutton Hoo inscriptions.   [2] Kitzinger (1940), 59.

[3] e.g. Painter (1965), pl. iii.

[4] McRoberts (1960–1), 307. Cf. *contra* Henderson (1967), 148 and fig. 35.

[5] McRoberts (1960–1), xxvi.

[6] Cf. Henderson (1967), 148 and fig. 35, who ignores McRoberts's suggestion.

[7] Baldwin Brown (1903–37), iv, pl. xciv, 1–2.

domestic context,[1] as part of a rich, silver table service. Otherwise objects of this form are normally found with spoons, as at Richborough, Kent,[2] at Dorchester, Dorset[3] (fig. 34 *b*), and at Canterbury[4], Kent. A Roman spoon from Kerch in the Crimea[5] and a ladle from Kaiseraugst[6] have terminals of roughly the same form as the claw-like objects quoted as parallels to the St. Ninian's Isle object. A similar feature occurs on a fiddle-shaped spoon from La Fortelle, Compiègne (S. et O.), France[7] (fig. 34 *a*), which is of an earlier date (3rd century) than those quoted above.

Formal parallels of similar date to the St. Ninian's Isle objects are rare. A pin from a late migration period grave from Darstadt, Ochsenfurt, Germany, has a finial of roughly similar form,[8] but the resemblance is almost certainly fortuitous as the finial probably represents a degenerate Style II animal head. A small, unprovenanced object from Ireland of similar form might just be functional (pl. xlix *b*); it is of bronze, 8·4 cm. long, has a baluster shaft and an incipient spur. It has a spiral-ornamented roundel and another roundel decorated with a herring-bone pattern. The tip is about 2 mm. thick and therefore would seem to be out of series with the Roman parallels quoted, which, like the St. Ninian's Isle example, are much slighter. This difference may, however, be due to the fact that the Irish object is made of bronze and the others of silver, which would lend itself to such treatment. Like the St. Ninian's Isle example it has a loop for suspension.

The late Roman prototypes of the St. Ninian's Isle object have been discussed by Professor Strong in his standard work on classical plate;[9] he has pointed out that they 'are thought to have been used for eating such foods as snails or shellfish'. The claw-like terminals of the Kerch and La Fortelle spoons can thus be seen as the successors of the simple pointed finials of the early Roman spoons which were certainly used for extracting shellfish.[10] Other uses have been suggested; they have been described, for example, as medical probes[11] and 'toilet implements'. The presence of an 'ear pick' on examples like those from Richborough and Canterbury may have been responsible for this latter designation, which can, I think, be dismissed.

In Roman contexts such objects have no apparent religious application; they are

[1] Laur-Belart (1963).

[2] Bushe-Fox (1949), pl. xxxvii, 126 and 127.

[3] Dalton (1922).

[4] Painter (1965).

[5] *Jahrbuch des kaiserlich deutschen archäologischen Instituts,* xxiii, 1908, 'Archäologischer Anzeiger', fig. 11.

[6] Laur-Belart (1963).

[7] St. Germain-en-Laye: Musée des antiquités nationales, reg. no. 28852. I owe this reference to Professor D. E. Strong, to whom I am most grateful for further discussion of this group of objects.

[8] Koch (1967), pl. 38.

[9] Strong (1966), 206 f.

[10] Ibid. 129, quotes the Martial epigram, xiv. 121, to demonstrate this point.

[11] *Instruments de chirugie greco-romains* (N. Rauch, Geneva, sale catalogue), 1961, nos. 2 and 86.

normally found, as has been pointed out, together with domestic plate. The chi-rho monogram which occurs on the Dorchester and Kaiseraugst examples has no ritual significance. Many secular objects bear this symbol,[1] which merely indicates the religion of the owner—no more. The association of many of these Roman claw-like objects with spoons suggests that they were used at table, perhaps in a highly mannered and delicate fashion, for eating some specialized food like shellfish.

The suggestion that the St. Ninian's Isle object was used in a Christian liturgical context in the ritual division of the host was first made tentatively by Dr. Bruce Mitford[2] and accepted without question by Monsignor McRoberts.[3] Neither scholar has, however, been able to provide satisfactory documentation for such a suggestion. The theory must rest on the occurrence of the find in a church—a theory which is discussed elsewhere.[4] They refer to the use of such an object in the Easter rite for cutting the bread. This is presumably the holy lance (*lancea*), which bears no resemblance to the St. Ninian's Isle object. It is in fact spear-shaped.[5]

Dr. Bruce Mitford has quoted the Stowe Missal treatise on the mass, with its complicated rules for the division of the host,[6] saying that the division into sixty-five particles implies that 'some form of implement must have been used for the dissection and picking up of the individual fragments, and it seems that the pronged implement in the St. Ninian's Isle hoard might serve this purpose ideally'.[2] However, the word *combach*, which is used here, means, I am assured by Professor David Greene, 'breaking' or 'crushing'. The passage, *in pars benar a hichtur ind lithe*[7] has been rendered 'the particle that is cut off from the bottom of the half'. The word *benaid* has many meanings, of which 'cut' is only one, and Professor Greene tells me that it would be perfectly legitimate to translate it as 'the particle which is removed from the bottom half'. This is the only place in the text where there is even a suspicion of evidence that an implement was used.

Arguments on grounds of common sense are liable to be received with little compassion by scholars, but I cannot refrain from the statement that the object would hardly be suitable for cutting bread, whether in the form of a wafer or a roll. It is hardly strong enough for such purposes. Dr. A. T. Lucas has told me that there is no evidence as to the form of bread used during the mass in the early Christian period, but the Stowe

---

[1] e.g. Toynbee (1953), *passim*.

[2] O'Dell *et al.* (1959), 259.

[3] McRoberts (1960–1), 307. It is also accepted by implication by Henderson (1967), 214.

[4] See p. 146.

[5] Cabrol and Leclercq (1907–53), viii. 1234 ff.

[6] Stokes and Strachan (1903), 253–5. I am grateful to Professor David Greene of the Dublin Institute of Advanced Studies for help in consideration of this text.

[7] Stokes and Strachan (1903), 254, line 3.

Missal description quoted above implies a wafer rather than ordinary bread.[1] Can one carve a wafer?

The St. Ninian's Isle object functioned as a pendant and this perhaps gives a clue to its original context. The pierced end and the remains of the ring are reminiscent of the pierced ornamental spoons which hung at the girdle of Anglo-Saxon ladies[2] often with a crystal ball. Indeed the moulding of the terminal of such spoons is not at all dissimilar to the moulding[3] of the St. Ninian's Isle object: the whole of the shaft, indeed, is similar. This undoubted parallel and the Roman parallels quoted must surely have its roots in a pagan context. As with the spoon from the treasure (no. 9), we can only say that there is no particle of evidence to suggest that it was ever used in the mass. Both objects have loops for suspension and presumably hung from the belt of some high-born Pict.

The interlace ornament of the object is completely unremarkable. The free ring is rather rare in Scottish ornament of the period, but the scrolled ends can be paralleled in a dozen places (cf., for example, pl. lv). The hatched background, perhaps with a hint of basketry ornament, need occasion no surprise in the face of such obvious technical parallels as the Birka bucket,[4] and the buckle from Valtos, Uig,[5] which are certainly of insular manufacture.

The pommel and chapes

The pommel (no. 11) and the two chapes (nos. 15 and 16) must be sword fittings. McRoberts's argument[6] that the pommel was the terminal of the handle of a *flabellum*, to which the three bosses (nos. 12–14) were also attached, does not stand up to detailed investigation. However, as this theory enters so considerably into arguments as to the nature of the hoard it must be investigated here in some detail.

McRoberts's statement, that 'the two great ostrich feather fans which are nowadays carried when the pope goes in solemn procession to the Vatican Basilica, are the sole modern survivors of the liturgical fans, which were in universal use throughout Western Christendom prior to the Middle Ages', shows a basic misunderstanding of the history and function of the *flabellum* in Christian liturgy. In the first place the two fans carried before the pope have nothing to do with *flabella*,[7] the true function of which was to keep flies away from consecrated wine. In eastern Christian contexts *flabella* occur at least as early as the fifth century,[8] but in the west their earliest recorded occurrence in

---

[1] For references to early bread in Ireland *vide* Lucas (1960–2), 10–14, and Power (1939–40).

[2] e.g. Baldwin Brown (1903–37), iv, pl. xciv. An unpublished spoon and curved pick of migration period type from Vidy in the Bern Museum adds point to this parallel.

[3] e.g. ibid., pl. xciv, 1.

[4] Arbman (1940), pl. 204, 2.

[5] Shetelig (1940), ii, fig. 43.

[6] McRoberts (1960–1), 308 ff.

[7] Braun (1932), 648, explains their origin.

[8] Ibid., 642 ff.

literature is in an inventory of 831. After this they are noticed but rarely until the eleventh century.[1]

A priori, therefore, it seems unlikely that a remote church in Shetland would produce a *flabellum* fifty years or so before the first recorded usage of such an object in the revived western Empire. Secondly, on purely practical grounds, the construction envisaged by Monsignor McRoberts[2] would be altogether too heavy to fulfill the true function of a *flabellum*.

The representations of *flabella* used by McRoberts to support his arguments are by no means convincing. The early Christian example from the catacombs[3] has no inherently eucharistic function and the same is true of the Langobardic representation on the Ferentillo altar canopy.[4] Nowhere can an illustration be found of a *flabellum* in use at an altar and some of the representations of alleged *flabella* cited by McRoberts have other, more reasonable, interpretations. The clerics on the St. Vigean's cross-slab for example,[5] certainly hold croziers and not *flabella*. Small croziers of comparative size are represented in the archaeological material by the insular crozier-head from Helgö, Ekerö, Sweden.[6] The '*flabella*' which McRoberts sees on the Whithorn and Raasay stones[7] must surely be interpreted as crosses; the Raasay example being very close in form to the famous Rupertus Cross of insular workmanship at Bischofshofen.[8] The angels in the Madonna-and-Child page of the Book of Kells[9] appear to be holding wands not *flabella*. The other representations quoted by McRoberts from this manuscript could in fact be *flabella*,[10] but their function, as liturgical implements, is by no means clear. One is held by the *imago hominis* of St. Matthew and the others appear in panels which portray the four evangelist symbols. The *flabella* cited by McRoberts on the altar frontal of the Langobardic church at Ferentillo in Umbria[11] could possibly be so interpreted. But these objects, which tower above the human figures and other embellishments of the frontal and in any case stand on feet, seem more likely to be formalized representations of crosses in honour of the three canonized popes to whom the altar was dedicated.

In his second article McRoberts expands his arguments by a more detailed consideration of Celtic sources referring to *flabella*,[12] in which he discusses the *flabellum* (*culebadh*) of Columcille, which is mentioned in an eleventh-century source. He, elsewhere,

---

[1] Ibid. 652.
[2] McRoberts (1960–1), fig. 6.
[3] Ibid., fig. 2.
[4] Ibid., fig. 3.
[5] Ibid., fig. 5.
[6] Holmqvist (1961), pls. B and C.
[7] McRoberts (1960–1), pl. xxvii.
[8] Jenny (n.d.).
[9] McRoberts (1960–1), pl. xxviii.
[10] Ibid., pls. xxix and xxx.
[11] Hubert *et al.*, fig. 278.
[12] McRoberts (1965), 245.

mentions other Celtic *flabella*,[1] but all the sources are late and of little value in the consideration of an eighth-century hoard.

In short, McRoberts seems to have failed in his attempt to document the use of the *flabellum* in the eighth-century Celtic church and to document the use of a liturgical *flabellum* (*sensu strictu*) in the western church of the eighth century. Further, although it is dangerous to rely on common-sense arguments, his reconstruction would produce an extremely heavy and clumsy object, completely at odds with the light medieval *flabellum*, which was made as a circular fan.[2] Further, his reconstruction of the function of the holes on the bosses (nos. 12–14), is completely at odds with the evidence of wear on these three objects (see p. 62).

If, however, one considers the form of the eighth-century insular sword-pommel, we are provided with such a striking parallel of form and method of attachment that there seems little reason to doubt the function of the pommel from St. Ninian's Isle. Bruce Mitford has already pointed out that the only surviving sword-pommel of this period from Scotland comes from Culbin Sands.[3] This rather paltry bronze object of seventh-century date cannot be compared in more than general terms with the St. Ninian's Isle pommel. If, on the other hand, we compare the St. Ninian's Isle object with the richer English example from Fetter Lane,[4] which is the only surviving Anglo-Saxon sword-pommel of the eighth century, we can see how the tripartite nature of the face is emphasized in a manner related to that on the St. Ninian's Isle object. If we further consider the general form of eighth- and ninth-century swords from Europe, we can see that this tripartite division is almost universal.[5]

The lack of pommel-guard and sword-guard need cause no real surprise. Anglo-Saxon swords of the pagan Anglo-Saxon period often only have a thin sheet of metal covering the base of a wooden guard which is crowned by a pommel.[6] One surviving Anglo-Saxon sword of this period, from Crundale, Kent,[7] has no such sheet at the base of its wooden pommel-guard, merely a gilt collar at the head of the grip. One method of attachment of the pommel to the hilt has been demonstrated in a number of ninth- and tenth-century contexts in recent years. Examples have been published from Viking graves in the Isle of Man[8] and on two late Anglo-Saxon swords, one of unknown provenance[9] and the other from Wallingford Bridge.[10] By this means of construction a

---

[1] McRoberts (1960–1), 313.

[2] Cf. Braun (1932), pls. 142, 563 and 141, 560.

[3] *Proceedings of the Society of Antiquaries of Scotland*, lxvii (1932–3), 33–4.

[4] Wilson (1964), pl. xxiii, 41.

[5] Cf. Dunning and Evison (1961), figs. 3–5.

[6] e.g. Hawkes and Page (1967), pls. I–II and figs. 2 and 3.

[7] Kendrick (1938), pl. xxxiii, 4.

[8] Bersu and Wilson (1966), 52, 70 and fig. 41.

[9] Wilson (1965), fig. 15.

[10] Evison (1967), fig. 8e.

bar passes through the pommel and guard, thus attaching it, by a method which is not clear, to the sword. The pin or bar found with the St. Ninian's Isle pommel (fig. 17 a), however, is equivalent to that shown in X-rays of the later examples just quoted.

To my knowledge not a single sword of pre-Viking, Christian Celtic origin has been found in Scotland. Study of them must rest at second-hand on representations of such objects on the carved stone monuments of the area. Details of sword-pommels are rarely encountered. On the face of the shrine from St. Andrews, Fife, three offensive weapons are portrayed: a scramasax and a spear, which need not concern us here, and a sword drawn from its scabbard and held in the right hand of the uppermost rider (pl. l a). This appears to have a comparatively small pommel and a longer pommel-guard, a feature which also occurs on the sword of Samson depicted on the stone from Inchbrayock, Perthshire.[1] The accuracy of this representation is open to question, but the actual form in both cases is not inconsistent with the appearance of the St. Ninian's Isle object. There can, however, be little doubt that the rider's scabbard on a slab of the St. Andrew's shrine (pl. l a) has a large chape. A similar feature can also be seen very clearly on stone no. 3 from Meigle, Perthshire (pl. liii), and possibly, but less certainly, on the Hilton of Cadboll stone (pl. lvi), on the stones from Benvie,[2] and Meigle (no. 6).[3] Many other scabbards represented on the sculptured stones admittedly have no such feature.[4] There seems little doubt, however, that the scabbards of some swords in the Pictish area in the eighth century had chapes not unlike objects nos. 15 and 16 from St. Ninian's Isle.

Large chapes are not unknown in Europe in the first millennium A.D. They are, for example, found in late Roman Iron Age contexts in Scandinavia,[5] where they normally take the form of large discs made of sheet metal. The opening in both the St. Ninian's Isle examples is not inconsistent with the presence of a scabbard. Openings of similar narrowness to that of the smaller chape (no. 16) are illustrated by Dr. Stjernqvist. It is impossible in logic to bridge the gap between the third and fourth centuries in Denmark and the eighth century in Scotland and we are not helped by the total absence of chapes in eighth-century contexts in the British Isles, nor by their rare occurrence in western Europe, where they are completely unlike the St. Ninian's Isle examples.[6] Although there may be some connection evidence must rest on the material provided by the Pictish sculpture.

[1] Stevenson (1955), pl. 11.
[2] Curle (1939–40), pl. xlviiia.
[3] Allen (1903), iii, fig. 315 B.
[4] e.g. Stevenson (1955), pl. 11 and Cruden (1964), pl. 7.

[5] e.g. Engelhardt (1866), pl. ix, 23, and Stjernqvist (1955), pls. xxii, xl, and xli.
[6] Cf. Behmer (1939), pls. xlvi and xlvii.

It might be argued that the inscription on no. 15 would presuppose a specifically Christian use for the object, but the inscription need only be taken as a pious platitude—secular objects quite commonly bear Christian symbols in this period.

While it is not impossible that the two objects are in fact strap-ends of unique form, their association with what can only be a sword-pommel, together with the evidence of sculpture, speaks strongly in favour of their use as chapes of sword-scabbards.[1] They would presumably be riveted, sewn, or fastened with glue or by the closing of the opening, or by a combination of any or all of these, to the leather of the scabbard.

The cones (nos. 12–14)

The use of one of these objects in the form of cones of spheroids (nos. 12, 13, and 14) is unknown. They are unique. The likelihood that they are parts of a *flabellum*, as was suggested by Monsignor McRoberts,[2] is slight in view of the arguments set out above (pp. 118 ff.). Bruce Mitford saw them as part of the sword-belt or as sword-fittings, citing the bosses and pyramidal studs on migration period scabbards as parallels,[3] giving as his reasons, 'a general similarity of gilding, ornamental style and wear to the pommel'. He felt, however, that no. 14 was odd: 'A slight difference in shape, a difference in ornamental theme, a greater degree of wear, and the different shape of its basal slots seem to indicate that No. 14 originally belonged to a different and somewhat earlier equipment.'

Before examining Bruce Mitford's proposals let us first consider a group of objects which might also be tentatively paralleled with nos. 12–14. From the Broch of Burrian, Sandwick, North Ronaldsay, Orkney, comes a thin bone disc (fig. 42 *a*) pierced with two holes of exactly the same form as the base of no. 13. Closely related examples occur on the same site (fig. 42 *b*) and at the Shetland site of Jarlshof (fig. 42 *c, d*). The circumstances of the finding of these objects is obscure, but there is a high probablity, particularly with regard to the Broch of Burrian examples,[4] that they are from Pictish levels. One of the discs from Burrian (fig. 42) has a ring-and-dot motif incised on one face. In size all the bone discs compare very closely with the base-plates of the St. Ninian's Isle objects: They vary in thickness between 1·8 and 3·8 mm., and in diameter between 3·3 and 3·8 cm. The diameter of the base-plates of the St. Ninian's Isle objects varies between 3·4 and 3·7 cm.—a striking coincidence! The use of the bone discs is also unknown, but it seems reasonably clear because of the striking similarity of the holes

---

[1] McRoberts (1960–1), 306–7, maintains that they are girdle ends, but adduces no real evidence in favour of this theory.

[2] McRoberts (1960–1) and (1965), 238 ff.

[3] O'Dell *et al.* (1959), 261.

[4] Traill (1890), 356.

in the two groups of objects, that the St. Ninian's Isle bosses are simply more elaborate versions of the bone discs from other parts of the northern isles of Scotland. If this is so, it would seem unlikely that they have any immediate relationship to the sword, although it is not impossible that they were attached to a sword belt.

It would seem likely that the bone objects functioned as dress- or girdle-fasteners. At this period it is unusual to find buckles in Celtic contexts and clothes must have been fastened with brooches, pins, toggles, and buttons, objects which are of reasonably common occurrence on Celtic settlement sites. The three St. Ninian's Isle objects must be seen as rather elaborate versions of a normal form of object.

The wear may help to indicate the way in which they were mounted. All three are heavily worn at the top—wear which would result from normal rubbing of the most exposed surface. The base-plate of no. 12 is buckled at the slots as though it has been attached to a yielding base of, say, leather. That of no. 14 has been strengthened with an internal bar and the area between the slots of the base-plate of no. 15 has been broken away. It would seem then that the mounts took some considerable strain at this point, a strain which they would not take if they had been firmly fixed to an unyielding surface—e.g. wood. It is also interesting that the slots are faceted on their outside edge, presumably so that they would not cut any cord or thong with which they were fastened. On at least two examples (nos. 12 and 14) there is also wear around the holes pierced in the walls: wear on the beaded wire ring round the base-plates occurs in a similar position. It would seem therefore that a thong or cord passed through the object and then under the base-plate to be fastened below the material on which the cone was laid. Such a thong would then add to the security of the fastening, ensuring that the valuable ornamental element would not be lost by accident, for the base-plate was only affixed by solder and could easily be ripped off. If my interpretation of the method of mounting these objects is correct, they could perhaps be regarded as belt buttons, perhaps for sword belts. I feel that Dr. Bruce Mitford's suggestion that they belonged to 'scabbard straps' as more likely than that they belonged to the scabbard itself, as I feel sure that they would have been affixed in a less clumsy way if the latter was the case.

The porpoise bone

The fact that a porpoise bone (no. 29) occurs in the hoard is puzzling. References in Celtic literature to porpoises are few and confusing and of no real significance.[1] There are hints, however, that the mammal was important in the early Christian period.

[1] I am grateful to my colleagues Mr. J. Stewart and Dr. D. M. Dixon for advice in this matter.

The dolphin, a creature of very similar appearance, which is rare in northern waters, frequently appears as an ornamental motif in western contexts and there is a hint in Anglo-Saxon documents that porpoises were in some demand.[1] The deeper meaning of this bone remains an enigma.

[1] Cf., e.g., Loyn (1962), 361. Cf. *mereswin* in Bosworth and Toller (1882), 680.

VI *A stylistic consideration of the miscellaneous objects*

THE St. Ninian's Isle hoard casts new light on the art of Britain in the eighth century. If I am correct in my contention (grounded on the typological premisses outlined above) that the hoard is of basically Pictish character, it must be seen as the first considerable body of evidence in metalwork of non-symbolic Pictish art. Further, the hoard provides a strong link with the art of both England and Ireland and illuminates a number of problems of Hiberno-Saxon ornament.

The argument of the chapter which follows is not strong because of the almost complete lack of non-lapidary material providing accurate stylistic parallels. The parallels which can be drawn are often only of general import due to differences of scale and material: in Scotland—apart from the brooches—there is little ornamental metalwork and no manuscript art, but a lot of sculpture. I shall, however, try to demonstrate in this chapter that most of the ornament of the St. Ninian's Isle hoard has its parallels in Pictland and that the style itself—though closely related in many details to the art of Ireland—is to a large extent influenced from Northumbria and the Anglo-Saxon area. There are some slight historical arguments to support such a supposition, for the east coast of north England and Scotland were at this period areas in contact with each other.[1]

In order to tackle this complicated subject the objects must be studied in groups or, occasionally, even singly; general stylistic conclusions based on this study will be found in the succeeding chapter.

The bowls

Two of the bowls (nos. 2 and 3, pls. xviii, xix and figs. 21, 22) bear friezes of punched animal ornament. No other animal friezes are known from Celtic vessels in Scotland and the only proper origin for the occurrence of such designs on similar vessels must be sought in Roman and Romano-British silver and pottery, where scenes of the chase are often displayed round a cup or bowl.[2] Such parallels are, because of the wide chronological

[1] Cf. Wilson (1970).
[2] e.g. British Museum, *Guide to the Antiquities of Roman* *Britain*, London, 1951, pls. iv, 15 and viii, 17.

gap, difficult to use and it is best to turn directly to the ornamental detail and consider the problem of the frieze below.[1]

Chronologically the most important parallel to these animals is that which was drawn by Bruce Mitford[2] to the animals executed in red dots on fol. 95ʳ of the Lindisfarne Gospels (fig. 35). The loop of the head and neck of one of the animals on bowl no. 2 is almost exactly paralleled here.[3] Other details of the bowls are to be seen in the Lindisfarne Gospels. The spiral formed by the rear legs on both bowls occurs on fol. 26ᵛ[4]—but in a much looser form—while the trick of twisting the legs when they have interlaced with the body, so that the nearside leg appears as the offside leg, occurs in a number of places on the bowls and in the manuscript (fig. 21).[5] Ornament executed in a dotted technique similar to that which occurs on the bowls is quite common in the pages of the Lindisfarne Gospels; it has its origin in the dotted outlines of ornament and letters in insular manuscripts of a much earlier period,[6] and is a feature which survives into the manuscript art of the ninth century.[7] The Lindisfarne Gospels provide a firm chronological peg in any discussion of this art. The date of 698 for its completion is perfectly acceptable, even though some would date it twenty years later. In view of other arguments which follow it seems reasonable to date the bowls to a period after the Lindisfarne Gospels had been completed.

The foliate element in the design of nos. 2 and 3 are difficult to parallel, although Bruce Mitford is surely correct in his supposition that 'the foliations of the tips of tails or tongues in the bowls are a post-Lindisfarne innovation'.[8] In general terms the phenomenon can be compared to that encountered in eighth-century Anglo-Saxon metalwork, on such objects as the Witham pins, where vine scrolls and animals are joined together in an organic pattern.[9] The projection of tongues and tails into foliate terminals is more common in southern English art of the late eighth and early ninth century, particularly in metalwork and manuscript illumination.[10] This might be slightly significant chronologically, but the stylistic link is slim. It might be interpolated that this feature occurs frequently in the Book of Kells;[11] but this provides the only major similarity between

---

[1] p. 132.

[2] O'Dell et al. (1959), 265.

[3] A derivative form of this animal is seen in another Anglo-Saxon context in a panel at the base of a page in the eighth-century Cologne *Collectio Canonum* (Cologne Cathedral Library MS. 213), but here the loop has become an angled knot—Henry (1965), pl. 63.

[4] Kendrick et al. (1960), fig. 41 b.

[5] Cf. also ibid., fig. 43 b and O'Dell et al. (1959), figs. 13 and 14.

[6] e.g. (The Cathach of St. Columba), Henry (1965), pl. 12.

[7] e.g. British Museum Royal I.E.VI., Zimmerman (1916), pl. 290.   [8] O'Dell et al. (1959), 265.

[9] Wilson (1964), pl. xviii.

[10] Cf., for example, ibid., figs. 8, 29, 40, 41–4, etc. Zimmermann (1916), pls. 290. Cf. also the eighth-century Anglo-Carolingian school typified by the Tassilo Chalice, Haseloff (1951), fig. 2.

[11] Henry (1967), pls. 32 and 33. See also fig. 37.

the ornament of Kells and that of the bowls, and one can only presume that the element is derived from a common source—the vine scroll. It must be admitted, however, that there seems to be little significance in any of these parallels, either stylistically or chronologically.

If we ignore this feature and turn to eastern Scotland we may see striking stylistic parallels for the ornament of the two bowls, so striking indeed that (even if they have little chronological significance) there can be little doubt that the bowls were manufactured in that area. The parallels occur in the flourishing stone sculpture of Pictland, which, in the almost complete absence of metalwork, provides practically the whole corpus of Pictish art. During the eighth century a number of Anglo-Saxon stylistic influences appear north of the Forth. Such motifs as zoomorphic and interlace ornament and (more rarely) inhabited vine-scroll motifs[1] appear for the first time on the Pictish sculptured monuments. It must be stressed that this ornament was not confined to southern Pictland; it is also found in the north, as, for example, in one of its finest expressions on the stone from Hilton of Cadboll in Ross,[2] which is usually dated to the late eighth century.[3] As a consequence of these influences the competent but stark ornament of the Pictish symbol stones was transformed into an elaborate and highly decorated style of many facets: but, as Dr. Henderson so rightly points out, this art is by no means 'a late or provincial reflection of the main developments in Hiberno-Saxon art',[4] it is a vital eclectic style which stands on its own feet. There is general agreement that there is little direct Irish influence in this phase of the stylistic history of the Pictish monuments. This is not the place to enter into arguments concerning the detailed origin of this art—suffice it to say that there was in Pictland in the eighth and early ninth centuries a considerable body of elaborate stone sculpture bearing zoomorphic and interlace ornament.

Among the motifs which appear on this sculpture are animals which are closely related to those on bowls nos. 2 and 3 from the St. Ninian's Isle hoard. The most striking parallels occur on the stones from Aberlemno (pl. lv) and Meigle nos. 1 (fig. 36) and 2.[5] Particularly noticeable are the animals with closely coiled hindquarters and reversed legs of the type which occurs on bowl no. 2.[6] There is also a hint on the Aberlemno stone of the foliate terminals encountered on the bowl, a feature otherwise practically impossible to parallel in the sculpture. Very approximate parallels to the

---

[1] For the vine-scroll in Pictland cf. Crawford (1937).
[2] Cruden (1964), pl. 19.
[3] Stevenson (1955), 116.
[4] Henderson (1967), 157.
[5] Allen and Anderson (1903), iii, fig. 311 A. The animals of this stone are drawn out in Curle (1939/40), fig. 11 b.
[6] It has been noted (p. 126) that the coiled hindquarters of similar animals in the Lindisfarne Gospels form a much looser spiral.

single animals on bowl no. 2 are to be seen on stones from Glamis (no. 1), Meigle (nos. 4 and 9),[1] and, more particularly, Lasswade (no. 2).[2]

The parallels quoted do not provide accurate parallels for all the zoomorphic features of the two bowls, but there are enough stylistic similarities and comparisons of detail to demonstrate the probability that the stone monuments and the bowls belong to the same artistic milieu. There seems little reason to deny that the treatment of the closely coiled hindquarters of the animals on the bowls and on the stones is a peculiarly Pictish element, especially as this feature occurs elsewhere in the hoard (e.g. fig. 31). Other details of the ornament of the bowls cannot be so firmly fixed in geographical or political contexts: the Anglo-Saxon parallels mentioned above must, for example, be seen as a reflection of the eclecticism of Pictish art.

It should, nevertheless, be mentioned that a parallel ornamental development occurred in Ireland. Animals with scrolled hindquarters appear in a number of eighth-century contexts in both the sculptural and manuscript ornament—as, for example, in MS. 51 at St. Gall,[3] in the British Museum Additional MS. 40618,[4] and on the Kilkieran and Bealin crosses.[5] In all these instances (with the exception of the last cited example, which is equivocal) the leg is bent sharply forward, from an underemphasized hip, at the knee joint in a manner completely foreign to that encountered in the Scottish series, where the legs are normally completely extended. Extended legs do, however, occur in one undoubtedly Irish metalwork context—a context which is probably earlier than the St. Ninian's Isle bowls—on the back of the Tara brooch.[6] Close examination of other apparently similar details shows that the joint is sharply bent, within a rather loose spiral. Much later the motif appears occasionally in Irish sources, but such occurrences are very much out of context.[7]

One may compare the ornament of the two bowls with that of certain other metal objects, the most important of which is undoubtedly the Monymusk reliquary.[8] This house-shaped casket, with its elaborate gilt-bronze mounts and red-and-yellow enamelled strap-hinge, has two thin silver plates on the front face which are decorated with incised animal ornament reserved against a *pointillé*—almost stippled—background. The *pointillé* and the incised lines are so fine, and the animals consequently so difficult to define, that it is almost impossible to achieve an accurate drawing of the ornament. The line-drawing reproduced here (fig. 41) may not be totally accurate[9] but it gives a

[1] Allen and Anderson (1903), iii, figs. 233 A, 313 A, 343 B.
[2] Ibid., fig. 442.
[3] Henry (1965), pl. 108.
[4] Ibid., pl. K.   [5] Ibid., figs. 25d and 26.
[6] Ibid., pl. 42.   [7] e.g. Henry (1967), pls. 46 and 47.

[8] Eeles (1933–4).
[9] I am most grateful to Mr. R. B. K. Stevenson for his help in my preparation of the drawing reproduced in fig. 41; without his co-operation such a drawing could not have been produced.

reasonably true impression of the type of ornament employed by the craftsmen who made the reliquary.[1] Although in many ways they are very closely related in technique to the animals of the St. Ninian's Isle bowls, the creatures on the reliquary are caught up in a more involved interlace, in a manner closely related to that found in the Lindisfarne Gospels. Here are none of the ornamental details peculiar to the St. Ninian's Isle bowls; the hindquarters (save for the occasional spiral hip) and necks are particularly different and, although there is obviously a close relationship between the two series of animals, the ornament of the Monymusk reliquary must be seen as less developed than that of the bowls.

On the left-hand side of the cross-slab from Shandwick in Ross-shire are a pair of balanced animals[2] which are perhaps related in compositional detail to the ornament of bowl no. 3, although in some ways they are closer to the creatures on the Monymusk reliquary. Facing and adorsed interlaced animals, related to that on bowl no. 3, are occasionally encountered in Scottish sculpture[3] and in Celtic metalwork, as on the Steeple Bumpstead boss.[4] The motif probably has its origin, however, in Anglo-Saxon and Germanic sources. The looped bodies of opposing animals, like those on bowl no. 3, may well be derived from the similar motif on the purse-lid and on the rim of the shield from Sutton Hoo;[5] indeed, it is possible that the two friezes have their origin in Germanic sources. They could be derived thence by way of Northumbria, where the manuscripts provide a series of interlaced animal friezes which are most conveniently drawn out by Bruce Mitford,[6] who has demonstrated the sequence from Sutton Hoo, by way of the Book of Durrow, to the Lindisfarne Gospels.

Returning, however, to the metalwork it is clear that the punched technique of executing the ornament is important in any consideration of these bowls. We have seen how it apparently originates in manuscript sources, where it occurs with relative frequency—although not in zoomorphic form. Its occurrence on the Monymusk reliquary has been mentioned, but the technique is rare in metalwork. The inscription and certain details of the ornament of the Ardagh chalice are executed in this technique;[7] but this is an object which provides no close stylistic parallel to the bowls. The unique penannular brooch from Bergøy, Rogaland, Norway (pl. xxxix *a*), exhibits a similar technique, but this object was almost certainly decorated in a Northumbrian workshop.[8]

---

[1] The reliquary is of normal insular form; cf. Swarzenski (1954).

[2] Allen and Anderson (1903), iii, fig. 66 B.

[3] e.g., ibid., fig. 322 A, 334 D, 351 B, and 397 A.

[4] Haseloff (1951), fig. 36 *d*.

[5] Bruce Mitford (1968), fig. 24 *a* and *b*.

[6] Kendrick *et al.* (1960), figs. 8 and 9.

[7] Henry (1965), pl. C.

[8] Kendrick *et al.* (1960), 253 and Bakka (1963), 26.

Zoomorphic ornament otherwise only occurs in this technique on the Monymusk reliquary and in the Lindisfarne Gospels.

Closely related to the punched background is engraved ornament set against hatching or basket-work. This ornamental element occurs frequently in the early Iron Age mirror style[1] and, although it seems to have been submerged during the Roman period, it re-emerges in Christian Celtic contexts. Stylistically one of the first early Christian Celtic objects to be decorated in this style was the Irish reliquary known as the *Domnach Airgid*,[2] which, by the analogy of its interlace with that of the Book of Durrow, is probably of late seventh-century date. Most other objects decorated in this technique have been found outside the British Isles and are conveniently assembled by Bakka in his study of Hiberno-Saxon animal ornament.[3] Bakka suggests that the majority of the objects decorated thus are Northumbrian, pointing to the presence of the vine-scroll as a deciding factor in his thesis.[4] It must also be remarked that the technique is found in a pagan Anglo-Saxon context on the back of the Fitzwilliam Museum's Faversham brooch,[5] which probably dates from the early seventh century.

The marigold pattern on the base of no. 3 is approximately paralleled in technique and design by the ornament behind the terminals of the brooch from Ervey, Co. Meath, Ireland (pl. xlii *e*), which despite the fact that it is truly penannular, is obviously out of series with the Pictish penannular brooches, although very much influenced by them.[6] The pattern of the border of this bowl is, to the best of my knowledge, unparalleled in the British Isles, although Bruce Mitford attempts to draw a parallel between this pattern and certain ornament in the sixth-century Italian Gospels of St. Augustine (Corpus Christi College, Cambridge, MS. 286).[7] I find this parallel a little far-fetched despite his statement that the 'detail on bowl no. 3 may be regarded as one of those Mediterranean elements absorbed with little change into Insular art with the introduction of Italian codices into Northumbria in the late seventh century'.

The pattern of the base of no. 2 consists of four developed triquetras, each set within a quadrant of a circle. The interlace in places is very muddled and, although one has parallels for the structure of the design in the bottom left panel of fig. 21,[8] they are of little chronological significance. The key-pattern on the base-ring, made up of inter-

---

[1] e.g. Kendrick (1938), fig. 2. Piggott and Daniel (1951), pl. 41.

[2] Henry (1965), pl. 55.

[3] Bakka (1963), figs. 23–9.

[4] Ibid., 32 ff.

[5] Kendrick (1938), fig. 14.

[6] A marigold pattern is compass drawn on the base of a bowl from Blystad, Vang, Hedemark, Norway (Shetelig, 1940, v. 85), which Norwegian scholars would interpret as an insular object. This is, however, such a common pattern that it is of little significance in this discussion.

[7] O'Dell *et al.* (1959), 265.

[8] Cf. Allen and Anderson (1903), ii, nos. 803 and 805.

locking Ls and interlocking Ts is reasonably common within the grammar of Celtic ornament,[1] but again there is no real chronological significance in such parallels.

Is it possible to draw any chronological conclusions from the parallels which have been made to the ornament of bowls 2 and 3? The only firm chronological point is provided by the Lindisfarne Gospels, which provide parallels which are undoubtedly striking, if not entirely accurate. Thus a date in the late seventh, or the beginning of the eighth, century would seem reasonable for the emergence of animals with a punched contour and with the strange treatment of the hindquarters and in one case (fig. 21) of the neck and head. The animals on the bowls from St. Ninian's Isle, however, seem to be more developed. The hindquarters have achieved a tight spiral, their heads have become less finely drawn and there has been the addition of the trefoil foliage to the tails and other appendages.[2]

The parallels which have been adduced, unsatisfactory though many of them are, all seem to point to a date later than the Lindisfarne Gospels. There is general agreement that the objects which provide close parallels of ornament to the St. Ninian's Isle bowls— the Aberlemno and Meigle stones and the Monymusk reliquary—are of eighth-century date: the consensus of opinion would probably date them to the late eighth century, the knotted head of bowl 2 with its exact parallel in the Lindisfarne Gospels being the only distinctly early feature—and this is equivocal in view of the occurrence of a modified form of the same detail in the Cologne *Collectio Canonum*. But such stylistic judgements are for the moment incapable of objective proof as there is no clearly definable evidence —such as inscriptions—on which to base a dating. Geographically most of the parallels in sculpture to the art of the St. Ninian's Isle bowls come from southern Pictland and belong to a school which Stevenson supposes to have developed in the middle of the eighth century.[3] Whether one can presume a similar origin or date for the St. Ninian's Isle bowls nos. 2 and 3 is open to question, but there is some evidence in its favour.

The four bowls, nos. 4–7 (pls. xx–xxiii and figs. 20, 25–7), are so close in technical detail and in quality of workmanship and material to the two discussed above that one might with some confidence assign them to the same workshop. The interlace ornament (figs. 25–7) and key-patterns which appear on these objects provide, however, little useful evidence of date or place of manufacture. Only the mount on the internal base of no. 6 has any extraordinary significance and one cannot guarantee that this is primary to the construction of the bowl.

[1] Ibid. ii, nos. 892 and 899.

[2] It is perhaps significant, and certainly worthy of mention, that such terminals occur on animals on the Tassilo Chalice (firmly dated to between 777 and 788)—

Haseloff (1951), fig. 2. This is another object made under Anglo-Saxon influence.

[3] Stevenson (1955), 112–15.

No other bowls of insular origin are known to have been decorated with zones of interlace. The nearest approach to such ornament occurs on the gilt-bronze chalice from Petöháza in Hungary which has a series of incised panels containing interlace ornament.[1] This parallel is too tenuous to be of any significance, beyond the fact that the chalice was made in the late eighth century in East Bavaria[2] under the influence of the Anglo-Carolingian school of ornament. In the absence, then, of purely ornamental parallels on similar objects we must turn to a detailed consideration of the ornament.

Again the most significant technical parallel to the ornament of the bowls, which is executed in a punched technique (sometimes reserved against a background of dots, sometimes not), is provided by the Lindisfarne Gospels[3] (where, however, such patterns are never reserved against a *pointillé* background). The technique of *pointillé* interlace continues in Anglo-Saxon manuscript material well into the ninth century—occurring for example in the late eighth-century Rome Gospels[4] and in the Canterbury Gospels (BM., MS. Royal I.E. VI),[5] a manuscript which probably dates from the early ninth century. The technique occurs in a Scottish context as a secondary interlace ornament on the back of the head of the pin from Dunipace, Stirlingshire.[6]

The interlace motifs on the bowls consisting of simple ribbons are hardly chronologically, or even culturally, significant. It is astonishingly difficult to date any particular interlace motif in insular art of the eighth and ninth centuries, for the patterns were almost universal—spread from one place to another through the medium of manuscripts and (possibly) textiles. This is true of the interlace with U-shaped bends which occurs on bowl 7,[7] as of practically every other pattern seen here. Until a corpus of dated interlace patterns has been worked out on the basis of Romilly Allen's analysis, it is unlikely that we shall be able to provide any firm dating of a particular pattern and, in view of the simple patterns provided by the St. Ninian's Isle bowl, it seems unlikely that such a corpus would help in a chronological or geographical study of the hoard. Suffice it to say that the interlace patterns on the bowls are also present in Anglo-Saxon and Celtic art.

This is true for the other patterns, key-patterns, whirls, and billets, which appear on the bowls. Only the ornament of the lower order of bowl no. 5 (pl. xxi) is difficult to parallel, but such a series of touching ovals is a pattern so simple as to be of little stylistic significance.

---

[1] Bóna (1966), fig. 4.
[2] Werner (1966).
[3] e.g. Kendrick *et al.* (1960), fig. 48 *h* and *g*.
[4] Zimmermann (1916), pls. 316 and 317. Cf. p. 134 below for dating.

[5] Kendrick (1938), pl. lxvi, 2.
[6] *Stirlingshire, an inventory of the Ancient Monuments* (RCHMS), i (1963), pl. 10D.
[7] Cf. the sites listed by Allen and Anderson (1903), ii, no. 533.

The internal mount of bowl no. 6 (pl. xxvi *e*) remains to be discussed. The originality or otherwise of its position is hard to estimate, but the object itself is of some stylistic and technical merit. Technically, openwork cast interlace of the quality seen within the frame cannot be paralleled in Celtic metalwork. The nearest parallel may well be with certain panels on the Ardagh Chalice, where openwork gold *Pressblech* is capped by interlace ornament in filigree,[1] which is often given (as in the case of the St. Ninian's Isle mount) zoomorphic character by the addition of animal heads. It might, on the basis of this parallel, be possible to date the bowl to the early eighth century. The small head of an animal which appears as the terminal of the interlace in one of the fields is directly paralleled elsewhere in the hoard—for example on the inscribed chape, no. 15 (pl. xxix) and on the brooches, e.g. no. 20 (pl. xxxii)—but stylistically the main use of this feature is to bind most of the objects in the hoard together within a small cultural area; it is of little chronological significance.

The human masks on the border are easily paralleled in insular metalwork; similar masks occur, in a slightly more elaborate form, for example, on a brooch from Co. Cavan[2] and on mounts found in Norway at Oseborg, Ørsta,[3] and Indre Eide, Nordalen, both in Møre.[4] In England masks appear—again in a slightly more elaborate form—at the terminals of an Hiberno-Saxon mount from Markyate, Hertfordshire,[5] which is probably of early eighth-century date.

The closest parallel to the structure of the whole mount was found in the far north of Norway. From an unpublished early Viking grave from Lurøy, Norland, comes a small rectangular mount which has four masks within the corners of a frame. The masks link the frame to a central circular field, which is decorated with interlace ornament round an empty setting.[6]

Of passing interest is the presence of red enamel in this mount. It is the only enamel in the hoard. Enamel is well documented in the Celtic area, although its significance there is minimal.[7] It was used in the Pictish area at least as early as the seventh century, for it occurs on plaques in the Norries Law, Fife, hoard[8] and on hand-pins with spiral ornament, some (but by no means all) of which are certainly of Pictish manufacture, as is demonstrated by the presence of a Pictish symbol on the back of an example[9] which also comes from Norries Law.[10]

---

[1] Henry (1965), pl. C.
[2] Ibid., pl. 44.
[3] Shetelig (1940), v, fig. 66.
[4] Ibid., fig. 64 *a*.
[5] Bruce Mitford (1964), pl. xl *f*.
[6] Shetelig (1940), v. 76.

[7] See, for example, the Monymusk reliquary—Eeles (1933–4).
[8] Henderson (1967), pl. 18.
[9] Ibid., pl. 16.
[10] For the most recent discussion of date and place of manufacture of these pins, cf. Fowler (1963), 127 ff.

From this discussion it may be seen that bowls nos. 4–7 cannot be dated with any degree of accuracy, nor can they be fitted into any strict geographical setting. The mount in no. 6 may help to date that particular bowl to the first half of the eighth century, but any other chronological statement would go beyond the limits of the evidence.

The ornament of bowl no. 1 (pl. xvii) is obviously related to that of some of the bowls discussed above, but its technical features and the motif employed are different and practically impossible to parallel. The main pattern consists of an incised line flanked by punched dots. I know of no technical parallel to this detail, although there are slight elements of it in the Anglo-Saxon manuscripts where occasionally—and perhaps accidentally—a line flanked by dots occurs as part of a complicated interlace pattern, as for example in the mid eighth-century Leningrad Gospels,[1] which is almost certainly Northumbrian. This parallel is, however, of little significance. The groups of dots in the interstices of the interlace on the bowl can perhaps be paralleled more easily. Such features occur in dotted lattice patterns in the Lindisfarne Gospels,[2] and at a later date in interlace patterns in the Rome Gospels (Vatican Barberini lat. 570),[3] a manuscript cautiously dated by Lowe to *saec. VIII*,[4] but one which was probably written in Mercia or south England in the late eighth or even early ninth century.[5] Triangular groups of dots also occur, without relationship to interlace patterns, in the Book of Cerne, a southern English manuscript possibly of the late eighth century.[6] Such parallels may perhaps suggest a late eighth-century date for this bowl, but it must be emphasized that the main design is unparalleled and is adapted with great ingenuity to the available surface.

The hanging-bowl

Without doubt the most difficult object to discuss in a stylistic context is the hanging-bowl (no. 8—pl. xxiv and fig. 23 *a*). Only one ornamental detail of the object—the decoration of the *Pressblech* plate (pl. xxv *b*) on the base—can be paralleled with any reasonable accuracy. This plate, which seems to be an original feature of the bowl, is close in design to a rectangular plate, executed in a similar technique, on the Moylough belt-shrine (pl. l *c*).[7] The detail of the plates on the belt-shrine, however, is much crisper than that of the St. Ninian's Isle examples. The only other definite example of the use of this technique in an Irish context occurs in four places on the lower foot-girdle of the Ardagh

[1] Zimmermann (1916), pl. 324.
[2] 139ʳ (facsimile edition).
[3] Zimmermann (1916), pls. 315 and 316.
[4] Lowe (1934), 20.
[5] I am particularly grateful to Professor T. J. Brown

for the great trouble he has taken to suggest this date for the manuscript.
[6] Zimmermann (1916), pls. 293 *a*, and 295 *b*.
[7] This is thoroughly published by O'Kelly (1965).

Chalice,[1] where the ornament takes the form of an interlace pattern. To many scholars the house-shaped shrine from Norway in the National Museum, Copenhagen,[2] and the similar object from Melhus, Norway,[3] would be considered Irish; they are certainly of either Irish or Scots origin and are mounted with roundels of bronze *Pressblech* which are decorated with spiral ornament of a simpler form than that encountered on the St. Ninian's Isle hanging-bowl.

Impressed plates of bronze and silver were quite common in Europe from the end of the Roman period,[4] and are not unknown in northern English contexts in the eighth century.[5] The technique is encountered, for example, on the seventh-century hanging-bowl from York (pl. xlix *a*), where, as in most of the other insular examples, the design takes the form of interlaced ribbon ornament. It would seem likely therefore that the technique spread to Ireland from England or Scotland and it is impossible on the basis of this mount alone to say whether it was of Anglo-Saxon or Celtic manufacture. Bruce Mitford[6] sees the St. Ninian's Isle mount as possibly the earliest element in the hoard (he considers it to have been used secondarily)[7] and compares it with the 'trumpet-pattern of ff. 3[r] (in the O of NOVUM) and 139[r] (in the Q of QUONIAM) and also with the rectangles of such pattern as f. 94[v], of the Lindisfarne Gospels'. These parallels seem reasonable and a date *circa* 700 for the inspiration of the design is perfectly possible. Bruce Mitford denies an earlier date, but there seems no good reason to suggest that the lower chronological limit should be 700. Dated spiral patterns are rare and this plate could well be as late as 750 or as early as 650.

The mount inside the base bears a procession of animals (fig. 38) which basically belong to Salin's Style II. The idea of such a procession round a disc was popular during the period in which Style II was dominant in England, being encountered for example on discs from Allington Hill[8] and Caenby.[9] The animals on these discs, on the Crundale sword pommel,[10] on the Sutton Hoo gold buckle (fig. 38), in the Book of Durrow (fig. 38), and elsewhere in seventh-century contexts provide close, if not altogether satisfactory, parallels to the animals on the internal mount of the St. Ninian's Isle

[1] Mahr (1932), pl. 52.

[2] Henry (1965), pl. 20 (bottom).

[3] Marstrander (1963), fig. 3.

[4] Cf. Arwidsson (1942), 13–17, for earlier examples; *Karl de Grosse, Werk und Wirkung*, Aachen 1965, pls. 22, 23, 108, for later examples.

[5] Listed Wilson (1961), 211–12. A seventh-century example comes from Caenby, Lincolnshire: *British Museum, Guide to Anglo-Saxon Antiquities*, London, 1923, fig. 102.

[6] O'Dell *et al.* (1959), 262.

[7] I see no reason for this suggestion. There is no evidence for any previous mount on the St. Ninian's Isle bowl and the York hanging-bowl demonstrates the use of *Pressblech* on such objects (pl. xlix *a*), as in a minor way does one of the Sutton Hoo hanging-bowls (cf. Bruce Mitford (1968), pl. 21 *a*), where *Pressblech* panels appear in the foot-ring.

[8] Kendrick (1938), pl. xxxvi, 3.

[9] Bruce Mitford (1968), fig. 23 *b*.

[10] Ibid., fig. 23 *c*.

hanging-bowl.[1] The stance of the animals is similar in all cases and the variations of detail are merely, in my opinion, reflections of differences in technique and material. A particularly significant detail is the fact that the animals on the bowl mount bite across their front legs in a manner entirely similar to that encountered on the Sutton Hoo buckle and in the Book of Durrow. The bent aspect of the hind leg, while not quite so significant is a noticeable detail of this phase of Style II ornament.[2] Again the panelled hip and double-contoured body form reasonable parallels and the only real difference is in the form of the feet which are not over-emphasized. The unique feature of the ornament of the mount is the use of basket-work hatching. This is the only place in this group of animals where this feature occurs. Herring-bone hatching[3] and cross-hatching[4] do occur in Style II ornament and it is not too far-fetched to compare this type of filling with the basket-work of the bowl mount, especially in view of the popularity of hatching which was to occur in the succeeding Hiberno-Saxon style.[5] In a similar technique basket-work hatching can be seen in the central roundel of one of the gilt-bronze mounts from the great Norwegian ship-burial from Oseberg.[6]

A minor ornamental element of this mount—the interlace ornament which forms the tail—is entirely without stylistic or chronological significance.

The third important ornamental element of the hanging-bowl is provided by the boar-shaped ribs. The idea of a displayed animal seen from above is not uncommon in eighth-century metalwork, but Bruce Mitford[7] has provided the best detailed parallel in the ribs of the Steeple Bumpstead boss (fig. 39), an object which was found nailed to the door of the church in the Essex village of that name. The most striking parallel of ornament is the series of panels of curled hair on either side of the backbone of the animals on the two objects. Otherwise, as Bruce Mitford rightly points out, the other details of the animal are not deeply significant as parallels. In Celtic metalwork displayed plastic beasts seen from above occur on a small number of mounts found in Norway,[8] but these bear little relationship to the ribs of the St. Ninian's Isle hanging-bowl. In Anglo-Saxon metalwork displayed animals occur on the Witham pins,[9] on a ring without provenance,[10] and on a ring from York;[11] but again these are of little significance

[1] The nearest parallel in Scottish sculpture occurs on the rather elaborate symbol stone from Rosemarkie—Allen and Anderson (1903), iii, fig. 62. Here the animal bites the hind leg.

[2] Cf. Bruce Mitford (1968), fig. 23.

[3] Ibid., fig. 23 f.

[4] Kendrick (1938), fig. 19.

[5] Bakka (1963), figs. 25–8.

[6] Bruce Mitford (1964), pl. xl a (cf. also pl. xl b, where

snake-like bodies are similarly treated).

[7] O'Dell et al. (1959), 263.

[8] Cf., for example, Shetelig (1940), v, pls. 46 and 86. Also in stone, cf. the Inchbrayock slab: Allen and Anderson (1903), iii, fig. 235 A.

[9] Wilson (1964), pl. xviii.

[10] Ibid., fig. 48.

[11] Cramp (1967), pl. vii.

in this context. Small details are easily paralleled. The animal heads, for example, are typical in this position on hanging-bowls, while the trumpet-spiral element of the front hips is paralleled on the animal head of the spoon in this hoard (pl. xxvi *a*); again, the interlace between the legs is easily paralleled in Anglo-Saxon and Celtic contexts. But no significant stylistic or chronological judgement can really be made on the basis of these unique ribs.

If the few elements which are susceptible to chronological judgement are assembled it seems that the bowl should be dated to the late seventh century, a view which is supported by the typological considerations outlined above. This date is based mainly on the presence of a developed Style II animal ornament on the internal escutcheon. If Bruce Mitford's judgement, that the spiral-ornamented *Pressblech* plate is closer in design to the spirals of the Lindisfarne Gospels than to those of the Book of Durrow, is correct, then a date nearer 700 would seem acceptable. If this dating is accepted it is likely that the hanging-bowl is the earliest object in the hoard.

The spoon and the claw-like object

The stylistic consideration of nos. 9 and 10 is of little significance in the general stylistic history of the hoard. As the ornament is to a large extent inextricably bound up with the discussion of the function and typological development of these objects, it has seemed easier to consider the stylistic aspects in the broader context above (pp. 113 ff.).

The pommel and the chapes

The animal ornament of the pommel (no. 11) (fig. 31) and of the uninscribed chape (no. 16) (fig. 30) are closely related, and to this extent they should be considered together. The animals on both objects have the same speckled bodies and similar feet and heads. There is a certain wildness about the contortions and interlacing of their limbs which is unparalleled elsewhere in the hoard. The animals are, for example, far removed from the more clumsy animals, so close to Style II, which are to be seen on the internal mount of the hanging-bowl (pl. xxiv), and, at the same time, they are also completely distinct from the well-disciplined creatures of the sub-conical objects nos. 12 and 13 (pl. xxviii *b*, fig. 32). In some of their technical and stylistic detail they are very close to the art of the Anglo-Saxon metalworker of the eighth century; but there are over-riding stylistic reasons which relate these creatures to Celtic and perhaps even to Pictish art. The most striking of these is the treatment of the hindquarters of the animals on the pommel; they are formed into spirals which are very close in design of those encountered on bowls nos. 2 and 3; here again can be seen the reversal of the two legs as they cross the spiralled body. These are features which have convincing parallels in Pictish sculpture and are difficult to parallel in other insular contexts, where the hips tend not to be reversed in the interlacing and the spirals appear to be looser.

There is a specious similarity between these animals and that on a finger-ring from the River Thames at Chelsea (pl. 1 d); a similarity which on detailed examination proves to be false. The points of comparison are obvious; the speckling and the panelling of the heads are easily compared; but such likenesses are due to a common source for the animal ornament, for there are too many dissimilarities of detail. For instance, the spiral front hips which occur on the St. Ninian's Isle objects are missing in the Chelsea finger-ring, as are the loops or contortions of the bodies of the animals, the clearly drawn pair of hindquarters, and the ragged (almost floral) quality of the feet. The uncontorted animal of the Chelsea finger-ring is much closer to the Anglo-Saxon tradition which stems from the Witham Pins to the Trewhiddle horn mounts.[1]

There are, however, sufficient points of comparison between the ornament on the objects from the St. Ninian's Isle hoard and that on the Chelsea finger-ring for us to look to the southern Anglo-Saxon area for the origin of certain details of style. The form of animal head and the speckled body are undoubtedly of southern Anglo-Saxon origin of late eighth or early ninth-century date; the Chelsea ring and the Fetter Lane sword being the earliest English objects to exhibit these features.[2] The other details of the animals, however, are all Pictish or Northumbrian—the spiral hips, the treatment of the hindquarters, the contortion of the animal's body,[3] and the large ragged feet.[4]

If we turn to the other ornamental details of the uninscribed chape we must at the same time consider the general form of the animal head terminals of the two chapes (nos. 15 and 16). On both examples the rilled snout and the gaping jaws of the animals, with their teeth biting in one case a fish and in another the tongue, relate the chapes to a mount found in the Thames at London which bears an incised runic inscription (pl. lii b).[5] All that can be said about this object is that it is of Anglo-Saxon origin. Apart from the perhaps insignificant parallels of the gaping animal head cast in the round, the blue glass eyes, the basket-work hatching, and even the pointed teeth, an unequivocal ornamental parallel is provided by the rilling. The median line on the top of the rilling of the inscribed pommel also occurs on the back of the Thames mount. It is difficult to date this object, but it provides yet another Anglo-Saxon parallel to the ornament of this small group of animal motif.

[1] Cf. Wilson (1964), passim.

[2] Cf. ibid. 26 ff.

[3] This contortion of the body of the animal is clearly seen on the Pictish stone from Shandwick, Ross-shire. Allen and Anderson (1903), iii, fig. 66 B.

[4] For similar feet see the Meigle stone (no. 4); ibid. fig. 313 A.

[5] For inscription see R. I. Page in Wilson (1964). 77 ff.

For further parallels it is necessary to turn to the Celtic world. The form of the animal head on the uninscribed mount with its teeth meeting at the extended tongue is paralleled on a complete animal on one of the Ardagh brooches.[1] This brooch is difficult to date; but, on the basis of the panels of brambling which occur on the brooch, it might be related to the thistle-head brooches which cannot be dated earlier than the ninth century (indeed one such brooch occurs in the Ardagh hoard).[2] On the Celtic crozier from Helgö, Ekerö, Sweden,[3] the tongue is replaced by a human mask, while the tongue on the inscribed chape in this hoard (pl. xxix) is replaced by a fish. Fish are occasionally found in insular sources as coincidentally, for example, on Pictish symbol stones[4] (which cannot be compared to the fish on the chape) and in the Book of Kells. The fish is a popular ornamental element in Merovingian manuscript art[5] and was present in the insular repertoire at an earlier date,[6] but its Christian significance normally invests the creature with a meaning which is certainly not present on the chape. Fish are not unknown in Celtic metalwork, occurring in a slightly more elaborate form on another of the Ardagh brooches[7] and possibly on a damaged object in the great Norwegian find from Gausel.[8] In some respects a more significant parallel may be the interlaced fish on the Markyate mount;[9] where the style of the creatures is very much the same as that on the St. Ninian's Isle object; but whether this is of any real chronological meaning is difficult to determine, although the presence of a similar mount at Oseberg,[10] may help to date the Markyate object to the end of the eighth or the beginning of the ninth century.

Certain filling ornament on both chapes can be paralleled. The key-pattern on the crest and behind the terminals of the uninscribed chape occurs only on the tenth century cross from Penmon, Anglesey,[11] but both this motif and the unique spiral triangle key-pattern on the back of the chape are well within the range of patterns which the insular craftsman of the Dark Ages would produce.[12] Such details are, however, both chronologically and geographically meaningless.

The animal heads which form a frieze along the crest of the inscribed chape are similar to heads found on other objects in the hoard; the panelled eye-socket and open mouth of these couped heads occur, for example, on brooch no. 20 (pl. xxxii). They are probably to be derived from the Northumbrian animal heads seen, for example, on such objects

[1] Mahr (1932), pl. 56, left.
[2] Ibid., pl. 55, 2.
[3] Holmqvist (1961,) pl. B.
[4] Allen and Anderson (1903), ii, figs. *passim.*
[5] e.g. Zimmermann (1916), pls. 105, 106, *et passim.*
[6] Cf., for example, Jessup (1950), pl. xix, 4.

[7] Mahr (1932), pl. 56, right.
[8] Ibid., pl. 24, top left.
[9] Bruce Mitford (1963), pl. xl *f.*
[10] Ibid., pl. xl *b.*
[11] Baldwin Brown (1903–37), vi, part 2, pl. xxvii.
[12] Allen and Anderson (1903), ii. 334–61.

as the Bjørke mount (but see above, p. 99),[1] or even from the heads on the bezel of the Chelsea finger-ring (pl. 1 *d*), which we have seen to be of southern English origin.

The last remaining ornamental element of the chapes is the inscription on no. 15; it appears to be the only Celtic uncial inscription in Scotland executed on metal. It can, therefore, in no way be regarded as typical. The inscription is dealt with in its linguistic and epigraphic character by Professor Jackson in Appendix A (pp. 167 ff.), which follows up work previously published by himself[2] and Professor T. J. Brown.[3] His conclusion that it is probably Pictish and should be dated to the eighth or early ninth century chimes with the evidence presented here.

To sum up, it would seem that the parallels adduced for all these three objects—and it should be remembered that no. 16 is in practically mint condition—would suggest a date late in the eighth century. The parallels, particularly with the Chelsea finger-ring, tenuous though they are, would in some respects tend to force the dating of no. 16 to the very end of the eighth century.

The three objects in the form of truncated spheroids
These three objects (nos. 12–14), which are so close in form to each other, are ornamented with two distinctly different patterns. No. 14 bears an over-all design of developed trumpet spirals, while the other two bear ornament which is largely zoomorphic.

The animal ornament on nos. 12 and 13 (pls. xxvii *a*, *b*, xxviii *b* and fig. 32) is very closely related. The grotesquely contorted animals bear a striking resemblance to those found on the two bowls decorated with zoomorphic motifs. Here again can be seen the tightly coiled spiral hindquarters and the spiral hip which are such a familiar feature of the ornamental repertoire of the hoard. Other features of the ornament have distinct parallels in the Pictish area: for example, the fore-part of the animal on no. 12 (fig. 32, left) is very closely paralleled on stone no. 4 from Meigle, where a very similarly shaped portion of an animal forms the upper frame of one face of the slab.[4] A similar feature occurs, for what it is worth, in manuscript art, at the base of the *Xpi*-monogram in the Rome Gospels, a late eighth- or early ninth-century South England product.[5]

The whole animal design, however, with the elaborately looped body (which has already been noticed in our consideration of the pommel—no. 11), is very much in keeping with the kind of motif which is found in the late eighth-century Book of

[1] Wilson (1964), pl. 1 *c*.
[2] Jackson (1960).
[3] O'Dell *et al.* (1959), 250–5.

[4] Allen and Anderson (1903), iii, fig. 313 A.
[5] Henry (1967), pl. 34. For dating see above, p. 134.

Kells—a manuscript generally considered to be Irish, a thesis which may soon be challenged by palaeographers. In the highly mobile and sophisticated draughtsmanship of the Book of Kells the body of an animal is quite frequently seen to be divided by a series of loops. This can be seen, for example, in the animal which forms the lower letter *a* in the initial on fol. 250ᵛ (fig. 37). Basically this development is only one step further from the normal looped animal so frequently found in insular metalwork in the previous century[1] and the main difference seems to be that, while the animals in the Book of Kells often bite themselves or are bitten by other animals, this feature never occurs in the St. Ninian's Isle menagerie and is certainly absent from the two objects at present under discussion. This parallel and many others with this manuscript are important in any consideration of the relative date of the St. Ninian's Isle hoard.

The disciplined, symmetrical organization of the animals is in many respects closer to that found on some of the Pictish sculpture. On the central panel of the slab from Nigg, Ross-shire (pl. lvi), for example, are interlaced animals with their heads and front hips widely separated from their bodies by long ribbon-like extensions in a manner close to that of object no. 7.

An interesting area of comparison is perhaps to be found amongst the material of Hiberno-Saxon origin discussed by Mr. Bakka. On a mount from Lilleby, Buskerud, Norway[2] (itself of domed shape) is an animal with a loop in its body of a very similar form to those encountered at St. Ninian's Isle, both on this object and the pommel (no. 11). This animal is repeated twice and the two fields alternate with a stylized tree motif of a type normally considered to be Northumbrian. However, the presence of plastic whirling snakes emerging from bosses on the flange of the Lilleby object relate to objects with similar motifs (with more formalized snakes) from Gausel, Norway,[3] and on mounts in the Musée des Antiquités Nationales at Saint Germain-en-Laye,[4] objects which are normally considered to be Irish. The only proper home for the Lilleby mount would seem to be Pictland, where the boss style, the animals, and the foliate motifs would all be perfectly acceptable to the eclectic taste of this area towards the end of the eighth century.

The simple or herring-bone hatching of the bodies of the animals is different from the basket-work hatching seen on the mount of the hanging-bowl (pl. xxiv). It is found frequently in eighth-century metalwork of the Hiberno-Saxon or plainly Celtic School of ornament[5] and seems to be without chronological significance.

---

[1] e.g. Henry (1965), pl. 41 (the Tara brooch): or even the more complicated looped animal bodies seen in the Lindisfarne Gospels; Kendrick *et al.* (1960), figs. 43 *i* and *k*.

[2] Bakka (1963), figs. 40 and 43.
[3] Bakka (1965), pl. 4 *b*.
[4] Ibid., pl. 5.
[5] e.g. Henry (1965), pls. 66, 69, 90, etc.

Another element of the ornament of these bosses is provided by the interlace panels of no. 13. This ship-carved technique of representing such a feature is common in Celtic metalwork and occurs in one of its grandest contexts, on the knop of the Ardagh Chalice.[1] It can also be seen on numerous other Celtic objects, and, in a modified form, on other objects in the St. Ninian's Isle hoard itself—for example, on the brooches (cf. pls. xxxi–xxxv). It is entirely without chronological or cultural significance.

The same is probably true of the interlocking spiral pattern of the third object (no. 14, pl. xxvii c, fig. 33). There seems to be little detail here which is at all significant in relation to date or place of origin. The general design of the motif is frequently seen in the flat. For example, on the mounts from the St. Germain museum[2] only the frond-like terminal elements are missing, all the other details of the ornament, as well as one or two more, occur. The only variations are of technique and scale; for example, the hatching of the ornament on the St. Ninian's object does not occur on the St. Germain object. The frond-like terminals are hardly significant and the only general judgement that can be made is that the pattern is more closely paralleled in eighth-rather than seventh-century contexts.

The fact that the spirals are placed on a curved surface need occasion no surprise. Spirals are similarly placed on the top of the strange object from Vinjum, Vangen, Aurland, Norway,[3] which may even be of Northumbrian or, at any rate, Hiberno-Saxon origin.[4] More significant parallels may perhaps be sought in the 'boss style', which Mr. Stevenson suggests must have flourished at the end of the eighth and the beginning of the ninth century.[5] Two of the surviving bosses at the head of the stone from Nigg, Ross, are covered with spiral ornament in the same way as the St. Ninian's Isle object.[6]

The boss style itself may be a significant factor in the origin and ornament of this group of objects. Metal bosses—free standing and otherwise—are quite common in the corpus of Celtic metalwork. The grandest example is the Steeple Bumpstead boss,[7] but other smaller mounts are known.[8] Other objects have bosses cast in with them, as for example the St. Germain plates and the Gausel fragments.[9] This style is known in sculpture, both in Scotland[10] and Ireland,[11] and, although the chronology of the style in the two areas is open to argument, there can be little doubt that it flourished from the

---

[1] Henry (1965), pl. D.
[2] Particularly Mahr (1932), pl. 25, middle.
[3] Mahr (1932), pl. 30, 2 b.
[4] Bakka (1963), 33.
[5] Stevenson (1955), 117 ff.
[6] Allen and Anderson (1903), iii, figs. 72 and 75.

[7] Mahr (1932), pl. 24, 5.
[8] e.g., ibid., pl. 24, 1 and 3, and Wilson (1955).
[9] Bakka (1965), pl. 4 b and 5.
[10] Stevenson (1955), 117 f.
[11] Henry (1965), pls. 84, 85, and 96.

late eighth century onwards. Is it possible that this interest in the decoration of domes and bosses in any way influenced the unique form of the three objects from St. Ninian's Isle?

In general terms the ornament of these three objects, and particularly the animal motifs, would seem to indicate a date in the late eighth century. Such a date would tie in very nicely with the boss style parallels and also with the date of the chapes and pommel, which are, in some technical respects, closely related to them.

VII *The treasure: summary and conclusions*

The art of the hoard

Apart from the hanging-bowl, which is quite possibly of Northumbrian origin and is earlier in date than any other object in the hoard, the nationality of the art of the St. Ninian's Isle treasure seems to be Pictish. This judgement is based in the first instance on the theory that one may, by a close study of the material in this hoard and elsewhere, recognize a Pictish type of brooch; in so far as it is possible to link together the brooches and other objects of the St. Ninian's Isle hoard in a common artistic milieu—and this is possible in certain cases—we have a strong presumption of a Pictish origin for the other objects in the hoard. In the second place this judgement is based on certain details of zoomorphic ornament which are best paralleled in indubitably Pictish sources. Such details are the tightly spiralled hindquarters of the animals on the bowls and other objects, the reversal of the legs in the interlace of this feature (although this latter does occur elsewhere—fig. 35) and the use of spirals on a boss. In the third place it seems reasonably certain that the inscription on one of the chapes (no. 15) is Pictish (see Appendix A). In the fourth place this judgement rests on the supposition in geographical terms that in an area that was in all probability Pictish—the Shetland Isles—any homogeneous treasure is likely to be of Pictish origin.

The difficulty of such a definite identification of the nationality of the style is exaggerated by the lack of recognizably Pictish metalwork in any period after that which produced the mounts decorated with symbols and the great Pictish chains. I have attempted here to provide a basic corpus of metalwork which might be considered Pictish. This corpus I take to be contemporary with the more elaborate Pictish stones, embellished with complicated ornamental elements, which derive from the south and west and which can presumably be dated to the eighth and early ninth centuries.

Even if my conclusions concerning the nationality of the art are not acceptable, the art itself is of great intrinsic interest; for gathered into the compass of the twenty-eight silver objects which make up this hoard are elements from all the major areas of insular art, forming a grammar of motifs of extraordinary value to the stylistic historian of the eighth and early ninth centuries. I have, indeed, tried to demonstrate in the course of this study the relationship of stylistic elements in the hoard with the art of Ireland, Pictland, Northumbria, Mercia, and even southern England. The art of the hoard seems to have its origin primarily in England and seems to stand in the same relationship to the art of the Anglo-Saxons as does contemporary Anglo-Carolingian style of upper Austria and south Germany. There is also in the art of the St. Ninian's Isle hoard a considerable non-Anglo-Saxon element (which may be distinguished as Celtic) part of which may have come directly from Ireland (some possibly by way of Northumbria), and part being indigenous to the area in which the hoard was made. I think it can be said, without fear of contradiction, that these objects were not produced in Ireland;[1] but it is clear that for many years to come argument will rage concerning the actual content and nature of Irish influence in the hoard. In the present climate of opinion concerning British art of the eighth century one can only make tentative judgements; it is for this reason that I have been careful to separate the facts of description from the theories of interpretation in this section of the book.

The nature of the hoard

It has been argued by Monsignor McRoberts that the hoard is an ecclesiastical treasure. I have attempted to show by a piecemeal examination of each individual item that this is highly unlikely. It differs completely from the other hoards of an ecclesiastical nature found in the British Isles—those from Ardagh[2] and Trewhiddle[3]—in that it does not include any definitely ecclesiastical object. I can see no individual item in the St. Ninian's Isle hoard that has a specifically Christian function in relation to our knowledge of church plate at this time.[4] The absence of the only really major and stereotyped piece of ecclesiastical plate of this period—the chalice—seems to me to give the lie to this theory. It is an undoubted fact that churches and monasteries at this period would often have rich secular material—this is demonstrated, for example, in the inventories and wills of Anglo-Saxon England[5]—and there seems no reason to suppose that the treasure of a Celtic church need be less secular in character than that of other contemporary churches. It would, however, be an extremely odd community that would not include precious vessels of a specifically and uncontrovertibly ecclesiastical nature in its treasure.[6] If this

[1] Cf. Henry (1965), 106.
[2] Mahr (1932), pls. 51–6.
[3] Wilson and Blunt (1961).
[4] The nature of the inscription is dealt with by Professor Jackson in Appendix A.
[5] Cf., for example, Whitelock (1955), 549.

[6] Collingwood (1908), 73 f., relates the account of Walafrid Strabo of Reichenau who tells that when the sails of the Vikings were sighted off Iona 'the jewelled shrine that held the sacred relics of Columba was hastily buried'. Such must have been the story in churches throughout Scotland.

hoard did originally belong to a church it must be seen as the secular portion of a rich treasury.

Why, therefore, was the hoard buried in a church? The answer may well lie in the tradition documented at a later period, both in the Celtic and non-Celtic areas of Britain, whereby the church acted as a place of refuge for both people and goods in time of danger. The church was often the most imposing and most easily defended building in the area; it was also a sacred place, inviolate and supernaturally protected. It would therefore be natural that families from surrounding areas would bring their treasure to the church for safe-keeping in times of trouble. Dr. Lucas has documented this practice in Ireland in both the Viking and post-Viking period.[1] It would seem reasonable to suppose that the hoard from St. Ninian's Isle represents the treasure of a family brought for sanctuary to the church in the time of threatened attack and never reclaimed by its owners for obvious reasons. The possibility that it formed a secular and minor portion of the church's treasure which was kept buried against sudden attack by raiders, presumably Vikings, seems slight. The homogeneity of the hoard militates against it being the gradually accumulated treasure of a Viking marauder; there is no hack-silver in the hoard and no ingots, no exotic pieces (other than the hanging-bowl), and no coins.[2]

One further possibility remains; that the hoard belonged to a jeweller. The fresh state of the uninscribed chape (no. 16) and the fact that it has not been gilded might argue in favour of such a theory. However, it is very unlike the only such hoard of this period known from the British Isles—the ninth-century hoard from Sevington, Wiltshire, which included coins, pieces of finished and unfinished jewellery, and broken pieces of metal.[3] The differing states of wear on the objects must be seen to indicate the accumulation of a family, rather than the stock-in-trade of a craftsman.

The setting of the hoard

The history and archaeology of the Shetland Islands in the period before written history is obscure. Dr. Henderson probably expresses the general opinion of most modern scholars when she says that, up to the time when the Scandinavians arrived in the ninth century, 'Shetland was in all likelihood part of the kingdom of the Picts'.[4] Traces of this settlement are rare, but the excavations at Jarlshof, at the southern-most tip of

---

[1] Lucas (1967), 194 ff.

[2] The only exotic element connected with the hoard was the larch-wood box in which it was enclosed. Larch was not, apparently, introduced into the British Isles until the late sixteenth century (it is mentioned in John Evelyn's diary) and it could be argued, with some weight, that the box or the wood was imported from central Europe which was at that time its natural habitat. I am grateful to Dr. J. Fletcher for this information. On the other hand, the wood could have come as driftwood.

[3] Wilson (1964), 167 ff.

[4] Henderson (1967), 24.

Shetland have clothed the period in some substance, if slightly equivocally from the point of view of cultural definition.[1] However, there are just sufficient remains of settlement and other cultural traits, such as symbol stones and oghams,[2] to enable us to assume that Shetland was not to all intents and purposes *terra deserta* immediately before the Viking Age, as was suggested by Brøgger[3] and Shetelig.[4]

The problem of whether this treasure was the property of a Pictish Shetlander is imponderable. The taste represented by the art of the hoard seems to be Pictish and it might be assumed, with all caution, that it would have belonged to a Pictish chieftain (possibly even Resad) who held land in the southern part of the islands. Unless it was hidden during some unrecorded internecine Celtic war, it must be postulated that the hoard was laid down at the time of a Viking raid in the late eighth or early ninth century.

The date of the hoard

It is difficult to estimate an accurate date for the deposition of the hoard in the face of the lack of fixed chronological points for the material culture of the Celtic world. Any such estimate is liable to a margin of error which is likely to be anything up to fifty or even a hundred years. Before examining the tenuous evidence which does exist it must be emphasized that not all the objects in the hoard are coeval. The earliest object is undoubtedly the hanging-bowl (no. 8), which exhibits many stylistic features of the late seventh century; it would be difficult to date this object to a period much later than 700. The later objects present greater problems as the comparative evidence in Britain is founded on a much shakier chronological basis at the end of the eighth century than *c.* 700; however, the uninscribed chape (no. 16) and the pommel (no. 11) are, on stylistic grounds, among the latest objects in the hoard and should be dated to within twenty-five years, one way or the other, of 800.

If the theory that this hoard was laid down in the face of Viking attack is accepted, it seems reasonable to suppose that it cannot have been laid down at an earlier date than the last quarter of the eighth century. The date of the earliest Viking antiquities found in the north of Scotland, the date of contexts in which insular objects are discovered in the Viking graves of Norway, and the tenuous historical sources available for the appearance of the Scandinavians in western waters, would support such a supposition. Further, it need not be taken as axiomatic that the Shetland Isles were amongst the earliest areas to be settled by the Scandinavian raiders because they are within two days' sailing from Norway. In fact it is likely that the first bases of the Vikings in the northern

[1] Hamilton (1956), 90 ff.
[2] Cf. Wainwright (1962), 94 ff.
[3] Brøgger (1929), 63 ff.

[4] Shetelig (1940), i. 21. For a modern estimate, cf. Wainwright (1962), 91 ff.

isles would be in Orkney, which presents (and must always have presented) a much richer economic potential. Further, it should not be presumed that the first contacts of the Vikings with Shetland were necessarily warlike; there is some slight, but tenuous, evidence that the Scandinavian take-over of these islands may not have been too bloody.[1] There is no reason, on grounds of political probability, why a hoard such as this should not have been deposited until the end of the first quarter of the ninth century.

The hoard is difficult to date by means of the ornament which appears on its component parts. In general terms, as I have shown in the previous chapter, I see the hoard as being a collection of silver formed in the course of three or more generations, the latest objects being dated to about 800, with a margin of error of about twenty-five years on either side. Its deposition could have taken place within the same bracket. Such a suggestion would be supported by the evidence provided by the brooches, which are a remarkable homogeneous collection. I have stated that they seem to be earlier than brooches in the hoards containing similar material from Croy and Rogart and have dated them within the wide bracket of the late eighth century.

In the face of all these intangibles and on the basis of the available comparative material the situation must be left in this most unsatisfactory state. I would suggest that the importance of the hoard lies in the light of future inquiries and finds. Once we begin to understand more about the manuscript art of Northumbria in the second half of the ninth century, once we can assign the Book of Kells to a definite scriptorium, and once we have available to us a certain amount of settlement-site evidence from the Pictish kingdoms, our understanding of this hoard will be illuminated and it will achieve its true value as an archaeological document.

[1] Cf. Wainwright (1962), 115.

VIII *The law relating to the treasure*

T. B. SMITH

AT the outset it seems expedient to summarize the legal issues involved in *Lord Advocate* v. *Aberdeen University and Budge*[1] before proceeding to examine the background.

Soon after the finding of the St. Ninian's Isle Treasure the Queen's and Lord Treasurer's Remembrancer claimed it for the Crown from the University of Aberdeen, which remained in possession with the consent of Mr. James Budge, on whose land the cache had been found. When this claim was rejected the Lord Advocate on behalf of the Crown raised an action in the Court of Session against the University for declarator (*scil.* a declaration) that the treasure belonged to the Crown and for delivery by the University to the Crown of the treasure, and Mr. Budge was added as defender for any interest which he might have. The Solicitor-General for Scotland and Mr. J. P. H. Mackay appeared for the Crown; and the University was represented by the Dean of the Faculty of Advocates (Mr. W. I. R. Fraser, Q.C.)[2] and Mr. C. K. Davidson. Mr. Davidson also acted as junior counsel for Mr. Budge on whose behalf an argument was presented by T. B. Smith, Q.C.,[3] when the action reached the Inner House. The action was heard by Lord Hunter in the Outer House in September 1962 and a reclaiming motion (appeal from his interlocutor) was heard by the Second Division in June 1963.

The basis of the Crown claim was that because the objects comprising the treasure had once been owned but had no longer any identifiable owner, they fell into the ownership of the Crown according to the legal principle embodied in the brocard *quod nullius est fit domini regis*—namely that things which no longer have an owner belong to the Crown. Moreover, the Crown claimed the objects as treasure—a special aspect of the more general doctrine. It may be explained that Scots law recognizes certain prerogative rights to be vested in the Crown. Those which belong to the Crown as representing the State, and held on trust for the people, are designated *regalia majora* and are inalienable, while a miscellaneous selection of property rights which may be alienated are classified

---

[1] 1963 Session Cases at p. 533.   [2] Now Lord Fraser.   [3] See note at end of chapter.

as *regalia minora*. Among *regalia minora* are included rights to things which no longer are in private ownership, such as lost or abandoned things and treasure.

The defenders resisted the Crown's claim on various grounds which may be broadly distinguished as 'the negative case' and 'the positive case'. Only certain aspects of the negative case were argued before the Lord Ordinary, while argument on the positive case was presented, after amendment of the record, only before the Second Division. The negative case was based on arguments that, whoever might be the owner, the grounds of the Crown's claim were unjustified in law; while the positive case rested on propositions of law which, if sustained, would have established that the defenders had definite title to participate in the ownership of the treasure.

So far as their case depended on merely resisting the Crown's grounds of claim as unsound, the defenders argued that, though the claim might have been justified had the objects been found on land subject to feudal tenure, as is the general rule in Scots law, the claim could not be asserted when the property was found on udal or allodial land, of which the Crown was not ultimate feudal superior or overlord. Though the defenders conceded that the treasure consisted of moveables, their argument at times—especially in the Outer House—tended to aequiparate buried treasure with the actual content of land such as minerals. A plenary landowner owned everything in or on his land. Again, on the negative case, the defenders argued that the law regarding treasure was a discrete category; that the objects which had been found had not been 'hidden'—and that the porpoise bone could not be 'treasure' because it did not consist of precious metal. Before the Inner House the second defender (Mr. Budge) also argued that by accepted rules of public international and British constitutional law the prerogative rights of the Crown which are merely concerned with property perquisites do not extend even to conquered or annexed territory unless or until the acquiring State alters the law of such territory.

So far as the defender's positive case was concerned, it was argued, after amendment of the record subsequent to the Lord Ordinary's decision, that by the code of the Norwegian King Magnus Håkonsson (known as the Law-Mender) which came into force in about 1274 and which, it was asserted, applied in Shetland until repealed or superseded, the landowner, the finders, and the Crown were each entitled to a one-third interest in the treasure.

Lord Hunter, the Lord Ordinary, held that, since the dispute concerned moveable objects, the defenders' arguments based on the nature of landownership were irrelevant, and the ordinary rules of Scots law regarding lost, stolen, or abandoned property applied. On the principle embodied in the brocard *quod nullius est fit domini regis* the

Crown's claim was justified. So far as the special plea regarding treasure was concerned, he was prepared to allow proof on the issue of hiding. The Second Division sustained his opinion on the negative case and agreed that all property which no longer had an identifiable owner belonged to the Crown. Moreover, they thought that, though the question of right to treasure as such was academic because the greater included the less, any speciality regarding the law of treasure could not depend upon the issue whether it had been deliberately 'hidden'. On the public international and constitutional law question regarding the extension of the Crown's property prerogatives, the Court expressed no view whatsoever, despite the fact that the Crown had adduced no counter argument.[1] So far as the contentions of the defenders on the positive case were concerned—based on the proposition that the code of King Magnus the Law-Mender still has effect in Shetland—the judges of the Second Division were of opinion that these could no longer be sustained. The code, if it formerly applied in Shetland, had been eroded. Moreover, its terms could not be proved in a Scottish Court of Law. Accordingly the Crown's claim to the treasure was upheld.

So much for the decision itself. The contest between the parties must now be set in the context of a basic conflict between two systems of law—Scots law and Old Norse law—and between national and international law.

In a penetrating and scholarly paper *Odal Rights and Feudal Wrongs*[2] the late Professor Croft Dickinson has traced the steps by which the Orkneys and Shetlands were brought under the sovereignty of the Scottish Crown. In 1468 Christian I of Norway and Denmark impignorated (i.e. pledged) the sovereignty of the Orkneys together with the Crown property there in security of an unpaid portion of the dowry of his daughter Princess Margaret who married James III of Scotland. He also and for the same purpose in 1469 impignorated the Crown lands in Shetland and his sovereign rights as well. The legal position of the Shetlands was substantially the same as that of the Orkneys after the impignoration, though doubts on this point were only resolved in 1968 when Mrs. Barbara E. Crawford made generally known in Britain a sixteenth-century copy of the document impignorating Shetland in the Royal Collection in the British Museum.[3] Though the terms of the Orkney impignoration could be ascertained from contemporary documents, the detail of those concerning Shetland could, until Mrs. Crawford's discovery, only be the subject of conjecture. Under both impignorations the right to

---

[1] In the circumstances, the actual decision is not a conclusive precedent even in the Court of Session were similar facts to be litigated again.

[2] Dickinson (1965).

[3] See (1969) *Scottish Historical Review*, 48, pp. 35–53, 'The Pawning of Orkney and Shetland'. Scandinavian scholars had already discussed this text; e.g. *Sveriges Traktater*, ed. O. S. Rydberg, iii (Stockholm, 1895), 674–5; *Norges Gamle Love*, second series, II. i (Oslo, 1914–18), 184–5, no. 116.

redeem is expressed, and has in fact been asserted on at least seven occasions including the negotiation of the Peace of Breda, 1667.

The rights which Christian impignorated require some explanation. Crown lands in the Orkneys were pledged for 50,000 florins and those in the Shetlands for 8,000. So far as 'sovereign rights' were pledged, those of cash value include *skat* (a yearly tribute for the support of the State), and claims to *participate* in the proceeds of (i.e. part of the *value* of) wreck, stranded whales, treasure, and so forth. Unlike the feudal system which prevailed in Scotland, in Norse law the King was not universal landlord as well as sovereign. The King of Norway owned some lands in the Shetlands—but other land-owning men or udallers were full owners of their own properties holding from no superior and those not so holding did not hold as vassals in the feudal hierarchy. On the law of the *odel*[1] much of the argument of the defenders in the *Treasure Case* depended.

In fact the King of Scotland acquired under the impignoration or pledge a relatively small amount of the lands in the Northern Isles. The most substantial landowners there were the Jarl and the Bishop. In 1470, however, William Sinclair, Earl of Orkney, agreed with the King of Scotland to excamb or exchange his Earldom and the Lordship of Shetland for Ravenscraig in Fife and certain other lands on the Scottish mainland. In 1471 an Act of the Scottish Parliament 'annexed and united the Earldom of Orkney and the Lordship of Shetland to the crown'.[2] It was in this way and later through a deal regarding the bishopric and the forfeiture of Earl Patrick Stewart—*not* as the direct result of the impignoration—that the Scottish Crown gained control of so much of the soil of the Nordreys.[3] To avoid the confusion into which so many Scots lawyers and laymen have fallen, one may stress that *the 'annexation' just mentioned has nothing whatsoever to do with the international law concept of annexing territory of another State.* Neither Scotland nor Great Britain has ever expressly 'annexed' in this sense, nor has Norway ever surrendered her right to redemption, except presumably latterly by tacitly acquiescing so long in the exercise of *de facto* Scottish and later British sovereignty. An *estate*, an Earldom and Lordship with their lands and privileges were made part of the patrimony of the Crown by the Act of 1471. They became part of the Royal Domain comparable in theory to the Stewartry.[4] This acquisition threw open to un-restrained Scottish exploitation and avarice the lands and property of the islanders—of which there was some evidence even before the impignoration. The way was clear for piecemeal confiscation and forced feudalization of odal (or udal) lands, arbitrary

---

[1] i.e. the rights associated with udal landholding. See especially title 'Udal Law' in *Encyclopaedia of the Laws of Scotland*.

[2] A.P.S. ii. 102. Dickinson dates the Act 1472.

[3] For the extent of the Earl's rights see *Encyclopaedia of the Laws of Scotland*, xv, § 689.

[4] The hereditary private patrimony of the Scottish royal house.

exactions and fines, forced services, and the eventual subversion of the old established legal order in such matters as succession and conveyance. Most of the literature on Scottish rule in the Shetlands is polemical in expression,[1] and it may be salutary for Scots irked by anglicization to remember the beam in their own eye. The Sinclairs, Bothwell, Robert and Patrick Stewart, the Mortons, Sir Lawrence Dundas and others maintained—directly or through their creatures—an unenviable tradition over the centuries. The Scottish—later British—Crown has a particularly infamous record for its exactions and for facilitating the exploitation of the islanders by Crown nominees or donatories. As Balfour in his *Oppressions* writes[2] of the Islands (the Crown's golden acre), 'Five times have they been formally annexed to the Crown by Act of Parliament and fourteen times committed in defiance of such Acts and without protection and redress to one needy and rapacious courtier after another. . . . The Crown might do justice on the oppressor, but it invariably appropriated his plunder and adopted his profitable exactions as prescribing rights and precedents for further claims. . . . Much of the evil still exists uncorrected and unredressed in this 23rd year of Victoria.' One instance he cites is mid-nineteenth century: 'Church lands were vested in the Scottish Exchequer and ultimately transferred to the British Board of Woods and Forests, by whom in Imperial contempt of all nationalities Scandinavian or Scottish the Orkney Bishopric has been sold (1854–6) and the price expended in the adornment and luxury of London.' This 'luxury and adornment' was the laying out of a park in the Central London area.

The oppressions under which Shetland suffered after the annexation were largely inflicted under form of law—the law of the Scottish incomer administered, it would seem, in defiance of international obligation and national legislation. No time limit was stated for redeeming the pledge, and it would seem to follow that the system of law in operation there at the time of impignoration was to be continued—at least basically—pending redemption. By contrast, when the Sudreys (the Hebrides or Western Isles) were ceded by Norway to Scotland in 1266, the treaty of cession expressly provided that the inhabitants should be subject to the law of Scotland. Certainly well after the impignoration there is clear evidence that the Shetlands still looked to Norway for legal direction. In 1485 an agreement regarding land in Shetland was made in the Court at Bergen with a lawrightman from Shetland present, and in 1538 a judgement given in Shetland according to 'Gulathing law', i.e. the Gulathing version of the Magnus Code, was confirmed in Bergen.[3] An Act of the Parliament of Scotland in

[1] e.g. Colville (1804), Balfour (1859), Hibbert (1822), i. 169, Mackenzie (1836), Peterkin (1822).

[2] Balfour (1859), xi.

[3] Dickinson (1965).

1567[1] 'found' that both Orkney and Shetland should continue to enjoy their own laws and should not be subject to the common law of Scotland. Yet long before that time there had been a fairly steady infiltration of Scots into the Islands, knowing little and caring less about the legal institutions of the Norse inhabitants. The former thought in feudal terms and looked to Edinburgh; the latter thought in terms of Norse law and looked to Bergen. The Crown likewise was not concerned to preserve Norse institutions, and by feudal grants of land and jurisdiction and by other means constantly subverted them. 'Law and administration', to quote Croft Dickinson,[2] 'are apt to regard exceptions with disfavour', and Scots well know that English politicians and lawyers have viewed Scottish institutions in that light since the Union. Scots have seldom thought of themselves as the imposers of their own institutions on others.

In fact there were two legal and cultural orders in competition and sometimes in combination, Norse and Scots, that of Scotland having the advantage of support from Edinburgh and from the more influential element of the population. The Crown-appointed Earls in particular constantly sought to establish themselves as feudal superiors over the udallers. Under the Earls Robert and Patrick Stewart (1565–1609) this process was carried far, especially as the Stewarts held the estates of the Lordship and Bishopric in an undivided tyranny. They were thus in a very strong position indeed to impose feudal tenures and to adjudicate through Sheriffs and Justiciars. Earl Patrick pressed feudal privileges, but invoked the Norse law when it operated to his advantage, thus aggravating the confusion. His misrule led eventually to his undoing. He was committed to Edinburgh Castle in 1609 and in 1615 suffered forfeiture and execution. Four years before his death the Privy Council (in 1611) recorded[3] that 'Some people . . . within the bounds of Orkney and Yetland have these divers years bygone most unlawfully taken upon them for their own private gain and commodity to judge the inhabitants of the said countries by foreign laws, making choice sometimes of foreign laws and sometimes of the proper laws of this kingdom as they find matters of gain and commodity.' The Council then purported to proscribe 'the said foreign laws in all time comine'. In 1615 a Thing or Court at Scalloway exercising legislative powers also denounced 'foreign laws'[4] and enjoined obedience to the King's laws. Following on this in 1624 the Court of Session decided[5] that udal lands 'behoved to be bruiked by some lawful title and that naked kindliness and possession were not sufficient to possess them'—a decision which led to further widespread expropriation of the udallers because of the difficulty

---

[1] A.P.S. iii. 41, c. 48.

[2] Dickinson (1965), 142.

[3] R.P.C. ix, pp. 181–2.

[4] 1 Aug. 1615. Donaldson (1958).

[5] *Sinclair* v. *Hawick* (1694), Mor. 16393.

of proving title. Only in 1690[1] did the Scottish Parliament give express protection to certain udal lands—that is where the value did not exceed £20 Scots.

In the result very little land is now held on udal title in Shetland. Professor Croft Dickinson concluded[2] that the Act of the Privy Council of 1611 proscribing foreign laws in Shetland was in effect 'the end of ane auld sang' so far as Norse law was concerned except for certain foreshore and fishing rights. The Shetland Court Book which begins in 1612[3] seems to disclose a more or less general substitution of Scots for Norse law and procedure. Nevertheless, despite all this, the refrain of the 'auld sang' has persisted faintly but obstinately for over 350 years since the *ultra vires* Act of the Privy Council of 1611. As stated earlier, most writing on the Shetlands is polemical. Whatever the immediate result *de facto*, it is strange doctrine to a lawyer that an Act of the Scots Privy Council could at a stroke—and in contradiction of an apparent Act of Parliament—abrogate a system of law and substitute another. This view is more robustly stated by Sheriff Peterkin in his *Notes on Orkney and Zetland*:[4] '. . . The only warrant which can be discovered for repealing the ancient laws of Orkney and Zetland was the Act of Privy Council, 6th Dec. 1611, an Act, it will now be generally admitted, of no authority whatever. . . . No monarch ever maintained higher doctrines as to royal prerogative than James VI, but even during his reign of despotism and buffoonery, it would not have been maintained openly that the Privy Council could abrogate, by an arbitrary and latent fiat, the whole statute law and chartered rights of the realm. It is impossible that the proceedings now alluded to can be vindicated upon any other principle than an assumption that such a power did lawfully reside in the Privy Council. . . . I beg leave to suggest . . . that the act now referred to was null and nugatory from the first . . . that the ancient laws, usages and rights of Orkney and Zetland as contra-distinguished from the municipal law of Scotland are not in any degree impaired by that Act of the Privy Council, but that the peculiar tenures and privileges of the inhabitants are preserved entire to them, except in so far as since altered by express Parliamentary statute or modified by inveterate usage and acquiescence of individuals in the innovations.' It may be that the learned Sheriff is right in law—but the Sheriffs of the Northern Isles in the early seventeenth century were men of a different stamp, and heritable jurisdictions continued until the mid eighteenth century. Salvage work on the Norse legal tradition in Orkney and Shetland began in the mid eighteenth century in the Parliament House. There were protracted lawsuits between the udallers of Orkney and the Earl

---

[1] A.P.S. ix, 200 c. 61. Lord Patrick in the *Treasure Case*, 1963 S.C. at p. 556, seems to have envisaged that an Act of the Privy Council might have effectively suppressed Norse Law—but see the vigorously expressed contrary view by the Lord Ordinary (Hunter) 1963 S.C. at p. 540.

[2] Dickinson (1965), 156.

[3] Ibid. 155.

[4] Peterkin (1822), 132–3.

of Morton, and though the actual published law reports are laconic, the papers bound and preserved in the Signet Library[1] are rich repositories of learning and research. The most important decisions vindicating the status of Norse law are of the nineteenth and twentieth centuries. Lord Lee observed in *Bruce* v. *Smith*,[2] 'the whole system of law in Shetland is different from the common law of Scotland except in so far as it has been assimilated by legislative enactments or gradual adoption'. While conceding this view in theory, however, Lord Hunter said in the *Treasure Case*: 'As a practical matter it is probably more accurate to say that the ordinary statute and municipal law of Scotland operates except in so far as there is some speciality still extant in Orkney and Shetland which modifies it. But, whatever may be the point of view from which one approaches the question, the important point is to discover what are the survivals.'

Though the Court in the *Treasure Case* as a matter of convenience, difficult to justify in law or logic, placed the burden of establishing that Norse and not Scots law applies on him who so asserts,[3] it may be argued that in principle at least the basic Norse law survives except as abrogated by Statute or by contrary usage acquiesced in generally. If there has been no occasion for acquiescence to be tested on a particular matter, abrogation should not be presumed to operate. In short, the onus should be on the party asserting that the Old Norse law has been superseded. One is, however, immediately confronted with the problem—what is the basic law of Shetland which survives until abrogated or superseded? This problem is formidable, since the Law Book of Shetland disappeared and is thought to have been burnt in the early seventeenth century during the misrule of Earl Patrick. Until recently the surviving rules of Norse or udal law have depended on oral tradition. This is paradoxical, since the Norse were remarkable for their early concern with codification of law, which they developed by custom.

Perhaps it would be appropriate to attempt a basic and skeletal reconstruction.

It is known for certain that at the time of impignoration and for a long time thereafter the system of law and its administration corresponded to the Norwegian pattern. The Foud was the chief administrator and presided in the Lawthing which legislated and adjudicated, but the oracle of the law was the Lawman chosen for his learning. There were twelve under-fouds and twelve lawrightmen—one of each in each parish. The Thing of Shetland continued as a court and small legislature until 1670—though its traditional Norse character had been superseded at the beginning of the century, by

---

[1] e.g. (1751) *Earl of Morton's Case*, 152 Session Papers.

[2] (1890) 17 R. 1000 at p. 1014; cf. Lord Hunter (L.O.) 1963 S.C. 533 at p. 540.

[3] See Lord Patrick 1963 S.C. at p. 556 and Lord Mackintosh at p. 563.

which time legal institutions had been largely feudalized. The Norse, as has been noted, were remarkable for their interest in codification at a relatively early stage of civilization. These ancient codifications were accepted and promulgated by the Things or assemblies of the various provinces—each Thing exercising judicial and legislative functions. The Gulathing was the assembly for western and southern Norway (in which Bergen is situated). Until the time of King Magnus Håkonsson each Province had its own code, but he devised a new code—hence his designation the Law-Mender. This code, based on older precedents, was accepted by the Gulathing in 1274 and subsequently by the other Norwegian Lawthings. The Code of Magnus thus became the one and unifying lawbook for all the four law districts of Norway, though, as it had to be accepted independently by each district, one may refer, for example, to the Gulathing *edition* of Magnus Law. It is improper to refer to 'the younger Gulathing Law', which would imply merely a revision of the old Gulathing law which preceded Magnus's codification. Nevertheless, sometimes one encounters a loose reference to 'Gulathing Law' or 'St. Ola's Law' in the Shetlands after 1274. This need not deflect an inquiry into the true sources.[1] There was certainly a written version of the law applicable in Shetland. It was produced to the Scottish Privy Council in the early sixteenth century, while the Court Book of Shetland 1602-4[2] refers to the Thing engaged in 'long and mature deliberatioun by the inspection of the chapteris of the law book'. Shetland's Lawbook, it may safely be assumed, was the codification of Magnus the Law-Mender either imposed directly from metropolitan Norway or more likely (by analogy with Iceland) accepted by the Thing of Shetland as the four Things of Norway had accepted it. Basically the Law Book of Shetland was Magnus Law—with, no doubt, some local variations based on customary developments and legislation by the Thing at Tingwall. Appeals were carried to the Gulathing at Bergen even after the impignoration to be decided according to 'Gulathing Law'—that is, the Gulathing edition of King Magnus's Code.[3] This procedure would only make sense if the same laws applied in Shetland and Norway. Time and again before the impignoration Norwegian edicts from the Norwegian King required justice to be done according to the laws of Norway, and when Scottish rulers as late as 1589 ordered that the laws of Shetland should be enforced these laws were basically those of Norway.

[1] The greatest living authority on this question, Professor Knut Robberstad of Oslo, contributed a memorandum in the *Treasure Case* which should convince scholars at least of the application of the Code of King Magnus in the Shetlands at the time of impignoration.

[2] Donaldson (1954), 43.

[3] Taranger considered that the Gulathing code in force before Magnus might have applied at the time of the impignoration—*Rets Historie*, ii, p. 154. This view conflicts with that of Robberstad which is preferred—though in the *Treasure Case* the defenders would have been better off under the original Gulathing Law, which gave no right in treasure to the Crown at all.

The law of Shetland at the time of impignoration was one devised for udallers, and the udal system in Shetland (unlike Orkney) lasted widespread until the late eighteenth century. In 1716 over three-quarters of the land in Shetland was udal, though by the middle of the nineteenth century most had become tenants at will liable to be ejected at forty days' notice. The udaller did not hold his land from any superior nor did he owe services to the Crown.[1] He was liable for *skat*—a tax for upkeep of the State. Strictly speaking the udaller had management and control of the land on behalf of the family. Thus he could only sell with their consent and they (the other udalmen) could redeem family land even after sale. Rights of inheritance (which were indefeasible) allowed both sons and daughters to participate (the daughters taking half the share of a son). (There is a single word for the brother–sister relationship in this context, *sutchkins*.) Scottish feudal encroachment has eroded most of this system, though in 1893 in *Hawick* v. *Hawick*[2] a Sheriff of independent mind upheld the udal law of inheritance. So far as udal holding of land survives there is no doubt that the Scottish Courts still recognize that the Crown has no rights of superiority in it at all.

Yet there were Crown rights under udal or Norse law—the Code of Magnus the Law-Mender. As kings or other rulers established their authority over communities in Europe from the Middle Ages onwards, they claimed prerogative powers as supreme executive officers. Also—to augment their revenues—they asserted other so-called prerogative rights or privileges affecting property known to feudal law as *regalia minora*. Some claims—such as those to royal birds or fish—reflect whim or caprice. Others, such as rights to treasure, wreck, and whales, are more obviously of money value, and the prince often granted his rights in these things to a subject for hard cash. Though the rulers of other Scandinavian countries followed the fashion of feathering their nests in this way, the independent attitude of the Norwegians curbed to some extent such claims in metropolitan Norway and in her overseas territories—Iceland, the Faroes, Orkney and Shetland, and Man.[3] The oldest Norse Codes excluded the Crown's claim to treasure completely—the original Gulathing code giving it to the landowner and that of Frostathing to the finder. The Code of Magnus provided that in cases of un-claimed wreck or cargo, one-third of the value should go to the finder, one-third to the udaller on to whose land it was washed or driven ashore, and one-third to the

---

[1] See generally W. P. Drever in *Encyclopaedia of the Laws of Scotland*, vol. 15, title 'Udal Law', and references there cited.

[2] Dickinson (1965), 159.

[3] The author is obliged to the Attorney-General for the Isle of Man for the information that the Deemsters and Keys of Man upheld the right of the Lord of Man to treasure in 1585 (Stats., vol. i, p. 60). By the early fifteenth century the Lord's prerogative to whale and wreck had already been recognized. *Bona vacantia* are dealt with in the Act of Settlement, 1704, c. 16 (Stats., vol. i, p. 168).

Crown. The finder was entitled to the property under burden of paying the value of the others' claims. So far as whales were concerned, apart from the larger ones which were claimed by the Crown, a similar tripartite division was prescribed. Scott in *The Pirate* describes in detail a 'whale drive', which was an important event in Shetland life in past times. Caaing whales, when they appeared off the coast, were driven inshore and up a voe by the assembled community, who then dispatched them with any weapon to hand. In such a case the udaller on whose land the whales were drawn up was entitled to his third, the Crown (or his donatory) to a third, and the hunters participating divided among them the value of the remaining third. Now, though in Magnus's Code for Iceland treasure was equally divided between landowner and finder, the Law Book of Magnus's Code for Norway provided that when a man, digging with permission, found treasure hidden in the land of another, the udal man (the landowner) owned a third, the finder was entitled to a third of the value, and the king also took a third of the value as, in effect, a tax. These provisions were almost certainly contained in the Law Book of Shetland which disappeared in the early seventeenth century. There seems to have been no recorded occasion to raise the question of rights in treasure, but folk memory of the threefold division survived, at least in the cases of wreck and whales. Though this division was of written origin, latterly lawyers tended to think of it as local custom—because until very recently the idea of comparing legislative texts with Norway had apparently not been considered. Since there had been no known case of a dispute about treasure until 1958, argument regarding it must rest on analogy. It seems a reasonably strong one. Scott in Chapter 30 of *The Pirate* discusses the association of the three situations when Triptolemus is rejoicing in his windfall—the silver and gold found underneath the hearthstone. 'Yes, but you forget, Jarto Claud', said the Udaller, 'that the Factor was only counting over the money for my Lord the Chamberlain. As he is so keen for his Lordship's rights in whales and wrecks he would surely not forget him in treasure trove.' It may be observed in parenthesis that, especially after the Law Book of Shetland disappeared, the Crown's donatories did their utmost to exact what could be claimed by the Crown on the mainland of feudal Scotland—and therefore the basic Norse law was always under challenge unless the gentry had an interest in asserting it. Thus the Mortons—as Hibbert shows[1]—endeavoured to sweep away every vestige of udal tenure. Yet in one case in 1752[2] Morton claimed that (as donatory of the Crown) he was entitled to exact skat from the Udalmen of Orkney. The udallers (pursuers in the action) had asserted that this payment was not analogous to feu duty but to a land tax, and that, as they had been subjected to a new land tax by British statute law, they

---

[1] Hibbert (1822), 58 ff.   [2] *Earl of Galloway* v. *Earl of Morton*, 1 July 1752, F.C.

should not be mulcted twice. They lost, however, by the doctrine of prescription without any decision by the Court of Session as to what the position would have been had
they raised the issue sooner. The same pursuers asserted that the weights and measures
of Norway were applicable in Orkney and Shetland, and evidence on affidavit from
the Mayor of Bergen and other Norwegian officials was obtained.[1] The Court of Session
seemed more indulgent then than now in allowing proof of Norse law in Shetland by
reference to Norwegian sources.

Gifford, who was Steward Depute of Shetland and Lord Morton's Chamberlain
and Factor for much of the eighteenth century, had succeeded in his father's place.
Though clearly concerned to uphold his master's interests as Crown Donatory, he is
explicit in his *Historical Description of the Zetland Islands* in recognizing and describing
the tripartite division of the value of stranded whales.[2] His description of practice in the
case of wreck (which now, of course, is regulated by the Merchant Shipping Act, 1894)
also recognizes a threefold interest—though clearly there had been a conflict between what
the salvors asserted as their rights and what the authorities conceded. Dr. Samuel Hibbert
in 1822 notes that the tradition of equal threefold division of wreck died hard.[3] 'This law
I was taught three miles west of Onzie Firth. A little girl was tempted with the offer of a
shilling to take a mile's walk and find an umbrella that I had left on the shore. . . . She
brought it back with an intimation from her father that by the law of the country she was
entitled to a third of its value for salvage. I next expected a similar demand of a third of
this *wreck* from the proprietor of the ground, but the claim was graciously waived.'

In *Bruce v. Smith*[4] a majority of the Second Division refused to uphold what they
described as 'the custom' of conceding one-third of the value of whales landed in a whale
drive to the landowner. There was no argument that the right had a firmer basis than
custom, and the very extensive research made by counsel had not extended (as had
their predecessors' in the eighteenth century) to Norse sources. The so-called 'custom'
was rejected on the grounds that it was inequitable—and it was noted (a striking contrast with the Crown attitude in the *St. Ninian's Treasure* case) that the Crown had long
ceased to assert a claim for its share. The decision—which was not unanimous and rejected an earlier Outer House precedent[5]—was unfortunate from the viewpoint of the
defenders in the *Treasure Case*. Had things gone differently in 1890 prospects would
have been brighter in 1963. Lord Mackintosh did note[6] the remarkable similarity of

---

[1] *Udallers and Heritors of Orkney v. Earl of Morton*, 1750 (not reported). (The relevant correspondence is kept in the Scottish Record Office.)

[2] Gifford (1780), 27.

[3] Hibbert (1822), 544.

[4] (1890) 17 R. 1000.

[5] *Scott v. Reid* (1838) unreported, but Lord Cockburn's note is printed in *Bruce v. Smith* at p. 1003.

[6] *Lord Advocate v. University of Aberdeen*, 1963 S.C. at p. 563.

the whale case to the tripartite discussion of treasure which was argued. He concluded, however, that since the diligence of counsel in 1890 had not led them to the Code of Magnus, it could scarcely be invoked now. Yet it may be observed that during the present century until the *Treasure Case* and indeed from the case of *Sir Lawrence Dundas*[1] in 1777, the Court of Session has been favourable to the rehabilitation of Norse or udal legal principles—as in *Lord Advocate* v. *Balfour*[2] in 1907 (a dispute over salmon fishings) and *Smith* v. *Lerwick Harbour Trustees*[3] (1903), where the Crown's claims over the foreshore in Shetland were rejected. Lord Mackintosh's assumption that the research of counsel in 1962 could not have been more diligent than that of their predecessors in 1890 was not necessarily well founded.

In the *Treasure Case* the Crown claimed the hoard as treasure trove or alternatively on the principle that all ownerless things belong to the Crown. The defenders before the Lord Ordinary argued primarily that as the objects were found in udal land (of which the proprietor had full ownership) they belonged to the proprietor. Lord Hunter found for the Crown,[4] applying the general principles which he considered applicable to the law of moveables on the mainland of Scotland. Only at a later stage before appeal to the Second Division did the defenders amend their defences to assert that the appropriate solution was the threefold division prescribed by the Code of Magnus which they contended must have applied in the Shetlands. In the opinion of one leading Old Norse law scholar of our time,[5] the udal man's right to treasure is clearly *part of his ownership of land*; by permitting another to search on his land he can determine who will be entitled to the second third of the *value*; while the Crown's right is in the *nature of tax* or prerogative claim. The provisions regarding treasure are, significantly, contained in Chapter 16 of the Law Book dealing with the Law of the Odel. Under the laws of Magnus, even if the articles found as treasure should be regarded as moveables, title to them depended on land law as did the claims of others to a share of their value.

The Court of Session concluded, correctly no doubt according to the law of Scotland (though the defenders argued to the contrary), that the law of treasure trove is an aspect of the law of moveables and that the Crown's prerogative right to *regalia minora* is as sovereign and not as feudal overlord. The defence laboured under the great

---

[1] (1777), 5 Br. Sup. 609.

[2] 1907 S.C. 1360.

[3] (1903) 5 F. 680.

[4] 1963 S.C. at p. 533. The Inner House did not accept the Lord Ordinary's one reservation—namely whether the record disclosed a sufficient admission of 'hiding' to

satisfy the technical requirements of the law of treasure trove—though this, in his general view of the law regarding ownerless property, did not have any practical significance.

[5] Professor Knut Robberstad—to whose memorial the author is deeply in debt.

difficulty that they could only assert what was *probably* the law—since Norse law had never given a greater right to the Crown than one-third of the value of the treasure. The Law Book of Shetland had disappeared, and the judges were clearly anxious to avoid difficulty by applying the general law of Scotland. Yet if the old Scots Act of 1567 preserved Norse law, except as repealed expressly, or by desuetude and contrary use, there was no evidence of contrary use. There is a basic maxim or fiction of law—*curia novit jura*, i.e. the Court knows the law applicable. Counsel's arguments are designed in theory merely to refresh the dormant memory. Only foreign law must be averred or proved—because regarded as a question of fact. It was probably technically a mistake that both defenders asked to be allowed to *prove* their averments as to Norse law in the Shetlands. Perhaps they should have taken opposite courses and one at least have asked the Court to accept Norse law as within its 'knowledge'. The Scottish Courts were bound to take judicial knowledge of the law of Shetland—but the fiction that they knew it already was manifestly absurd. Did it necessarily follow that they should apply Scots law in an entirely novel situation? Even if the Norse rule applicable in Norway had not existed in Shetland, was it justified to introduce a novel Crown exaction by judicial fiat? Though the Crown as claimant could point to no instance in which a prerogative demand for treasure had succeeded in the islands and were driven lamely to instance an uncontested seizure by the Crown of a mummified corpse found in a bog, the Solicitor-General asserted that the general law of Scotland regarding *regalia* or prerogative rights applied unless the defenders could positively prove otherwise. If, however, the prerogative rights of the Crown *must* be the same in Shetland as elsewhere in Britain, then logically Britain generally should be subject to the Norse prerogative right of *skat*.

In International Law and Constitutional Law it is certainly not assumed[1] that the *property* prerogative rights even of an annexing State (as contrasted with prerogative rights essential for government) extend to acquired territory without statutory or other sanction—which was certainly lacking in Shetland (even treating Shetland as 'annexed' territory in the sense of international law).[2] When Britain annexed Cape Province[3] and Ceylon,[4] though the prerogatives essential for *government* came into operation, the Roman-Dutch property prerogatives continued; equivalent English prerogative claims were not regarded as exigible. Similarly on the annexation of what

---

[1] O'Connell, *The Law of State Succession*, pp. 94–5; Schwarzenberger, *Private International Law*, p. 170; *Campbell* v. *Hall* (1774), 20 St. Tr. 239; *Case of German Settlers in Poland*, P.C.I.J., 1923, Ser. B, No. 6.

[2] Which may now be the case, *de facto* exercise of sovereignty having been long acquiesced in.

[3] Hahlo and Kahn, *Union of South Africa* (British Commonwealth Series, vol. 5), p. 587.

[4] Jennings and Tambiah, *Ceylon* (same series, vol. 7), p. 82.

is now the Province of Quebec,[1] though the prerogative rights concerned with *government* came into operation, those concerned with property claims, e.g. treasure, did not. The Second Division did not deal with this argument on State succession, and indeed it remains unanswered. It may be regretted that it was not tested by appeal to the House of Lords. The present author considers it unanswerable as well as unanswered. In holding that the ordinary law of Scotland regarding treasure applied in Shetland the Court of Session seemed also to lay down that the only survivals of Norse law which will be recognized by our Courts are those which have already been recognized. This restrictive attitude contrasts with the apparent benevolence of the Court of Session to assertions of Norse law over the past two centuries, and the *obiter* observations of the judges in the *Treasure Case* do not necessarily establish a rigid precedent for the future.

In the *Treasure Case* their Lordships awarded not only the silver treasure to the Crown, but also the porpoise bone, and they seem to have taken the view that all ownerless things belong to the Crown—giving wider extension to this alleged principle than ever before—indeed, superseding the need for any law on treasure trove at all, since the greater includes the less.[2] On this view the Crown owns and can claim any derelict thing during the prescriptive period of twenty years. What chance now has the rag picker against the Royal Rummager of Dustbins?—for the St. Ninian's treasure in law seems to stand in no different position from any other abandoned thing.[3] The brocard *quod nullius est fit domini regis* represents the feudal outlook (in the broad sense of feudal), contrasting with the rule of the Civil or Roman law, *quod nullius est fit occupantis*, which latter certainly still applies in Scotland to the appropriation of wild animals. In the *Treasure Case* the second defenders submitted unsuccessfully that the feudal brocard —which in terms favours the Crown's claim to all other ownerless property—is in fact merely a general expression covering a number of discrete categories such as treasure, wreck, *ultimus haeres*, waifs, and so forth. The last word may not have been said on these matters as far as the general law of Scotland regarding moveables is concerned. Since 1846[4] the Queen's and Lord Treasurer's Remembrancer has been laying claims to finds of *all* articles of antiquity whether or not of precious metal and whether or not hidden on the basis of the feudal maxim—but the legal ground for such claims may yet be questioned and re-examined in a fuller or higher Court. For years archaeologists

---

[1] Baudouin, *Le Droit Civil de la Province de Québec*, p. 469. The Fifth Report of the Commissioners who drafted the Quebec Civil Code emphatically rejected the idea that they should incorporate the English prerogative claim to treasure.

[2] For a contrary view see D. Murray (1896), esp. 62 ff.

[3] But see now the Local Government (Development and Finance) (Scotland) Act, 1964, and H. McN. Henderson, 1965 S.L.T. (News), 81, on the powers of local authorities in respect of 'litter'.

[4] See *Report on the Operation of the Law of Treasure Trove* (presented to the Society of Antiquaries of Scotland by the Secretaries), 1905, p. 10.

such as Dr. David Murray in *An Archaeological Survey of the United Kingdom*[1] have wished (as would be most reasonable) modern legislation to regulate rights over objects of antiquarian interest, since the law of treasure trove seems technical and anachronistic and was not concerned with values other than mercenary values. However, in *Lord Advocate* v. *The University of Aberdeen* the judges of Scotland have cut the Gordian knot with a vengeance.

The judges in effect adopted the wide statement contained in Bell's *Principles*, s. 1291 (3), as summarizing the thought of the earlier institutional writers—'Things already appropriated, but lost, forgotten, or abandoned fall under a different rule from that which regulates things that have never been appropriated. The rule is "*Quod nullius est fit domini regis*".' The underlying justification offered was to avoid fraud, contests, or litigation, and to benefit the revenue. Thus Lord Hunter commented:[2] 'My reading of the institutional writers leaves me with the strong impression that such rights as treasure, waif and stray goods, and wreck are, or were, like things lost or derelict, and for that matter the Crown right as *ultimus haeres*, illustrations of a general principle which in relation to moveable property is in no sense an incident of feudal law and which, in relation to heritage, in at least one respect modified the strict feudal rule almost out of recognition—Stair I, vii, 3, II, i, 5, III, iii, 27, III, iii, 47; Bankton I, iii, 14–16, I, viii, 2–9, II, i, 8, III, iii, 91; Erskine II, i, 12–13, II, iii, 7, III, x, 2.' Similarly Lord Patrick relied[3] on Bell's statement (eliding the difficulties of two passages in Stair which, though they could be construed as complementary, he regarded as contradictory). His Lordship concluded that if the proper inference today is that the objects are ownerless, they belong to the Crown by virtue of the maxim *Quod nullius est fit domini regis*. To like effect is Lord Mackintosh's opinion[4] which stated that the pursuer claimed the treasure

as moveable objects which have become ownerless and so fall to the Crown under its prerogative right to appropriate ownerless property—and he also claims them under the specialised form of ownerless property known to our law as treasure or treasure trove. This claim is based on the Crown's right as sovereign and . . . has nothing to do with overlordship of land. That the law of treasure is . . . just a specialised instance of the rule *quod nullius est fit domini regis* clearly appears from the treatment of this topic by Erskine.

It may be observed that this use of 'Occam's razor' scarcely explains why the earlier institutional writers bothered to particularize rules for different kinds of ownerless

---

[1] Murray (1896).
[2] 1963 S.C. at pp. 549–50.
[3] At p. 554. It is thought that the references to Stair should have been III. iii. 27 and II. i. 5 and not as quoted by his Lordship.
[4] At p. 561.

property as do writers on the English and pre-codification European systems. The Scots law on the current interpretation is substantially more favourable to the Crown in the context of both treasure trove and abandoned property than is English law.

In conclusion, one may raise, but leave unanswered, certain further questions concerning this fascinating case. Professor Wilson has argued a formidable case for regarding the hoard as the treasure of the household of a local chief. When, however, the action was raised the defenders believed and averred that the objects were part of the wealth of an early Celtic Church and were used in connections with its ritual. The identification of the silver as religious objects has also been argued by Monsignor McRoberts.[1] Had the defenders' assumption been correct, there might well have been some ecclesiastical successor to the original owners—*Ecclesia vivit aeterna*. Were the last owners a community of the Celtic rite acknowledging no superior hierarchy, or had they acknowledged the authority of Rome? Were they a daughter community of some Irish religious house? Further, the former interests of the Norwegian Church in the Shetlands, which continued long after the impignoration, cannot be overlooked. Certain Church property rights have devolved on the General Trustees of the Church of Scotland—who certainly do not regard the Queen as holding any special ecclesiastical status as in England. The Crown in its action against the University of Aberdeen and the udal proprietor called no other defenders, and the rights (if any) of third parties are not necessarily extinguished. In theory there might have been some very unecumenical litigation, albeit based on a dubious archaeological assumption.

As the Lord Ordinary observed,[2] however, the defenders 'so far from suggesting that the owner was some successor of the Celtic Church referred to in the defences maintained that the owner was the second named defender (the udal proprietor)'. In retrospect it may be regretted that the defenders did not include a plea of 'all parties not called'. Lastly, it may be recalled that the Law Book of Shetland, which is known to have existed, has been lost for centuries. So also had the treasure. The text of the impignoration of the Shetlands was not available when the *Treasure Case* was argued, and only came to light in 1968. Should the Law Book ever be traced would its probable vindication of the defenders' arguments in the *Treasure Case* have more than academic interest? These possible questions for the future are as difficult as those which concern the past. There may yet be laughter in Valhalla.

NOTE. In normal circumstances the author, who was professionally concerned with

---

[1] McRoberts (1965).   [2] At p. 549.

the *Treasure Case*, would have been reluctant to publish at all. The unusual nature of the litigation, and the desire to see that the extensive and intensive research required for its preparation should not be left unrecorded, seem to justify him in undertaking—in default of others prepared to undertake the task—the unusual course of acting as author as well as counsel.

Appendix A *The inscriptions*

KENNETH JACKSON

O F the two objects which have been regarded variously as the chapes of sword-scabbards, or strap-ends, or the ends of an ecclesiastical stole or girdle, one (no. 15) bears two inscriptions, one on each side. The reading of both is perfectly plain, though doubts have been raised about two letters in the second inscription, doubts which are nevertheless quite unnecessary.

There is no question about the first inscription, which reads INNOMINEDS; that is, *in nomine d[ei] s[ummi]*, 'in the name of God the highest'. This is a known Latin formula which occurs five or six times elsewhere in the early Celtic inscriptions of Britain, as follows:

1. On a stone from Faenor, Breconshire, illustrated in Gibson's *Camden* but since lost; IN NOMINE DI SUMMI.[1] Nash-Williams dates it '7th–9th century (?)', but the lettering suggests rather seventh–eighth century.

2. On a cross-shaft at Llantwit Major, Glamorganshire: IN NOMINE DI SUMMI.[2] Dated tenth–eleventh century by Nash-Williams.

3. On a pillar-cross at Margam, Glamorganshire: I NOMINE DI SUMI.[3] Also tenth–eleventh century, according to Nash-Williams.

4. On a cross-slab from Kenfig, Glamorganshire, now at Margam. The reading is highly doubtful, hence 'five *or* six times' above, but Rhys made it [IN NOMI]NE DI SUM[MI],[4] and Macalister gives I[N] NOMINE [. . .].[5] Nash-Williams attempts no reading, but puts the cross in the late tenth–eleventh centuries on the evidence of the decoration.[6]

5. On a cross-slab at Margam: I[N] NOMINE DI SUMMI. Nash-Williams makes this eleventh century.[7]

[1] Nash-Williams (1950), 82, no. 72, and pl. XVI.
[2] Nash-Williams (1950), 144, no. 223, and fig. 156, pl. XLVII.
[3] Nash-Williams (1950), 148, no. 233, and fig. 167, pl. XLVIII.
[4] Rhys (1899), 144.
[5] Macalister (1949), 160, no. 1020.
[6] Nash-Williams (1950), 133, no. 200, and pl. LVIII.
[7] Nash-Williams (1950), 152, no. 237, and fig. 162, pl. LVII.

6. On the base of a cross-shaft at Ogmore, Glamorganshire: [IN NOMINE] DI SUMI. Nash-Williams ascribes it to the same date as the preceding.[1]

In addition to these there are two others in Glamorganshire, respectively of the late ninth and of the eleventh century, with the fuller formula *in nomine dei patris et fili et spiritus sancti*.[2] Finally one may mention a small stone disc from Dunadd in Argyll, now in the National Museum of Antiquities, Edinburgh, with an apparently unfinished inscription scratched on it: I NOMINE. The lettering suggests an eighth-century date.

The second inscription, on the reverse side of the same 'chape', reads RESADFILIS-PUSSCIO. It is, of course, tempting to regard this as following immediately from the other side and as representing in some form the same continuation *patris et fili et spiritus sancti* as in the two Glamorganshire inscriptions just mentioned; particularly since *spus* and *sci* are known abbreviations for *spiritus* and *sancti*. The whole would therefore be *In nomine dei summi—patris et fili et spiritus sancti*, 'In the name of God the highest—of the Father and the Son and the Holy Ghost'. But attractive as this is, there are objections to it so serious as to militate conclusively against it. First, the complete absence of *patris*, the presence of '*resad*', the final *o*, and even the lack of the two *et*'s, would be quite inexplicable. It really will not do to try to explain away *resad* as a bungling attempt by an illiterate craftsman 'intended to read as some form of PATRIS', as Monsignor McRoberts tentatively suggests that we might.[3] RESAD, which is perfectly clearly engraved, has five letters, not six; not one of them is remotely like any letter of *patris* coming near the same place in the word; and the rest of the inscription does not suggest that the engraver could possibly have been so incompetent. As to the *o*, to explain this as a 'filler' is a counsel of despair. Two other suggestions are that it stands for *omega*, assuming a lost *alpha* at the beginning; and that it is an abbreviation for *omnipotentis*. But in the *alpha et omega* formula, which occurs a number of times in inscriptions in the British Isles,[4] the second letter is invariably an elaborate *omega*, not an *omicron*; and in any case the 'lost *alpha*' is most unsatisfactory. As for *omnipotentis*, if this were a recognized part of the *patris et filii* formula, as *dei summi* is of the *in nomine* one, it would be convincing, but it is not (indeed it never occurs), and hence it is not. Still another objection to *patris et filii et spiritus sancti* is the fact that the two inscriptions appear to be in two different hands (as is discussed below), but this would be inexplicable if the second

[1] Nash-Williams (1950), 160, no. 255, and fig. 173, pl. XLI.

[2] Nash-Williams (1950), 140, no. 220, and figs. 151, 152, pl. XXXVII; and 154, no. 240, and fig. 170, pl. XLIV.

[3] McRoberts (1965), 236 f.

[4] e.g. Macalister (1945), 446, no. 469; 460, no. 481; (1949), 30, no. 578, pl. VII; 81, no. 878, pl. XXXVII; 98, no. 916, pl. XLIII; Nash-Williams (1950), 210, no. 382, fig. 238, pl. LVI; and 215, no. 392, fig. 244, pl. LII.

inscription was simply the second half of one single inscription of which the first was the first half. Two other tentative interpretations, '[The property of] Resadfil (*or* Resadkil, *or* Resad and Kil), priest(s), servant(s) of St. John', and 'The thing of Adkil, servant of St. John',[1] have been shown to be wholly impossible for several reasons which need not be repeated here,[2] and the same objections apply to 'The thing of Adkil the holy priest' (in which moreover the final *o* is once again ignored).

To the Celticist, the interpretation seems quite obvious; it is the name of the owner. In the Celtic world a man's full name was cast as an unvarying formula, 'X son of Y', and this formula appears hundreds of times in inscriptions in the British Isles and endlessly in texts. In purely Celtic contexts the Celtic word for 'son' is used, but in Latin contexts the Latin word, and it is significant here that the early Celtic inscriptions of Britain are generally (though not always) Latin contexts. That is, the names are of course Celtic or Latinized Celtic but the rest is Latin. Now, in these inscriptions it is normal throughout the British Isles, though not wholly invariable, that the 'X son of Y' formula is in the genitive, which means that in a Latin context it appears as 'X *fili* Y'. On a gravestone, '[This is the grave]' or '[This is the epitaph]' is understood before the names, and on a portable object '[This is the property]'. Hence, *a priori*, our *resadfilispusscio* can only be one thing, '[This is the property] of Resad son of Spusscio'. There is only one difficulty here, that neither name is a known one, not to mention that the second perhaps looks a little queer. But this is of no real importance. The St. Ninian's Isle treasure appears to be of Scottish origin, or at any rate to have belonged to Scottish owners, and if so, Resad and his father may perfectly well have been Picts, particularly since Shetland was pretty certainly Pictish rather than Gaelic before it was Norse. Now, rather little is known about Pictish nomenclature, but what is known indicates that quite often it was very queer indeed—far more so than either of these names. One may mention *Canutulachama*, *Bliesblituth*, *Usconbuts*, *Uipoignamet*, *Uumpopual*, and *Dorornauch Nerales*, names which must surely stem from the pre-Celtic peoples of Pictland,[3] and were adopted through intermarriage by the immigrant Celts. Indeed there is a Pictish inscription from St. Ninian's Isle itself, *besmeqqnanammovvez*, in which the genitive *meqq* is exactly *fili*,[4] and Bes and Nanammovvez seem therefore to be Pictish names. If so, there is no reason at all why Resad and Spusscio should not be so too; Spusscio is, if anything, less 'peculiar' than Nanammovvez.

There is no difficulty about a text of Pictish origin being in Latin. The Pictish church must of course always have used Latin as its written language, from the time it

---

[1] O'Dell *et al.* (1959), 253 f.

[2] Jackson (1960), 41 f.

[3] On this whole question see Jackson (1955), 144 ff.

[4] Jackson (1955), 140.

was set up in the fifth and sixth centuries, and the document known as 'The Pictish Chronicle' appears to have drawn on various Pictish ecclesiastical records in Latin of which some may have been as old as the sixth century. Nor is there any objection to a valuable piece of property being identified by the name of the owner inscribed on it.[1] An interesting parallel to an owner's name being engraved on part of a scabbard is seen in a runic inscription on a bronze plate from Greenmount in County Louth: 'Donald Seal's-Head owns this sword.'[2] Here the owner bears an Irish or Scottish name. As to the other inscription, *in nomine dei summi* is not in the least unnatural even if the object is a chape. It simply means that Resad was a pious Christian who drew his sword in the Lord's name, or invoked his protection when he did so.

As Professor Brown has pointed out, the two inscriptions are in different 'hands', the *in nomine* one being what he calls 'bold and stately' and the other 'less formal', more cursive.[3] In theory this could mean, of course, that they were engraved by two different craftsmen, at two different times and even in two different places; but it does not necessarily do so. It is not at all inappropriate that the formula invoking God should be in a more formal script than that naming the owner. One may compare the way in which works of devotion print, or used to print, certain words and phrases in more elaborate type, or in red, and the fact that it is still usual to refer to God as *He* and *Him* rather than as *he* and *him*. If we suppose that the second inscription was added later and quite independently of the first we should also have to suppose that the space in which it stands had been left wholly blank and was not originally intended to bear an inscription at all. But this is most improbable, in the light of the very complete decoration of the treasure as a whole and of the other 'chape' in particular. It is obvious that the space occupied by the second inscription was intended for this purpose from the start, and highly probable that both were meant to be, and were, inscribed at the same time though not necessarily by the same person.

All discussion of the lettering must start from the fact that this is a problem in epigraphy; that these are *inscriptions* cut on metal with an engraving tool, not written with pen and ink on parchment. Of course the script is essentially a handwritten type and not a monumental one, but it is a handwritten one transferred to a much less tractable material and instrument, and the difficulties involved must be borne in mind.

---

[1] Cf. O'Dell *et al.* (1959), 254; and Macalister (1945), 32, no. 27, and Macalister (1949), 25 f., no. 573.

[2] Macalister (1949), 29 f., no. 576. The blade of the Anglo-Saxon scramasax from Sittingbourne, Kent, is inscribed s. GEBEREHT MEẠH, Wilson (1964), pl. XXX, 80. Another Anglo-Saxon inscription may be of incidental interest as it occurs on a sixth-century scabbard; executed in runic characters; it is apparently meaningless, cf. *British Museum Guide to Anglo-Saxon . . . Antiquities*, London, 1923, fig. 74.

[3] O'Dell *et al.* (1959), 250 f.

Moreover the Celtic metal craftsmen and monumental engravers had worked out a tradition of how to deal with manuscript letters, which had to some degree a life of its own by no means always necessarily directly dependent on scribal usage, and there-fore properly called epigraphic; which tradition is illustrated in a mass of inscriptions belonging to the seventh to eleventh centuries found in the Celtic regions of the British Isles. It is to these inscriptions that we must turn in the first place for parallels to those in the St. Ninian's Isle treasure.

The striking things about the first inscription are three: the exaggerated curved 'hooks' in the *i*, *n*'s, *m*, and *s*; the way in which the engraver seems to have been rather uncertain how to join up his minims, so that at first glance it looks rather like *mnonnneds*; and the fact that the *m* is split by the central boss with the first two minims to the left of it and the last one to the right. Also that the *o* is much smaller than the other letters, and that the *e* has a very long cross-stroke. 'Hooks' like these are extremely rare in inscriptions from the Celtic regions, but not unique. They are found in the L of the Stowford inscription in Devon[1] (eighth or ninth century) and of the *Deniel* inscription at Wareham in Dorset[2] (late eighth century), as well as the *n* of the *Gongorie* inscription also at Wareham[2] (eighth–ninth century). Something analogous is seen in the hollow 'wedges' of the *i nomine* inscription from Dunadd mentioned above, perhaps eighth century, and of the Kilnasaggart stone in Co. Armagh, the date of which is about 715;[3] and the large rectangular substitutes for wedges in the eighth-century Welsh inscription at Towyn[4] and in other Welsh examples may perhaps be compared. The failure to join the minims is similar to the failure to join the cross-stroke of the *e* in *resad* and the diagonal stroke of the *f* in *fili*, though this only just misses the upright. This may arise from an excess of caution, the engraver being anxious that his tool should not slip on the metal and cut through the line it was supposed to join; but such things are also found, particularly with *e*, where it is common,[5] on stone monuments, and it may simply be part of the epigraphic convention inherited by the engraver.

Nevertheless one has an impression that the man who inscribed *in nomine* may not have been very competent or experienced, or else possibly that he did not know Latin and was not really certain what the letters meant, but was merely copying what was given him, this exemplar itself not being very clear. If so, this would certainly explain the way he cut his *m* in two round the central boss, though mere incompetence would also account for this; but it can be paralleled in the Irish Shrine of St. Patrick's Bell,[6]

[1] Macalister (1949), 187, no. 1060, and pl. LXII (where it is wrongly numbered).

[2] Radford and Jackson (1970), II. ii. 308, 312.

[3] See Macalister (1949), 114, no. 946, and pl. XLVI.

[4] Nash-Williams (1950), 172, no. 287, and fig. 188, pl. XXIII.

[5] e.g. in the Stowford inscription just mentioned.

[6] See Mahr (1932), pl. 80.

where an *m* is similarly divided on either side of a rivet by an engraver who was far from unskilled. The fact that the *o* is so much smaller than the other letters may well be due to bad spacing, not enough room being left for a full-sized letter; but again, similar small *o*'s are found quite often in other early Celtic inscriptions,[1] and moreover, inscriptions where this consideration of available space does not apply. As to the elongated cross-stroke of the *e*, this is not at all rare, as for instance on the Llanllwyni stone,[2] probably eighth century, or on one from Clonmacnois in Ireland[3] with a forked serif at the end analogous to the well-marked serif of our text. The uncial *d* is of a type well known in Celtic inscriptions of the seventh–eleventh centuries. The letters have small or very small neat serifs, apart from the one just mentioned. I cannot agree with the claim[4] that there is any special likeness between the *in nomine* inscription and the hands of the Books of Lindisfarne and Kells, but merely a very broad general similarity arising from the fact that all are insular work of a very roughly similar date.

The second inscription has one or two interesting features in addition to its being more cursive, less formal than the first. The *r*, which is perfectly normal otherwise, has a peculiar crook (not really a 'blob') at the end which is unique in inscriptions so far as I know. It may have been meant as a large thickened serif, somewhat comparable to those on the *r*'s and *s*'s in the seventh-century North Welsh Catamanus inscription.[5] Parallels to most of the other letters can be found in Celtic inscriptions all through the series from the seventh to the eleventh centuries. The *e* with separate cross-stroke is familiar in these inscriptions throughout the period, as already noted. There is really nothing notable about the first *s*. The last two, and above all the first of these, make the join of the two arms rather low. One may compare some of the cursive *s*'s in the Boniface Gospels of the first half of the eighth century illustrated by Lindsay in his *Early Irish Minuscule Script*,[6] pl. III, though these have the normal curve at the top of the second stroke which is so remarkably lacking in the last three here, where the line is almost straight. Particularly also the first *s* of the Samson inscription of the late tenth century at Llantwit Major,[7] in which the deep (though not the wide) angle and the absence of curve are both found. The half-uncial horned *a* is a familiar letter which has some specially close relatives in inscriptions of the tenth and eleventh centuries, but is of course also found very much earlier. There is nothing particularly remarkable about the *d*; even the fact that the bow approaches the stem so near the top has various

---

[1] e.g. the *Petri apustoli* stone at Whithorn, late sixth or early seventh century; see Macalister (1945), 497 ff., no. 519.

[2] Nash-Williams (1950), 116, no. 164, fig. 123, pl. XXIX.

[3] Macalister (1949), 58, no. 738, pl. XXXIII.

[4] O'Dell *et al.* (1959), 250 f.

[5] Nash-Williams (1950), 55 f., no. 13, fig. 21, pl. VII.

[6] Lindsay (1910).

[7] Nash-Williams (1950), 142, no. 222, fig. 155, pl. XL.

epigraphic parallels.[1] The *f* has been taken for a *k*,[2] on rather unclear grounds but apparently because the second stroke does not quite join the stem, a phenomenon which has already been explained above. Like those of the last three *s*'s, this stroke has no curve at the top, though it is much less deeply engraved. In fact *k* is impossible, because (1) *k* is a letter wholly unknown in Celtic inscriptions and virtually so in manuscripts apart from the abbreviations for Latin *kalendae*; and (2) the cross-stroke is horizontal as in *f*, and not sloping downwards as in *k*. In fact the letter is a cursive minuscule *f*, like the *s*'s, but adapted to engraving on metal, and there is no shadow of reason to regard it as anything else. The sloping second stroke is very like that of the *f*'s in, for instance, the Vat. Pal. Lat. 68 psalter, eighth or beginning of the ninth century, illustrated by Lindsay;[3] which MS. is significantly of Northumbrian Irish provenance. The cursive *p* calls for no remark. The *u* has been taken for a *b*, but it has been shown elsewhere[4] that this epigraphic 'square' *u* is perfectly well known in the Celtic inscriptions of the period, notably in the eighth century ones at Towyn and Llanlleonfel,[5] and that the letter cannot be a *b*. There are very small serifs similar to those of the other inscription though smaller, with some of the letters; but they are larger and more distinct at the bottoms of the last two *s*'s and the last *i*.

It appears then that both inscriptions fall well within the range of what is reasonably familiar in the Celtic epigraphy and, allowing for the difference of technique dictated by the material and tools, the palaeography of the seventh–eleventh centuries, apart from the 'hooks' in the first and the 'crook' on the *r* of the second; neither of which features, however, is wholly without parallel. The *in nomine* inscription is in a somewhat more formal lettering than the other; which is easily explained by the difference in tone if the second is the owner's name, the first being a solemn invocation to God, but could not be so explained if the whole were one single invocation of this kind. It may be that two separate craftsmen were at work, though this is not certain. Perhaps there was only one, supplied with exemplars in two different scripts, but that given him for the first inscription was unclear and he himself was not sufficiently competent in Latin to be sure about the minims. It is not likely that the two were engraved at different times in different workshops. As to the date, individually the letters cannot really be closely pinned down, but as a whole, particularly in view of the 'hooks' and one or two other features mentioned, the eighth or early ninth century seems probable.

[1] e.g. in the Llanllyr inscription, Nash-Williams (1950), 100, no. 124, fig. 98, pl. XVI; dated by him seventh–ninth century.

[2] O'Dell *et al.* (1959), 252.

[3] Lindsay (1910), pl. XII.

[4] Jackson (1960), 40.

[5] Nash-Williams (1950), 77, no. 62, fig. 51, pl. XXI. On the date see also Jackson (1953), 294 n. 1.

Appendix B *Chemical analyses of the silver objects*

HUGH McKERRELL

MISCELLANEOUS OBJECTS

Catalogue no.	%Ag	%Cu	%Sn	%Pb	%Zn	%Au	%Bi	%Sb	%As	%Fe	%Ni
9	36	57	4	2·4	0·8	0·05	0·1	0·06	<0·05	0·08	<0·005
10	17	73	7	2·0	1·0	0·04	0·09	0·09	<0·05	0·06	0·06
11	32	58	8	1·3	0·7	0·07	0·06	0·03	<0·05	0·05	0·03
12	54	31	13	1·6	0·7	0·1	0·03	0·02	<0·05	0·02	0·05
13	44	48	6	1·5	0·8	0·09	0·07	0·08	<0·05	0·02	0·02
14	47	46	5	1·7	1·1	0·1	0·1	0·06	<0·05	0·04	0·02
15	25	62	10	1·6	1·0	0·08	0·1	0·1	<0·05	0·01	0·04
16[1]	36	57	6	1·5	0·5	0·08	0·08	0·07	<0·05	0·01	0·02

[1] Rivet.

BROOCHES

Catalogue no.	%Ag	%Cu	%Sn	%Pb	%Zn	%Au	%Bi	%Sb	%As	%Fe	%Ni
17	41	50	6	2·0	0·7	0·05	0·04	0·04	<0·05	0·02	0·02
18	44	49	4	2·0	0·9	0·12	0·05	0·07	0·07	0·09	0·03
19	37	57	3	1·8	0·9	0·04	0·01	0·04	<0·05	0·04	0·02
20	46	48	3	1·1	1·3	0·06	0·08	0·02	<0·05	0·04	<0·005
21	30	57	9	3·0	0·8	0·05	0·01	0·09	<0·05	0·06	0·05
22	44	45	9	1·2	0·9	0·12	0·11	0·07	<0·05	0·03	0·03
23	47	44	7	1·4	0·8	0·12	0·04	0·06	<0·05	0·04	0·04
24	32	60	5	1·9	1·0	0·04	0·02	0·08	0·06	0·06	0·02
25	82	14	2	1·1	0·5	0·07	0·13	0·02	<0·05	0·04	<0·005
26	61	33	5	1·3	0·8	0·06	0·03	0·03	<0·05	0·07	0·04
27	65	29	3	2·6	0·4	0·09	0·03	0·07	<0·05	0·09	0·02
28	35	58	4	2·0	1·1	0·06	0·12	0·09	<0·05	0·1	0·05

PINS OF BROOCHES

Catalogue no.	%Ag	%Cu	%Sn	%Pb	%Zn	%Au	%Bi	%Sb	%As	%Fe	%Ni
17	19	75	4	2·0	0·5	0·06	0·1	0·03	<0·05	0·05	0·05
18	61	30	6	1·3	1·7	0·1	0·1	0·09	<0·05	0·07	0·01
19	26	70	2	1·4	1·0	0·06	0·03	0·03	<0·05	0·08	0·04
20	70	26	2	1·0	0·6	0·1	0·1	0·05	<0·05	0·1	0·05
21	18	73	6	2·9	0·8	0·04	0·02	0·04	0·06	0·01	0·03
22	59	32	7	1·3	0·4	0·1	0·09	0·02	<0·05	0·04	<0·005
23	48	37	13	1·3	0·6	0·09	0·08	0·08	0·06	0·09	0·04
24	35	53	9	1·4	0·6	0·07	0·09	0·02	<0·05	0·1	<0·005
25	91	5	3	1·1	0·1	0·1	0·1	0·03	<0·05	0·05	0·06
26	58	37	3	1·1	0·6	0·04	0·1	0·04	<0·05	0·04	0·02
27	73	23	3	1·1	0·7	0·1	0·1	0·03	<0·05	0·1	0·02
28	34	59	5	1·4	0·9	0·08	0·09	0·09	0·07	0·08	0·02

COMPARISON OF ANALYTICAL METHODS USED

%Zinc			%Tin	
Sylloge no.[1]	Atomic absorption	Spectro-graphic	Colori-metric	Spectro-graphic
58	0·02	0·08	<0·01	<0·01
86	0·1	0·1	0·09	0·05
105	0·1	0·2	0·3	0·4
139	0·8	1·0	0·5	0·4
610	0·2	0·1	0·06	0·2
597	2·0	1·6	0·3	0·3
455b	2·4	1·0	0·2	0·3
13	1·7	1·6	0·5	0·7
151	0·2	0·3	0·3	0·2

[1] This refers to coins in the National Museum of Antiquities of Scotland catalogued by Stevenson (1966): The numbers are those used there.

List of Sources

ADAMS, J. H.   (1967)   'A New Type of Cresset Stone?', *Cornish Archaeology*, vi. 47–56.

ALCOCK, L.   (1963)   'Pottery and settlements in Wales and the March A.D. 400–700', *Culture and Environment* (ed. Foster, I. LL. and Alcock, L.), London, 281–302.

ALLEN, J. R.   (1894)   'The Celtic Brooch, and how it was worn', *Illustrated Archaeologist*, i. 162–75.

ALLEN, J. R., and ANDERSON, J. O.   (1903)   *The Early Christian Monuments of Scotland*, Edinburgh.

ANDERSON, J.   (1874–6)   'Notice of a Find of Silver ornaments, &c., at Croy, Inverness-shire . . .', *Proceedings of the Society of Antiquaries of Scotland*, xi. 588–92.

     (1879–80)   'Notice of a fragment of a silver penannular brooch . . .', *Proceedings of the Society of Antiquaries of Scotland*, xiv. 445–52.

     (1881)   *Scotland in Early Christian times* (second series), Edinburgh.

     (1906–7)   'Ship-burial of the Viking time at Kiloran Bay, Colonsay', *Proceedings of the Society of Antiquaries of Scotland*, xli. 443–9.

ARBMAN, H.   (1940)   *Birka I*, Uppsala.

ARWIDSSON, G.   (1942)   *Vendelstile*, Uppsala.

BAKKA, E.   (1963)   'Some English Decorated Metal Objects found in Norwegian Graves', *Årbok for Universitetet i Bergen, Humanistisk serie*, i.

     (1965)   'Some decorated Anglo-Saxon and Irish metalwork found in Norwegian Viking graves', *The Fourth Viking Congress* (ed. Small, A.), Edinburgh and London, 32–40.

BALDWIN BROWN, G.   (1903–37)   *The Arts in Early England*, London.

BALFOUR, D.   (1859)   *Oppressions of the Sixteenth Century in the Islands of Orkney and Zetland*, Glasgow.

BATTISCOMBE, C. F. (ed.)   (1956)   *The Relics of St. Cuthbert; studies by various authors*, Oxford.

BEHMER, E.   (1939)   *Das zweischneidige Schwert der germanischen Völkerwanderungszeit*, Stockholm.

BERSU, G., and WILSON, D. M.   (1966)   *Three Viking Graves in the Isle of Man* (Society for Medieval Archaeology, Monograph Series: No. 1), London.

BLUNT, C. E.   (1949–50)   'The Date of the Croy Hoard', *Proceedings of the Society of Antiquaries of Scotland*, lxxxiv. 217.

BÓNA, I.   (1966)   'Cundpald Fecit', *Acta Archaeologica . . . Hungarica*, xviii. 279–325.

BOSWORTH, J., and TOLLER, T. N.   (1882)   *An Anglo-Saxon Dictionary*, Oxford.

BRAND, J.   (1701)   *A Brief Description of Orkney, Zetland, Pightland Firth and Couthness*, Edinburgh.

BRAUN, J.   (1932)   *Das christliche Altargerät in seinem Sein und in seiner Entwicklung*, München.

BRØGGER, A. W.   (1929)   *Ancient Emigrants*, Oxford.

BRUCE MITFORD, R. L. S.   (1960)   'The treasure of St. Ninian's', *Scientific American*, cciii. 154–66.

       (1964)   'A Hiberno-Saxon bronze mounting from Markyate, Hertfordshire', *Antiquity*, xxxviii. 219–20.

       (1968)   *The Sutton Hoo Ship-burial, a handbook*, London.

       (1969)   'The Art of the Codex Amiatinus', *The Journal of the British Archaeological Association*, 3rd ser., xxxii. 1–25.

BUSHE-FOX, J. P.   (1949)   *Excavations of the Roman Fort at Richborough Kent*, iv, London.

CABROL, F., and LECLERCQ, H.   (1907–53)   *Dictionnaire d'archéologie chrétienne et de liturgie*, Paris.

CAMPBELL, A. (ed.)   (1967)   *Æthelwulf, de abbatibus*, Oxford.

CAMPBELL of KILBERRY, M., and SANDEMAN, M.   (1962–3)   'Mid-Argyll; an archaeological survey', *Proceedings of the Society of Antiquaries of Scotland*, xcv. 1–125.

CLAPHAM, A. W.   (1934)   'Notes on the Origins of Hiberno-Saxon Art', *Antiquity*, viii. 43–57.

COFFEY, G.   (1910)   *Royal Irish Academy Collection: Guide to the Celtic Antiquities of the Christian Period presented in the National Museum, Dublin*, 2nd ed., Dublin.

COLLINGWOOD, W. G.   (1908)   *Scandinavian Britain*, London.

       (1927)   *Norman Crosses of the Pre-Norman Age*, London.

COLVILLE, J.   (1804)   *Historie and Life King James the Sext*, Edinburgh.

CRAMP, R.   (1967)   *Anglian and Viking York (Borthwick Papers, 33)*, York.

CRAW, J. H.   (1929–30)   'Excavations at Dunadd and at other sites on the Poltalloch Estates, Argyll', *Proceedings of the Society of Antiquaries of Scotland*, lxiv. 111–46.

CRAWFORD, O. G. S.   (1937)   'The Vine-scroll in Scotland', *Antiquity*, xi. 469–73.

CRUDEN, S. H.   (1964)   *The Early Christian and Pictish Monuments of Scotland*, 2nd ed., Edinburgh.

       (1965)   'Excavations at Birsay, Orkney' in: *The Fourth Viking Congress* (ed. Small, A.), Edinburgh and London, 22–31.

CURLE, A. O.   (1913–14)   'Report on the Excavation of . . . the Mote of Mark', *Proceedings of the Society of Antiquaries of Scotland*, xlviii. 125–68.

CURLE, A. O.   (1923–4)   'A Note on Four Silver Spoons and a Fillet of Gold found in The Nunnery at Iona . . .', *Proceedings of the Society of Antiquaries of Scotland*, lviii. 102–11.

                                (1938–9)   'A Viking settlement at Freswick, Caithness', *Proceedings of the Society of Antiquaries of Scotland*, lxxiii. 71–110.

CURLE, C. L.   (1939–40)   'The Chronology of the Early Christian Monuments of Scotland', *Proceedings of the Society of Antiquaries of Scotland*, lxxiv. 60–115.

CURSITER, J. W.   (1886–7)   'Notice of the bronze weapons of Orkney and Shetland and on an Iron Age deposit found in a cist at Moan, Harray', *Proceedings of the Society of Antiquaries of Scotland*, xxi. 339–45.

DALTON, O. M.   (1922)   'Roman Spoons from Dorchester', *The Antiquaries Journal*, ii. 89–92.

DANNHEIMER, H.   (1966)   'Der Holzbau am Rande des Reihengräberfeldes von München-Aubing', *Germania*, xliv. 326–37.

DE FLEURY, C. R.   (1883)   *La Messe*, i, Paris.

DE PALOL, P.   (1967)   *Arqueología Cristiana de la España Romana* (= España Cristiana, serie monográfica I), Madrid and Valladolid.

DICKINSON, W. C.   (1965)   'Odal Rights and Feudal Wrongs', *The Viking Congress* (ed. Simpson, W. D.), Aberdeen, 142–60.

DONALDSON, G.   (1954)   *The Court-book of Orkney and Shetland 1602–4*, Edinburgh.
                                (1958)   *Shetland Life under Earl Patrick*, Edinburgh.

DOPPELFELD, O., and   (1966)   *Fränkische Fürsten im Rheinland*, Düsseldorf.
  PIRLING, R.

DUNNING, G. C., and   (1961)   'The Palace of Westminster Sword', *Archaeologia*, xcviii. 123–58.
  EVISON, V. I.

EDMONDSTON, A.   (1809)   *The Ancient and Present State of the Zetland Islands*, Edinburgh.

EDWARDS, A. J. H.   (1939–40)   'A Brooch fragment from Freswick Links, Caithness', *Proceedings of the Society of Antiquaries of Scotland*, lxxiv. 138.

EELES, F. C.   (1933–4)   'The Monymusk Reliquary or Brecbennoch of St. Columba', *Proceedings of the Society of Antiquaries of Scotland*, lxviii. 433–8.

ELBERN, V. H.   (1964)   *Der eucharistische Kelch im frühen Mittelalter*, Berlin.

ENGELHARDT, C.   (1866)   *Denmark in the Early Iron Age*, London.

EVISON, V. I.   (1967)   'A sword from the Thames at Wallingford Bridge', *The Archaeological Journal*, cxxiv. 160–88.

FAIRHOLT, F. W.   (1848)   'Remarks on Irish Fibulæ', *Transactions of the British Archaeological Association at its third annual conference, 1846*, London.

FAIRHURST, H.   (1938–9)   'The Galleried Dūn at Kildonan Bay, Kintyre', *Proceedings of the Society of Antiquaries of Scotland*, lxxiii. 185–228.

FAUSSET, B.   (1856)   *Inventorium Sepulchrale*, London.

FEACHEM, R. W.   (1951)   'Dragonesque Fibulae', *The Antiquaries Journal*, xxxi. 32–44.

FETT, P.   (1939–40) 'Bergens Museums tilvekst av oldsaker 1939', *Bergens Museums Årbok, Hist.-Antik, rekke, nr. 3.*

FOWLER, E.   (1960)   'The origins and development of the Penannular Brooch in Europe', *Proceedings of the Prehistoric Society*, xxvi. 149–77.

                           (1963)   'Celtic Metalwork of the fifth and sixth centuries A.D.', *The Archaeological Journal*, cxx. 98–160.

                           (1968)   'Hanging bowls', *Studies in Ancient Europe* (ed. Coles, J. M., and Simpson, D. D. A.), Leicester, 288–310.

FRASER, T., and   (1874–6) 'Notice of a find of silver ornaments, &c., at Croy,
  ANDERSON, J.   Inverness-shire', *Proceedings of the Society of Antiquaries of Scotland*, xi. 588–92.

GIBSON, W. J.   (1933–4) 'Some prehistoric relics from Lewis', *Proceedings of the Society of Antiquaries of Scotland*, lxviii. 428–32.

GIFFORD, T.   (1780)   *An Historical Description of the Zetland Islands*, London.

GOUDIE, G.   (1880–1) 'Notice of a Sculptured Slab from the Island of Burra, Shetland', *Proceedings of the Society of Antiquaries of Scotland*, xv. 199–209.

                           (1904)   *The Celtic and Scandinavian Antiquities of Shetland*, London.

                           (1912)   'The Ecclesiastical Antiquities of the Southern Parishes of Shetland', *Transactions of the Scottish Ecclesiological Society*, iii, pt. 3, 36–50.

GRANT, F. J.   (1893)   *The County Families of the Zetland Islands*, Lerwick.

HAMILTON, J. R. C.   (1956)   *Excavations at Jarlshof, Shetland*, Edinburgh.

                           (1968)   *Excavations at Clickhimin, Shetland*, Edinburgh.

HASELOFF, G.   (1951)   *Der Tassilokelch*, München.

                           (1958)   'Fragments of a hanging-bowl from Bekesbourne, Kent, and some ornamental problems', *Medieval Archaeology*, ii. 72–103.

HAWKES, S. C., and   (1967)   'Swords and Runes in south-east England', *The Antiquaries Journal*, xlvii. 1–26.
  PAGE, R. I.

HENCKEN, H. O'N.   (1942)   'Ballinderry Crannog, no. 2', *Proceedings of the Royal Irish Academy*, xlvii, C. 1–77.

HENDERSON, I.   (1967)   *The Picts*, London.

HENRY, F.   (1936)   'Hanging Bowls', *Journal of the Royal Society of Antiquaries of Ireland*, lxvi. 209–46.

                           (1947)   'The Antiquities of Caher Island (Co. Mayo)', *Journal of the Royal Society of Antiquaries of Ireland*, lxxvii. 23–8.

                           (1956)   'Irish Enamels of the Dark Ages and their Relation to the Cloisonné Techniques', *Dark Age Britain. Studies presented to E. T. Leeds* (ed. Harden, D. B.), London, 71–90.

                           (1957)   'Early Monasteries, Beehive Huts, and Dry-stone Houses in the neighbourhood of Caherciveen and Waterville (Kerry)', *Proceedings of the Royal Irish Academy*, lviii, C. 45–166.

HENRY, F. (1965) *Irish Art in the Early Christian Period (to 800 A.D.)*, London.

(1967) *Irish Art during the Viking Invasions, 800–1020 A.D.*, London.

HIBBERT, S. (1822) *Description of the Shetland Isles*, London.

HILLGARTH, J. (1961) 'The East, Visigothic Spain, and the Irish', *Studia Patristica*, 4. 442.

(1962) 'Visigothic Spain and Early Christian Ireland', *Proceedings of the Royal Irish Academy*, lxii, C. 167–94.

HOLMQVIST, W. (1955) *Germanic Art during the first millenium A.D. (Kungl. vitterhets historie och antikvitets akademiens Handlingar, 90)*, Stockholm.

(1961) *Excavation at Helgö*, i, Stockholm.

(1963) *Övergångtidens metallkonst (Kungl. vitterhets historie och antikvitets akademiens Handlingar, Ant. Ser. xi)*, Stockholm.

HOPPE, G. (1965) 'Submarine Peat in the Shetland Islands', *Geografiska annaler*, Ser. A. 47. 4.

HOUGEN, B. (1936) *The Migration style in Norway*, Oslo.

HUBERT, J. *et al.* (1967) *L'Europe des invasions*, Paris.

HUGHES, K. (1966) *The Church in Early Irish Society*, London.

JACKSON, K. H. (1953) *Language and History in Early Britain*, Edinburgh.

(1955) 'The Pictish Language', *The Problem of the Picts* (ed. Wainwright, F. T.), Edinburgh, 129–66.

(1960) 'The St. Ninian's Isle Inscription, a Re-appraisal', *Antiquity*, xxxiv. 38–42.

JENNY, W. (n.d.) 'Das sogenannte Rupertus-Kreuz in Bischofshofen', *Arte del primo millenio (Atti del 2 convegno per lo studio dell'arte alto Medio Evo, Pavia 1950)*, Turin, 383 ff.

JESSUP, R. (1950) *Anglo-Saxon Jewellery*, London.

KASKE, R. E. (1967) 'The silver spoons of Sutton Hoo', *Speculum*, xlii. 670–2.

KAY, G. (1908) 'A Description of Dunrossness by G. Kay, minister thereof', *Description of ye Countrey of Zetland* (ed. G. Bruce), Edinburgh.

KENDRICK, T. D. (1932) 'British Hanging-Bowls', *Antiquity*, vi. 161–84.

(1938) *Anglo-Saxon art to A.D. 900*, London.

(1941) 'A late Saxon hanging-bowl', *The Antiquaries Journal*, xxi. 161–2.

KENDRICK, T. D., *et al.* (1960) *Evangeliorum Quattuor Codex Lindisfarnensis . . .*, Oltun et Lausanna.

KILBRIDE-JONES, H. E. (1935–7) 'The Evolution of Penannular Brooches with zoomorphic Terminals in Great Britain and Ireland', *Proceedings of the Royal Irish Academy*, xliii, C. 379–454.

(1936–7) 'A bronze hanging-bowl from Castle Tioram, Moidart: and a suggested absolute chronology for British hanging-bowls', *Proceedings of the Society of Antiquaries of Scotland*, lxxi. 206–47.

KITZINGER, E. (1940) 'The Silver', *Antiquity*, xiv. 40–63.

KOCH, R. (1967) *Bodenfunde der Völkerwanderungszeit aus dem Main-Tauber-Gebiet (Germanische Denkmäler der Völkerwanderungszeit, ser. A, VIII)*, Berlin.

LAUR-BELART, R. (1963) *Der spätrömische Silberschatz von Kaiseraugst (Argau)*, Augst.

LEEDS, E. T. (1933) *Celtic Ornament in the British Isles down to A.D. 700*, Oxford.

LIESTÖL, A. (1953) 'The Hanging Bowl, a Liturgical and Domestic Vessel', *Acta Archaeologica*, xxiv. 163–70.

LINDSAY, W. M. (1910) *Early Irish Minuscule Script*, Oxford.

LIONARD, P. (1961) 'Early Irish Grave Slabs', *Proceedings of the Royal Irish Academy*, lxi, C. 95–169.

LOW, G. (1879) *A Tour through the Islands of Orkney and Shetland*, Kirkwall.

LOWE, E. A. (1934) *Corpus Inscriptionum Latinorum*, i, Oxford.

LOWRY-CORRY, D. (1959) 'A newly-discovered statue at the church of White Island, Co. Fermanagh', *Ulster Journal of Archaeology*, 3 ser., xxii. 59–66.

LOYN, H. R. (1962) *Anglo-Saxon England and the Norman Conquest*, London.

LUCAS, A. T. (1960–2) 'Irish Food before the Potato', *Gwerin*, iii (2), 8–43.

(1967) 'The plundering and burning of churches in Ireland, 7th–16th century', *North Munster Studies* (ed. E. Rynne), Limerick, 172–229.

MACALISTER, R. A. S. (1945) *Corpus Inscriptionum Insularum Celticarum*, i, Dublin.

(1949) *Corpus Inscriptionum Insularum Celticarum*, ii, Dublin.

MACDONALD, A. D. S., and LAING, L. R. (1967–8) 'Early Ecclesiastical Sites in Scotland: a Field Survey. Part I', *Proceedings of the Society of Antiquaries of Scotland*, c. 123–34.

MACKENZIE, J. (1836) *The General Grievances and Oppressions in the Isles of Orkney and Shetland*, Edinburgh.

McROBERTS, D. (1960–1) 'The Ecclesiastical Significance of the St. Ninian's Isle Treasure', *Proceedings of the Society of Antiquaries of Scotland*, xciv. 301–13.

(1965) 'The ecclesiastical significance of the St. Ninian's Isle treasure', *The Fourth Viking Congress* (ed. Small, A.), Aberdeen, 224–46.

MAHR, A. (1932) *Christian Art in Ancient Ireland*, i, Dublin.

MARSTRANDER, S. (1963) 'A new Norwegian find from the Viking Period with Western European imported goods', *Lochlann*, iii. 1–36.

MARTIN, M. (1703) *Description of the Western Isles of Scotland*, London.

MOAR, P. (1951–2) 'Two Shetland Finds', *Proceedings of the Society of Antiquaries of Scotland*, lxxxvi. 206.

MOAR, P. and STEWART, J. (1943–4) 'Newly discovered Sculptured Stones from Papil, Shetland', *Proceedings of the Society of Antiquaries of Scotland*, lxxviii. 91–9.

MUIR, T. S. (1862) Shetland—An Ecclesiological Sketch. (Edinburgh.)

MURRAY, D.   (1896)   *An Archaeological Survey of the United Kingdom*, Glasgow.

NASH-WILLIAMS, V. E.   (1950)   *The Early Christian Monuments of Wales*, Cardiff.

NOLL, R.   (1958)   *Vom Altertum zum Mittelalter*, Wien.

O'DELL, A. C.   (1959)   'Excavations at St. Ninian's Isle', *The Scottish Geographical Magazine*, lxxv. 41–3.

     (1960)   *St. Ninian's Isle Treasure . . . (Aberdeen University Studies*, 141), Aberdeen.

O'DELL, A. C. *et al.*   (1959)   'The St. Ninian's Isle Silver Hoard', *Antiquity*, xxxiii. 241–68.

O'KELLY, M. J.   (1965)   'The Belt-shrine from Moylough, Co. Sligo', *Journal of the Royal Society of Antiquaries of Ireland*, xcv. 149–88.

ORGAN, R. M.   (1959)   'The Treatment of the St. Ninian's Hanging Bowl Complex', *Studies in Conservation*, iv. 41–50.

O'RÍORDÁIN, S. P.   (1942)   'The Excavation of a large earthern ring-fort at Garranes, Co. Cork', *Proceedings of the Royal Irish Academy*, xlvii, C. 77–150.

OZANNE, A.   (1962)   'The Context and Date of the Anglian Cemetery at Ipswich', *The Proceedings of the Suffolk Institute of Archaeology*, xxix, pt. 2, 208–12.

PAINTER, K. S.   (1965)   'A Roman silver treasure from Canterbury', *Journal of the British Archaeological Association*, 3rd ser., xxviii. 1–15.

PEERS, C., and RADFORD, C. A. R.   (1943)   'The Saxon Monastery of Whitby', *Archaeologia*, lxxxix. 27–88.

PETERKIN, A.   (1822)   *Notes on Orkney and Zetland*, Edinburgh.

     (1839)   *The Booke of the Universale Kirk of Scotland*, Edinburgh.

PETERSEN, J.   (1928)   *Vikingetidens smykker*, Stavanger.

PIGGOTT, S., and DANIEL, G. E.   (1951)   *A picture book of Ancient British Art*, Cambridge.

POWER, P.   (1939–40)   'A decorated Quern-stone and its symbolism', *Proceedings of the Royal Irish Academy*, xlv, C. 25–30.

RADFORD, C. A. R.   (1955*a*)   'An Early Cross at Staplegorton', *Transactions of the Dumfries and Galloway Natural History and Antiquarian Society*, xxxii. 178–9.

     (1955*b*)   'Two Scottish Shrines: Jedburgh and St. Andrews', *The Archaeological Journal*, cxii. 43–60.

     (1962)   'Art and Architecture, Celtic and Norse', *The Northern Isles* (ed. Wainwright, F. T.), Edinburgh, 163–87.

RADFORD, C. A. R., and JACKSON, K. H.   (1968)   Notes on the Wareham inscriptions in *Inventory of the Historical Monuments in the County of Dorset, II; the Royal Commission on Ancient Monuments*, London.

RAFTERY, J.   (1966)   'The Cuillard and other unpublished hanging bowls', *Journal of the Royal Society of Antiquaries of Ireland*, xcvi. 29–38.

RHYS, J.   (1899)   'Some Glamorgan Inscriptions', *Archaeologia Cambrensis*, fifth series, xvi. 132–68.

ROE, H. M.   (1959)   *The High Crosses of Kells*, n.p.
ROMILLY ALLEN, *see* ALLEN, J. R.
ROSS, A.   (1885–6) 'Notice of the Discovery of Portions of Two Penannular
                               Brooches of Silver . . .', *Proceedings of the Society of Anti-
                               quaries of Scotland*, n.s. viii. 91–6.
ROSS, A.   (1967)   *Pagan Celtic Britain*, London.
RYAN, J.   (1931)   *Irish Monasticism, Origins and Early Development*, Dublin
                               and Cork.
RYNNE, E.   (1965)   'A bronze ring brooch from Luce Sands, Wigtownshire:
                               its affinities and significance', *Transactions of the Dumfries-
                               shire and Galloway Natural History and Antiquarian Society*,
                               xlii. 99–113.

SCOTT, H.   (1915)   *Fasti Ecclesiae Scoticanae*, Edinburgh.
SCOTT, W.   (1822)   *The Pirate*, London.
SELLING, D.   (1945)   *Alexander Seton (1768–1828) som fornforskare (Kungl. vitter-
                               hets, historie och antikvitets akademiens Handlingar, 59. 3)*,
                               Stockholm.
SHETELIG, H. (ed.)   (1940)   *Viking Antiquities in Great Britain and Ireland*, i–v, Oslo.
                     (1954)   *Viking Antiquities in Great Britain and Ireland*, vi, Oslo.
SIBBALD, R.   (1711)   *The Description of the isles of Orkney and Zetland*, Edinburgh.
SIMPSON, M.   (1968)   'Massive Armlets in the North British Iron Age',
                               Studies in Ancient Europe (ed. Coles, J. M., and Simpson,
                               D. D. A.), Leicester, 233–54.
SIMPSON, W. D.   (1963)   'The Early Romanesque Tower at Restenneth Priory,
                               Angus', *The Antiquaries Journal*, xliii. 260–83.
SMALL, A.   (1966)   'Excavations at Underhoull, Unst, Shetland', *Proceedings
                               of the Society of Antiquaries of Scotland*, xcviii. 225–48.
SMITH, R. A.   (1914)   'Irish Brooches of Five Centuries', *Archaeologia*, lxiv. 223–
                               50.
                     (1925)   'Examples of Anglian Art', *Archaeologia*, lxxiv. 233–54.
STEVENSON, R. B. K. (1955)   'Pictish Art', *The Problem of the Picts* (ed. Wainwright,
                               F. T.), Edinburgh, 97–128.
                     (1955a) 'Pins and the Chronology of the Brochs', *Proceedings of the
                               Prehistoric Society*, xxi. 282–94.
                     (1958–9) 'The Inchyra Stone and other unpublished Early Christian
                               Monuments', *Proceedings of the Society of Antiquaries of
                               Scotland*, xcvi. 33–55.
                     (1966)   *Sylloge of Coins of the British Isles: National Museum of
                               Antiquities of Scotland*, pt. 1, London.
                     (1968)   'The Brooch from Westness, Orkney', *The Fifth Viking
                               Congress, Tórshavn, July 1965* (ed. Niclasen, B.), Tórshavn,
                               25–31.
STJERNQVIST, B.   (1955)   *Simris, on cultural connections of Scania in the Roman Iron
                               Age*, Bonn/Lund.

STOJKOVIC, I. N.   (1957)   'Rapport préliminaire sur . . . monuments chrétiens à Doclea', *Actes du V Congrès international d'archéologie chrétienne*, Rome/Paris, 567–72.

STOKES, W., and   (1903)   *Thesaurus Palaeohibernicus*, ii, Cambridge.
STRACHAN, J.

STRONG, D. E.   (1966)   *Greek and Roman Gold and Silver Plate*, London.

STUART, J.   (1867)   *Sculptured stones of Scotland*, ii, Edinburgh.

SWARZENSKI, G.   (1954)   'An Early Anglo-Irish Portable Shrine', *Bulletin of the Museum of Fine Arts, Boston*, lii. 50–62.

THOMAS, A. C.   (1961)   'The Animal Art of the Scottish Iron Age and its Origins', *The Archaeological Journal*, cxviii. 14–64.

    (1963)   'The interpretation of the Pictish symbols', *The Archaeological Journal*, cxx. 31–97.

    (1967a)   *Christian Antiquities of Camborne*, St. Austell.

    (1967b)   'An Early Christian Cemetery and Chapel on Ardwall Isle, Kirkcudbright', *Medieval Archaeology*, xi. 127–88.

    (1968)   'The Evidence from North Britain', *Christianity in Britain, 300–700* (ed. Barley, M. W., and Hanson, R. P. C.), Leicester, 93–122.

    (1971)   *Early Christian Archaeology of North Britain*, London.

TOYNBEE, J. M. C.   (1953)   'Christianity in Roman Britain', *The Journal of the British Archaeological Association*, 3rd ser., xvi. 1–24.

TRAILL, W.   (1890)   'Results of Excavations at the Broch of Burrian, North Ronaldsay, Orkney during the summer of 1870 and 1871', *Archaeologia Scotica*, v. 341–64.

VAN DER MEER, F., and   (1958)   *Atlas of the Early Christian World*, Edinburgh.
MOHRMANN, C.

VOLBACH, W. F.   (1961)   *Early Christian Art*, London.

WAINWRIGHT, F. T. (ed.)   (1962)   *The Northern Isles*, Edinburgh.

WERNER, J.   (1966)   'Zum Cundpald-Kelch von Petöháza', *Jahrbuch des Römisch-germanischen Zentral-Museums Mainz*, xiii. 265–78.

WHITELOCK, D.   (1955)   *English Historical Documents c. 500–1040*, i, London.

WILSON, D. M.   (1955)   'An Irish mounting in the National Museum, Copenhagen', *Acta Archaeologica*, xxvi. 163–72.

    (1956)   'An Anglo-Saxon grave near Dartford, Kent', *Archaeologia Cantiana*, lxx. 187–91.

    (1958)   'A group of penannular brooches of the Viking Period', *Árbók hins íslenzka fornleifafélags*, Fylgyrit, 95–100.

    (1960a)   'The Fejø cup', *Acta Archaeologica*, xxxi, 147–73.

    (1960b)   'Irsk-britisk import i Lejre', *Nationalmuseets Arbejdsmark*, 36–7.

    (1961)   'An Anglo-Saxon Bookbinding at Fulda', *The Antiquaries Journal*, xli. 199–217.

WILSON, D. M.   (1964)   *Anglo-Saxon Ornamental Metalwork, 700–1100, in the British Museum*, London.

                        (1965)   'Some neglected late Anglo-Saxon swords', *Medieval Archaeology*, ix. 32–54.

                        (1970)   *Reflections on the St. Ninian's Isle Treasure*, Jarrow.

WILSON, D. M., and   (1961)   'The Trewhiddle Hoard', *Archaeologia*, xcviii. 75–122.
  BLUNT, C. E.

WILSON, D. M., and   (1964)   'Medieval Britain in 1962 and 1963', *Medieval Archaeology*, viii. 231–99.
  HURST, D. G.

                        (1965)   'Medieval Britain in 1964', *Medieval Archaeology*, ix. 170–220.

WILSON, D. M., and   (1966)   *Viking Art*, London.
  KLINDT-JENSEN, O.

ZIMMERMANN, E. H.   (1916)   *Vorkarolingische Miniaturen*, Berlin.

Index